COMMUNICATING
Forgiveness

COMMUNICATING
Forgiveness

Vincent R. Waldron | Douglas L. Kelley

Arizona State University

SAGE Publications

Los Angeles • London • New Delhi • Singapore

For information:

Sage Publications, Inc.
2455 Teller Road
Thousand Oaks,
    California 91320
E-mail: order@sagepub.com

Sage Publications India Pvt. Ltd.
B 1/I 1 Mohan Cooperative
    Industrial Area
Mathura Road, New Delhi 110 044
India

Sage Publications Ltd.
1 Oliver's Yard
55 City Road
London EC1Y 1SP
United Kingdom

Sage Publications Asia-Pacific Pte. Ltd.
33 Pekin Street #02-01
Far East Square
Singapore 048763

Printed in the United States of America

Library of Congress Cataloging-in-Publication Data

Waldron, Vincent R.
Communicating forgiveness / Vincent R. Waldron, Douglas L. Kelley.
    p. cm.
Includes bibliographical references and index.
ISBN 978-1-4129-3970-6 (cloth)
ISBN 978-1-4129-3971-3 (pbk.)
    1. Forgiveness. 2. Interpersonal communication. I. Kelley, Douglas L.
II. Title.
BF637.F67W34 2008
155.9′2—dc22   2007014960

This book is printed on acid-free paper.

07   08   09   10   11   10   9   8   7   6   5   4   3   2   1

Acquisitions Editor:	Todd Armstrong
Editorial Assistant:	Katie Grim
Production Editor:	Astrid Virding
Copy Editor:	Barbara Ray
Typesetter:	C&M Digitals (P) Ltd.
Proofreader:	Dennis Webb
Indexer:	Juniee Oneida
Cover Designer:	Candice Harman
Marketing Manager:	Carmel Withers

Contents

Making Sense
Seeking Forgiveness
Granting Forgiveness
Relationship Negotiation and Transition
Concluding Thoughts

Five Reasons to Forgive
The Dark Side of Forgiveness
Prescriptive Models of Forgiveness
Communication Tasks of Forgiveness (CTF):
    A New Prescriptive Model
Reconciliation: A Possible Outcome
    of Forgiveness
Contributions From Long-Term Couples
Concluding Thoughts

Why Do We Study Forgiveness?
Conceptual Definition: What Is
    Forgiveness Anyway?
Picking Our Paradigm: Which Questions
    Matter Most?
How Do You Measure Forgiveness?
Transformations

Preface

To be honest, we needed to write this book, whether or not anyone published our ideas about the potentially powerful role that forgiveness plays in social life. As we write these pages, the news outlets broadcast a steady stream of jarring stories about the failings of human relationships: religious strife, workplace violence, school shootings, high divorce rates, stressed-out families, shrinking circles of social support. We know from our students and our interviews with couples, friends, and coworkers that nearly all of us at times suffer profound hurt and feel deep moral disappointment in our close relationships. Against this backdrop, we find forgiveness to be a vitally important and hopeful relational alternative to bitterness, vengeance, and disillusion. Studied as a *communication* process, forgiveness is a means by which distressed partners can negotiate improvements in relational justice, create a renewed sense of optimism and well-being, and potentially recover lost intimacy and trust.

Research on forgiveness has been accumulating for more than a decade, but communication scholars, practitioners, and students have yet to fully reap its benefits or shape its direction. This is puzzling, given that the discipline has been teaching and researching forgiveness-related processes for many years, including conflict management, repair and maintenance of romantic relationships and friendships, dysfunctional patterns of family communication, account-making, and problematic work relationships. *Communicating Forgiveness* remedies this situation in several ways. For *scholars and advanced students*, we provide a detailed synthesis of historical, theological, and contemporary forgiveness scholarship (Chapter 1). We demonstrate how communication theories can yield questions and answers that usefully reframe and supplement existing psychological approaches (Chapter 3). We also propose a new *Negotiated Morality Theory* (NMT), which we hope will fuel future investigations. For *students*, we developed a descriptive model of the forgiveness process, depicting it as a transgression-driven, relational, and morally negotiated process, embedded within a cultural and temporal context (Chapter 2). Drawing on our interviews with long-term couples (married 30–80 years) and other research, we provide a framework for effective application—the *Communication Tasks of Forgiveness* model. We also provide a personal account of our experiences as forgiveness researchers, with special emphasis on the methodological tradeoffs and personal transformations that accompany this kind of research (Chapter 6). Finally, for *researchers and students from all disciplines*, this volume offers rich qualitative data and detailed analysis of the specific *communication practices* that partners use to enact forgiveness. This is particularly in evidence in Chapter 4, which focuses heavily on interpersonal communication behaviors.

This book is intended to have broad applicability as a teaching tool for instructors from all of the disciplines that concern themselves with personal and work relationships. Colleagues intend to assign it in upper-division undergraduate courses in subjects such as *interpersonal communication, personal and family relationships, conflict management, relational justice, psychology of human relationships,* and *work relationships*. The chapters on communication theory will be a useful supplement in courses on *communication theory*. Chapter 6 was explicitly designed to provide students in *research methods* classes (at all levels) with a personal and rich account of the decisions (and emotions) that inform studies of personal relationships. The book may be particularly useful in graduate courses offered in such disciplines as communication studies, psychology, family studies, counseling, justice studies, and mediation.

Communicating Forgiveness is a unique book in several ways. First, it contributes to a rich intellectual discussion being conducted by scholars from multiple discipline and divergent research paradigms. For example, both Chapter 1, *Conceptual Foundations*, and Chapter 2, *Elements of the Forgiveness Process*, cast forgiveness as a phenomenon that is individual and relational, simultaneously psychological and interactional. Our desire is to address the interplay between communication practices, psychological states, religious and social context, and relational morality.

Regarding this last point, the development of a *Negotiated Morality Theory of Forgiveness* offers an alternative to familiar theories. In Chapter 3, we offer an extended exploration of dialectical, uncertainty management, and identity management frameworks for forgiveness research. However, we finish the chapter by addressing what many social scientists have shied away from in theory and research: *the role and function of values in interpersonal processes*. It is clear from our research that relational morality plays a key role in how people conceptualize forgiveness and, consequently, shapes their sense of its communicative possibilities and limitations. An advantage of this book is its sharing of the moral and justice concerns expressed in *quotes and narratives* reported by friends, coworkers, romantic partners, parents, sons, and daughters. Readers will see how communication is used to negotiate questions of relational justice and human dignity in the wake of serious transgressions, such as extramarital affairs and verbal abuse. NMT draws attention to the means by which moral standards are expressed, questioned, reinforced, and reevaluated as partners decide whether they should forgive and (possibly) reconcile.

A final theme that will be appreciated by most readers is our effort throughout the book, but in the last two chapters in particular, to make our research and theorizing useful. Chapter 5, *Practicing Forgiveness*, and Chapter 6, *Studying Forgiveness*, are designed to help both students and researchers think through the practical ramifications of this field of study. Our desire is that readers will be better informed about the *choices* they must make, as relational partners and as researchers of personal relationships.

Regarding choices. Although neither of us is typically inclined to read the end of a good book first, that is exactly what some readers may choose to do. Because it provides detailed information about us, our research participants, and how we conducted our research, Chapter 6 will be particularly useful for those interested in the research process. Some reviewers found this chapter an unusual and helpful addition to a book of this kind. They appreciated its personal account of the research process, communicated through vignettes we call *On the Drive Home*. We try to be honest in addressing the tradeoffs associated with various data collection methods and the effects this research had on us as people and friends.

We can say with great enthusiasm that researching, analyzing, and "talking through" the complex and hopeful process of forgiveness has been a highlight of our academic careers (and our own relationship). The personal stories shared so generously by numerous participants transformed our thinking about personal relationships; we hope it has a similar effect on at least some readers. The many couples we interviewed, the hours of conversations we have had over coffee and on the drive home, changed our lives forever. We hope that they will change yours as well.

❖   ACKNOWLEDGMENTS

The authors wish to thank the many graduate and undergraduate students who have shared our interest in the topic of forgiveness.

In numerous class discussions, they helped us articulate the ideas that appear in this book. Some wrote papers on the topic and analyzed our data for new meanings. There are simply too many to name, but we are grateful nonetheless. Several students provided invaluable, tangible assistance. These include Jessica Harvey, Melissa Powers, and Kathy Langford.

We are greatly indebted to the many people who shared their for-giveness narratives with us, including the long-term couples who wel-comed us into their homes and shared their intimate and inspiring stories.

We thank the Templeton Foundation for funding during the early phases of this work. Their support made it possible for us to interview the long-term couples who have been so helpful to our thinking about forgiveness.

Ann Kelley provided valuable research assistance and editing sug-gestions through out this project.

Vince Waldron also benefited from the generous support of the Bernard Osher Foundation, which partially funds his work with life-long learning programs. Discussions with seasoned learners enrolled in these programs were very helpful as we interpreted our interview data. They helped us understand how forgiveness sometimes unfolds over years and even decades.

Todd Armstrong at SAGE has been a pleasure to work with. We thank him for his guidance and support from the beginning to the end of the writing process.

Finally, Arizona State University provided small but essential grants and other support at various times. We are thankful to the administrators who supported this work, including Lesley Di Mare, Mark Searle, and John Hepburn.

SAGE Publications gratefully acknowledges the following reviewers: Jennifer L. Bevan, University of Nevada, Las Vegas; Kathleen M. Galvin, Northwestern University; Kristina Coop Gordon, The University of Tennessee, Knoxville; Janie M. Harden Fritz, Duquesne University; Jon A. Hess, University of Missouri-Columbia; Susanne M. Jones, University of Minnesota, Twin Cities; and Leanne K. Knobloch, University of Illinois at Urbana-Champaign.

1

Conceptual Foundations

That is where I draw the line. I just couldn't stay with him if he had sex with someone else. I don't see how anyone could. It's just not part of my moral code. Forget it!

—Aaron, age 26, engaged to Kevin

Are we willing to throw away 32 years, you know, just for a fling? I take it seriously; it crushed me. And it's probably changed me a lot . . . the marriage was on real shaky ground there for a while . . . If you're not willing to work through the hard times, you're just not going to make it.

—Jan, age 64, married to Art for 41 years

These quotes illustrate, in two very different ways, why forgiveness is such an important topic for those of us who study personal relationships. Aaron was one of our students when she offered her thoughts on what for many is the most unforgivable of relational transgressions. We know from our research that some partners *do* eventually negotiate forgiveness after affairs, but Aaron speaks for us in linking the choice to forgive to the moral values that govern relationships. Forgiveness is partly a process of identifying and rectifying wrongdoing in our relationships, whether it happens at work, in our families, or among friends. Aaron suggested further to her classmates that there would be "nothing more to talk about" if her fiancé cheated. Here, we would respectfully disagree. Even under the most dire circumstances, partners are compelled to communicate as they become aware of transgressions, express strong emotions, and explore causes and potential consequences of relational events. They may choose to hold a grudge, seek retribution, or start down the more hopeful and compassionate path that leads to forgiveness and, possibly, reconciliation. But, in each case, communicative acts signal intentions, redefine relational possibilities and limitations, and propel them toward the relational future.

As participants in one of our studies, Jan and her husband told their story one day over cups of coffee in their comfortable living room. They remind us of a second important theme, one that complements Aaron's emphasis on moral accountability: forgiveness can be a crucial step in the processes of repairing and maintaining the relationships we really care about. We interviewed nearly 60 couples like Jan and Art, most of whom had endured searing relational pain at some point in long relationships (most had lasted more than four decades). Confronted with a relational crisis, Art and Jan began a lengthy and painful process of forgiveness, one that continues today, but one that eventually restored their sense of relational justice, mutual respect, and love. Years after the affair, they are again happy. Jan is convinced that their relationship is stronger, in part because she eventually let go of her hostility and an understandable desire for revenge.

Most of us have committed less dramatic relational transgressions than those contemplated by Aaron and Jan—times when we sorely needed forgiveness because our behavior harmed a valued relationship. However, we have learned that people disagree about the very nature of forgiveness, when it is called for, and how it relates to other important concepts such as relational justice, atonement, and reconciliation. It turns out that theologians, philosophers, and scientists struggle with these issues too. They have for many years. In this first chapter, we explore these different conceptualizations of forgiveness, both as a theoretical construct and as an important element of human relationships. We do so with an eye on the larger goal of this book, which is to present forgiveness primarily as a communication phenomenon, a process that gets negotiated by those who have been hurt as well as those who have been responsible for the pain.

In later chapters, we describe the key elements of the forgiveness process (Chapter 2), and present communication theories that help us understand and explain how forgiveness is communicated (Chapter 3). In Chapter 4, we look closely at the communication behaviors partners use for identifying transgressions, managing emotion, making sense of their relational circumstances, seeking and granting forgiveness, and renegotiating the moral standards that define relationships. Chapter 5 helps the reader practice forgiveness more effectively, by drawing from the promising work of therapists and successful experiences shared by participants in our research projects. Finally, Chapter 6 draws heavily on our personal experiences as forgiveness researchers to illustrate the conundrums we faced and the methodological "tradeoffs" we made. This final chapter also shares the personal transformations that arose from this challenging and rewarding work.

❖ WHY IS FORGIVENESS IMPORTANT?

At the time of this writing, the newspaper headlines are shouting horrifying news about a disturbed man who invaded a one-room schoolhouse in rural Pennsylvania, taking hostage a group of schoolgirls. Inexplicably, the gunman methodically shot the young women in cold blood, then killed himself. At Virginia Tech University a disturbed student launched a murderous rampage against professors and fellow students. From a Colorado school comes a similar report: several teenaged girls sexually assaulted and at least one killed by a lone psychopath who also commits suicide. As stories of these chilling accounts fade, puzzling new ones emerge. Amish families in Pennsylvania break the silence of their grieving to make it known that, in keeping with their religious beliefs, they have forgiven the murderer and offered condolences to his family. In Colorado, parents of the slain girl quietly urge their neighbors to forgive and their community to heal. These acts of forgiveness made by families who have been victimized by horrific transgressions prompt wide admiration, but spur public comments by theologians, philosophers, and therapists. Is it appropriate for families to forgive on behalf of the murder victims? Is it good for a society when murder is forgiven? We take up these questions later, but clearly forgiveness is a matter of considerable public concern at this very moment.

Of course, for most of us the topic of forgiveness arises from less troubling circumstances, times when we sorely needed forgiveness because our behavior harmed a valued relationship. Moreover, nearly everyone has struggled to find the right response to the hurtful actions of a friend, coworker, family member, or romantic partner. Should I seek revenge? Hold a grudge? Try to "get over it"? Can I really forgive someone whose behavior caused me such emotional pain?

In the last decade, forgiveness has emerged as a vital topic as scholars and moral leaders have addressed the pain inflicted in human relationships and the means by which it can be healed. South African cleric Desmond Tutu's book, *No Future Without Forgiveness* (1999), documented the processes of the Truth and Reconciliation Commission in South Africa during the mid-1990s. For Tutu, forgiveness was a difficult but essential part of that country's recovery from the evils perpetrated in the name of racial apartheid. The re-release of Simon Wiesenthal's book (1969/1997), *The Sunflower: On the Possibilities and Limits of Forgiveness*, has catalyzed dialogue about forgiveness. This small book examines the true story of a Jew incarcerated in a concentration camp during World War II and his encounter with one of his persecutors, a dying Nazi SS man. Wiesenthal asks a variety of world leaders, religious and secular, whether they would have responded with forgiveness had they found themselves in the place of the Jewish Holocaust survivor. In the realm of social science, the recent *Handbook of Forgiveness* (Worthington, 2005a) presents the work of a growing cadre of forgiveness researchers. Some of their studies were funded by the Templeton Foundation, an influential organization that sees forgiveness as a fruitful intersection for theological and scientific inquiry. Forgiveness has also found its way into popular U.S. culture, as evidenced by recent episodes on the ever-popular *Oprah Winfrey Show* and a growing number of self-help books on the topic.

Although interest in forgiveness has increased rapidly everywhere, we are most encouraged that academics have begun to think seriously about the topic. The interest stems from the fact that forgiveness is a rich but not well-understood phenomenon, one with the potential to have real effects on the well-being of individuals, relationships, and communities. Worthington's (2005a) *Handbook of Forgiveness* signifies that research has expanded enough to warrant publication of a comprehensive synthesis of academic publications. Nevertheless, some scholars approach the topic with strong feelings of skepticism, because the concept strikes them as "fuzzy," unrealistically optimistic, or better suited to theological rather than scientific methods of study. We welcome these kinds of concerns because they force us to be clear about what forgiveness is, what it is not, and how forgiveness affects our own relationships.

As communication researchers, we emphasize the *socially negotiated* aspects of forgiveness rather than the psychological or sociological dimensions. One of us defines forgiveness from an understanding of its deep roots in Christian theology. The other takes a more secular and justice-oriented perspective, emphasizing forgiveness as an important component of relational ethics. We both share the desire of scientists to develop a deeper understanding of forgiveness processes and how people can use that knowledge to improve the quality of their relationships. To give the reader a sense of where we are headed in this first chapter, we offer our own definition here. We will address each of its elements after surveying the vast conceptual landscape that surrounds this complex construct.

Forgiveness is a relational process whereby harmful conduct is acknowledged by one or both partners; the harmed partner extends undeserved mercy to the perceived transgressor; one or both partners experience a transformation from negative to positive psychological states, and the meaning of the relationship is renegotiated, with the possibility of reconciliation.

❖ THEOLOGICAL FOUNDATIONS

Forgiveness has long been the subject of discussion by theologians and philosophers. In organizing this brief review, we examine the role of forgiveness in several religious traditions. The relationship between forgiveness, repentance, and reconciliation emerges as a primary historical concern. We then examine how some of these concepts have been updated and applied in a variety of contexts ranging from therapy to international diplomacy. In developing a contemporary definition of forgiveness, we look to the recent social science literature, with a particular interest in those studies that contrast definitions offered by scholars with those used by laypersons. Finally, we present our communicative definition, acknowledging its debt to the study of classical rhetoric, with a particular emphasis on the genre known as *apologia*.

Forgiveness is studied from both secular and spiritual perspectives, but its growing interest to scholars and laypersons may stem from its prominent role in familiar religious traditions. The complex and sometimes disturbing questions raised by modern relationships have encouraged some scholars to blend science and faith as they search for answers. Helmick (2001) is typical of those who are frustrated with the "intellectual mainstream," explaining:

> The devastating cruelty and violence of the twentieth century have finally taught the intellectual mainstream, so long alienated from religion, that the three holy icons of The Modern Age—science, rational enlightenment and liberal politics—have not in fact answered all the questions. (p. 84)

Postmodernists "now look to the wisdom traditions, including often the whole spectrum of traditional faiths, to supply what modernism has failed to provide" (Helmick, 2001, p. 84).

The notion of forgiveness surfaces in certain early Hindu texts (Rye et al., 2000). However, early Jewish and Christian writings place a more fully developed conceptual understanding of forgiveness between God and humankind. The sacred scriptures of each of these religions emphasize the centrality of forgiveness as a means of reconciliation between God and humankind. Kirkup (1993) argues:

> The root is the figure of Abraham, the founder of the three main western religions of Judaism, Christianity, and Islam. It was Abraham's departure from Mesopotamia, both literally and figuratively, that provided the foundation to these religions. This foundation involves three main concepts: (1) Creation is good. (2) God is merciful. (3) We, created in God's likeness, have a duty to imitate God and be merciful towards each other. (p. 83)

The Hebrew scriptures describe a sacrificial system whereby the high priest intercedes for the people and gains God's forgiveness. Through various sacrificial rites, the demands of justice are met (sin is paid for) and forgiveness is given (Israel's relationship to God is restored). Many contemporary Jews still celebrate Yom Kippur to commemorate God's forgiveness.

Early Christians, who were mostly Jewish, believed the crucifixion (sacrifice) of Christ was, once and for all, the act of justice that was needed to restore the relationship between God and humankind. In the Christian New Testament, Jesus emphasized the importance of God-human forgiveness, but he also linked the idea of God's forgiveness to the importance of human beings forgiving one another. Jesus taught his disciples to ask God to "forgive us our debts as we forgive our debtors" (Matthew 6:12). Perhaps the most magnanimous example of forgiveness comes from Jesus when he prayed for his persecutors while being crucified, saying, "Father forgive them, for they know not what they do" (Luke 23:34).

Islamic perspectives also view God as merciful. Islamic scripture expands on the contexts in which forgiveness is useful by showing the forgiving Muhammad to be a leader of the State (Rye et al., 2000). In Buddhist and Hindu writings, karma is a central tenet. These religions encourage forgiveness-like behavior because justice is maintained through karma. Knowing that justice is taken care of, for example, allows Buddhists to emphasize the practice of "forbearance" and "pity" (compassion) as a means of keeping others from suffering (Rye et al., 2000).

Repentance and Reconciliation

The connection between forgiveness and reconciliation is an important theme in traditional Christian and Jewish writings. Repentance is instrumental in the process of forgiveness. For example, Jesus makes the statement in Luke 17 (New International Version), "If your brother sins, rebuke him, and if he repents, forgive him." Jewish rabbis have gone to great lengths to specify the importance of repentance in the forgiveness process. Heschel (1996) states, "In Judaism . . . forgiveness requires both atonement and restitution" (p. 172). Atonement makes amends for the wrong done and restitution restores the damaged relationship to its original state.

According to Dorff (1998), the process of teshuva is "a full-blown return to the right path and to good standing with the community and, indeed, with God" (p. 38). It is not completely clear from rabbinic writings how teshuva is enacted; however, Dorff suggests an eight-step process based on work by the philosopher-rabbi Maimonides (1140–1204). Dorff notes the process varies with the type of offense. To begin, there must be acknowledgement that one has done something wrong. This could involve public confession and expressions of remorse as well as a commitment not to sin this way again. These are followed by an offer of compensation to the offended party and a request for forgiveness. Finally, the offender resolves to avoid the conditions that led to the offense and to act differently. Significantly, Dorff sees this process as one enacted between the offender and offended (and possibly the larger community) and considers all of these steps to be crucial elements of the larger forgiveness process (p. 43).

Kirkup (1993) conceptualizes the repentance process around three elements: admission, restitution, and discipline. *Admission* involves confession of one's wrongdoing. This confession may be general (as when it is a part of a religious ritual of confession) or specific (often when addressing the offended party directly). For example, a child's simple "sorry" is insufficient for a deep adult transgression. This confession may be public or private. Second, *restitution* may be physical (returning a stolen object) or symbolic (when physical restitution is impossible). Finally, *discipline* recognizes the offender's attempts to address the weakness that led to the offense.

In this tradition, once an offender has executed the steps of repentance, it is the duty of the offended party to forgive (Kirkup, 1993). Dorff (1998) states:

> forgiveness becomes the duty of the victim after the offender has done his or her best to make amends, act differently in the future, and has asked for forgiveness at most three times . . . where the offender has undergone the entire process of return, forgiveness is required, even when the wrong can never be righted fully. (p. 45)

In essence, then, from a Jewish perspective, forgiveness is an interpersonal process. That is, forgiveness involves public confession, restitution, and the rebuilding of trust through changed actions, all of which obligate forgiveness in return, often with reconciliation as the outcome.

Certain contemporary forgiveness scholars also embrace the relationship between forgiveness and reconciliation. North (1987), for example, holds that

> Typically an act of wrongdoing brings about a distancing of the wrongdoer from the one he has harmed. . . . Forgiveness is a way of healing the damage done to one's relations with the wrongdoer, or at least a first step towards a full reconciliation. (pp. 502–503)

Even stronger, Hargrave (1994) believes that "the work of forgiving demands that a victim enter back into the relationship with the very people that hurt him or her unjustly" (p. 345). Volf (2001) emphasizes the importance of reconciliation by distinguishing between reconciliation and cheap reconciliation: "cheap reconciliation sets 'justice' and 'peace' against each other as alternatives. To pursue cheap reconciliation means to give up on the struggle for freedom, to renounce the pursuit of justice, to put up with oppression" (p. 35). True reconciliation, on the other hand, recognizes that "forgiveness is an element . . . in which the search for justice is an integral and yet subordinate element" (p. 47).

Identifying justice as an important component of forgiveness and reconciliation (Botcharova, 2001; Volf, 2001) is consistent with Enright and Fitzgibbons's (2000) emphasis that reconciliation requires the reestablishment of trust. Worthington (2001) discusses this process in light of managing unforgiveness: "reconciliation is the restoration of trust in a relationship where trust has been violated, sometimes repeatedly. Reconciliation involves not just *forgiveness* but also many other ways of reducing *unforgiveness*" (p. 176). Unforgiveness consists of an emotional complex of resentment, bitterness, hatred, hostility, residual anger, and fear. Unforgiveness intensifies when people ruminate about the transgression. Forgiveness is but one way of managing unforgiveness and moving toward reconciliation. Others include justice-seeking strategies, conflict resolution, psychological mechanisms such as denial, and simply forbearing or accepting.

Overall, the concept of reconciliation has been underdeveloped in the literature. Often reconciliation is referenced in simplistic terms without definition. The reality is that reconciliation has various component parts and may take various forms or take place in various levels. For example, Mullet, Girard, and Bakhshi's (2004) work identifies lay perceptions of what constitutes repentance. Their repentance factor included items that represent the offender accepting his wrongs, righting his wrongs, behaving better in the future, making amends, and being more likely to forgive you in the future.

Kelley's (1998) early forgiveness work identifying relational consequences provides evidence that reconciliation may occur in stages or at various levels or types. For example, some narratives reported relationships returning to normal after forgiveness. This, of course, would be the standard understanding of reconciliation. Other relationships, however, changed in type (e.g., from dating partners to friends) or strengthened or weakened from their original state, indicating that although many relationships were "reconciled," they had changed in significant ways.

Contemporary applications

Its close association with religious traditions may be why many scholars and clinicians embrace the notion of forgiveness. It may also explain the skeptical reactions of others. Certainly many clients and practitioners are amenable to forgiveness-based therapy because of consistency with their spiritual beliefs (Mahoney, Rye, & Pargament, 2005). Rye et al. (2000) contended that because of their long history and extensive development, theological perspectives provide social scientists with a rich language for understanding how forgiveness might be enacted in contemporary relationships. For example, Mahoney et al. (2005) argue that from a spiritual perspective interpersonal violations may be seen as desecrations, or acts that violate a "sanctified aspect of life" (p. 58). The emotional trauma associated with transgressions might be better understood when they are framed as desecrations of valued spousal, family, or friend relationships.

Religious perspectives are being used to understand forgiveness in other social contexts. For example, Kirkup (1993) used religious principles to provide practical guidelines for mediation processes. He suggests three principles to a "truer definition of forgiveness" (p. 80). First, lasting peace involves forgiveness, no matter how minimal or covert. Second, a mature approach to forgiving will be neither naïve nor cynical. Finally, forgiveness requires hope. After reviewing the religious history and stories of forgiveness, Kirkup concludes with 14 guidelines for mediators to consider. These guidelines can be summed as follows. Forgiveness involves hope and work, and takes many shapes and degrees. Forgiveness is achieved through repentance, which involves taking the offense seriously, while at the same time not humiliating the offender. Serious conflicts require concrete actions toward peace. Forgiveness helps prevent conflicts from escalating and is typically a private process unless the conflict is so extensive as to involve the larger community.

Montville has argued for the significant role of religion in healing international conflicts through "track two" diplomacy (Montville, 1990). Track two diplomacy uses informal structures to accomplish peace. These nontraditional diplomats place less emphasis on political goals, but rather focus on psychosocial ends, including forgiveness. Botcharova (2001) has developed a model for track two diplomacy on the basis of her work with leaders of ethnic and religious communities in Bosnia, Serbia, Croatia, and other conflict professionals worldwide. For Botcharova, "The concept of forgiveness is at the core of the model and is seen as the culmination of a healing process that makes it possible for the parties in conflict to move forward to reconciliation" (p. 303).

❖ SOCIAL SCIENCE APPROACHES

Recently two leading forgiveness researchers argued that "no consensus exists on the dimensions of forgiveness or the steps and processes that it involves" (Kearns & Fincham, 2004, p. 838). This frustrating lack of conceptual clarity results from several factors. First, although the research has expanded rapidly over the last ten years or so, a decade is a relatively short time for researchers to forge agreement. A second problem is that forgiveness scholars find homes in multiple disciplines. Psychologists, counselors, theologians, justice studies scholars, and political scientists are among those who study the phenomenon. And, of course, two communication researchers are authors of the book you now hold in your hands. Unfortunately, researchers often fail to talk over the walls that separate neighboring disciplines. The third and, we believe, most important impediment is that forgiveness is simply a multifaceted social construct. Like those offered for love and friendship, forgiveness definitions are shaped by the purposes and perspectives of those using the term. For example, a marriage therapist sees forgiveness as a tool for relationship repair. Theologians conceptualize forgiveness as one component of a larger system of religious values or as a spiritual mandate from God. Psychological researchers view forgiveness as an individual decision influenced by motives, needs, and personality traits.

A Prototype Approach

Concepts that defy simple definition, such as love, commitment, jealousy, and, of course, forgiveness, have been studied fruitfully using a "prototype" approach (Fehr, 1988; Sharpsteen, 1993). In applying this approach to the "fuzzy" construct of intimacy, Prager (1995) identified five characteristics of good definitions. First, a useful definition will integrate current conceptualizations of the construct. Second, it will recognize the various loci in which the phenomenon is encountered. Regarding this point, there is considerable debate in forgiveness circles about whether forgiveness is a psychological or social phenomenon. Worthington (2005b) describes it thus: "Definitional squabbles concern whether the communication of forgiveness or talk and behavior about transgressions should be included within the definition or treated as a separate interpersonal process" (p. 5). Prager's third suggestion is to carefully distinguish the concept from those that are used similarly. In the case of forgiveness, it is critical, for both theoretical and applied purposes, to differentiate from such concepts as tolerance, acceptance, and reconciliation. Fourth, fuzzy constructs are characterized by a "shifting template of features" (p. 13). In the case of forgiveness, features may shift by culture and level of analysis (international conflict versus interpersonal conflict) among other factors. Fifth, Prager suggests that differences in research and lay definitions should be acknowledged. In fact, differences between lay and scholarly definitions contribute to the fuzziness of the forgiveness construct.

Integrating Definitions of Forgiveness

Scholars and laypersons mention certain characteristics of forgiveness with enough regularity to consider them central features. At the same time, laypersons equate forgiveness with similar but different relational concepts, such as acceptance or reconciliation.

Researcher definitions

In offering one of the early definitions, Enright and colleagues integrated the work of ancient and modern thinkers to offer this formulation: "[forgiveness involves] the casting off of deserved punishments, the abandonment of negative reactions, the imparting of love toward the other person, self-sacrificial nature, the potential restoration of the relationship, and positive benefits for the forgiver" (Enright, Eastin, Golden, Sarinopoulos, & Freedman, 1992, p. 88). Features of this definition resonate in later work, including the decision to forgo punishment and the replacement of negative reactions with more positive ones (see also Enright, Gassin, & Wu, 1992; Kearns & Fincham, 2004). McCullough, Pargament, and Thoresen (2000) argue that the transformation from positive to negative affect is one of the central features across definitions:

> A consensual definition might be more feasible than one might initially imagine. All existing definitions seem to be built on one core feature: When people forgive, their responses toward . . . people who offended or injured them become more positive and less negative. (p. 9)

McCullough et al. (2000) also emphasized additional characteristics of the forgiveness process. They defined forgiveness as "intra-individual, prosocial change toward a perceived transgressor that is situated within a specific interpersonal context" (p. 9). New here is a perception that a wrong has occurred. The authors note the importance of *perception*. In essence, the offended believe they have been wronged in some way, which may or may not be corroborated by the offender or observers. Finally, forgiveness is seen as an intra-individual process that takes place within an interpersonal context. Forgiveness is a cognitive and emotional process but it is oriented toward another person.

Lay definitions

As Kearns and Fincham (2004) argue, "It is possible that the lay conception of forgiveness plays a causal role in the events of forgiveness" (p. 853). Everyday understandings of forgiveness may limit or liberate relational partners. For example, those who believe that reconciliation is a necessary part of forgiveness may be more reluctant to forgive, simply because reconciliation is an unpalatable relationship alternative. It wasn't until we studied detailed reports provided by laypersons that we realized that time should be an essential component of any forgiveness model. For example, some participants emphasized the "passing of time" (sometimes minutes, sometimes years) as an essential element of forgiveness, because it allows emotions to cool, people to change, and memories to fade.

Two studies looked specifically at how laypeople define forgiveness. Zechmeister and Romero (2002) asked participants to write "forgiving" and "unforgiving" narratives. The former included more positive affect. They also yielded more positive outcomes and more event closure. In an earlier study, Kelley (1998, 2001) asked lay participants to write forgiveness narratives describing situations in which they forgave, were forgiven, or requested forgiveness. Participants described multiple types of forgiveness, including intellectual/emotional, conditional, and unilateral/ bilateral forgiveness. The intellectual/emotional distinction refers to the difference between decision-making and feeling components. Laypersons reported thinking about and choosing forgiveness, but they also discussed forgiveness as a change in feelings toward the transgressor. Worthington (2005b) has also addressed this distinction, using the term "decisional forgiveness" to represent changes in intentions. For Worthington, emotional forgiveness is, "a replacement of negative, unforgiving emotions with positive, other-oriented emotions" (p. 4).

"Conditional forgiveness" sets limits on when and how forgiveness will be exercised. In reference to her father, one young woman wrote, "I told him I would accept his apology, however, we both knew that there was the stipulation that he stay off of the booze." Others described "unconditional forgiveness," which is offered without contingency and is unretractable. Some of Kelley's respondents believed it was their religious duty to be unconditionally forgiving. One of our students told us, "It is not my job to play God. If God can forgive me, then I should forgive others. No questions asked."

"Unilateral" and "bilateral" forgiveness are distinguished by whether or not forgiveness is reciprocated. According to Kelley's (2001) respondents, when one party is clearly to blame, forgiveness can be offered only by the wounded party. In this unilateral conception, forgiveness is requested by the offender and granted by the victim. However, laypersons often describe forgiveness as a "two way street," usually because the parties share at least some of the blame. Bilateral forgiveness is reciprocal in nature, signaled by statements such as, "Well, I guess we both lost our tempers."

Other studies have focused on the *similarities and differences* in layperson and researcher definitions. For example, Kanz (2000) discovered that both researchers and laypeople believed that anger dissipates during forgiveness. Interestingly, only laypersons believed that reconciliation was an essential part of forgiveness. Kearns and Fincham (2004), in five separate studies, supported the idea that laypeople use a forgiveness prototype similar to that suggested by researchers. Both researchers and laypeople acknowledged that (1) forgivers' responses toward the offender become less negative, and (2) forgiveness involves cognition, affect, and behavior. However, they noted some differences between researcher and lay conceptualizations. In contrast to most scholarly definitions, 12% of lay participants listed condoning and excusing as an attribute of forgiveness, 28% believed that "forgetting" was central to forgiving, and 21% believed that reconciliation is a central feature of forgiveness. In addition, laypeople tended to agree that negative aspects of forgiveness include feelings of weakness, being a "pushover," and giving the other person permission to hurt you again.

What Forgiveness Is Not

McCullough et al. (2000) find general agreement that forgiveness is not pardoning, forgetting, condoning, excusing, denying, or reconciliation. The following section makes important distinctions between these concepts and forgiveness.

Forgiveness is not pardoning

Typically practiced in judicial proceedings, *pardons* differ from forgiveness in that they are issued by impartial judges, not victims (Enright et al., 1992). This of course raises an important question. Who has the "right" to forgive?

> ### The Right to Forgive?
>
> In 1997, a 14-year-old high school student opened fire at a Kentucky high school. Three teenage girls attending a Bible study were killed. Shortly after, several other students posted a sign for the murderer stating, "We forgive you, Michael." There was an outcry from people who claimed that the students couldn't forgive the murderer because they were not his victims. A subsequent article in the *Wall Street Journal* (Prager, 1997) condemned a "feel-good doctrine of automatic forgiveness." This story raises two related issues. First, can you forgive someone if you are not the victim? Second, is forgiveness a process that extends across social networks? In other words, the students (and the larger school community) are victims in the sense that they lost beloved friends and endured a horrible violation of the moral code that governed relations among community members. In this regard, the widely admired cleric Desmond Tutu describes the South African concept of "ubuntu"—the notion that what affects you must also affect me as a member of your community. From this perspective, even "secondary" victims have a right to seek and grant forgiveness to some degree.

Forgiveness is not forgetting

Perhaps the best known forgiveness maxim is "forgive and forget." This injunction is problematic for forgiveness theorists. Generally speaking, victims cannot forget painful experiences, even when they want to. Forgetting is not a simple act of the will. Yet, victims may still grant forgiveness. Second, forgetting implies that moral violations have been overlooked, that lessons learned from the incident may have been forgotten in the process. In fact, ongoing acknowledgment of the transgression may be the factor that most distinguishes forgiveness from other related concepts such as condoning, excusing, and denying.

Forgiveness is not condoning, excusing, or denying

Condoning differs from forgiveness in that it implies accepting a moral infraction, often because of circumstantial pressure. Enright and Fitzgibbons (2000) argue that condoners often continue to see offenders in a negative light, whereas forgivers view them as people worthy of respect. On the other hand, *excusing* an act reframes it so it is no longer perceived as a moral infraction. There is nothing to forgive because the offender escapes responsibility for the act. Imagine a situation in which a teenager with only a driver's permit loses control of the car and causes a fender bender. Forgiveness may be inapplicable in this situation (assuming the teen was being attentive) because the accident might be blamed on inexperience. Finally, *denying* makes forgiveness irrelevant by claiming that no transgression took place.

Additional conceptual distinctions

Enright and Fitzgibbons (2000) created a checklist of "philosopher's distinctions between forgiveness and related concepts," adding conciliation, justification, becoming less disappointed, balancing scales, self-centering, and reconciliation to the list (p. 38). They also noted that commonly expressed statements about forgiveness frequently oversimplify a complex and multifaceted concept (see the textbox for examples). *Conciliation* differs from forgiveness in trying to please the perceived offenders or placate them through self-condemnation. In the same way, a *justification* fails to fully acknowledge wrongdoing and hurt. There is no need to forgive an action that is truly justified. Instead, we accept that there was sufficient reason for the action. *Becoming less disappointed* is also an unsatisfying substitute for forgiveness. It merely suggests that the victim has, to a degree, accepted poor treatment.

Common (but Incomplete) Understandings of Forgiveness

I need to "forgive and forget"
I might forgive but I won't *ever* forget
Just get over it!
I've just accepted what happened and I am moving on
She doesn't *deserve* to be forgiven
Forgiveness is just a "feel good," quick fix
I didn't want him to stay upset, so I forgave him
He needed to be forgiven, so I just did it
Asking for forgiveness would be "giving in"
I can forgive her but God will punish her later
I won't let him *get to me*
I forgave her one time, but now she is in my debt
I just wanted to keep the peace in the family, so I forgave him

—adapted from Enright & Fitzgibbons, 2000 (p. 38)

Balancing the scales and self-centering, as described by Enright and Fitzgibbons (2000), may be part of a forgiveness process, but they are insufficient by themselves. *Balancing the scales* is essentially an attempt to restore fairness or justice to a relationship. The restoration of relational justice is essential to our own *Negotiated Morality Theory* (NMT) of forgiveness (see Chapter 3). However, balance can be achieved through responses that are antithetical to forgiveness, such as revenge. On the other hand, *self-centering* focuses on the therapeutic goal of repairing the self, while ignoring the offender's role and our relationship with the offender. For Enright and Fitzgibbons (2000), this "is one of the most serious misunderstandings of forgiveness" (p. 46). Although self-help is a positive goal, these clinicians believe that forgivers must acknowledge the perceived offender's responsibility as well as his or her humanity. For them, forgiveness ultimately requires compassion for those who hurt us, whenever that is possible.

Forgiveness is distinct from reconciliation

Historically, forgiveness and reconciliation have often been linked. The role of compassion in forgiveness makes reconciliation something to at least be considered. Yet, the relationship between these two concepts has generated considerable debate. Marriage therapists often emphasize the reconciliation potential of forgiveness-based interventions. For example, Hargrave and Sells (1997) define forgiveness to include "the release of blame and reconciliation" (p. 43). Hargrave's (1994) forgiveness model identifies two central steps: "exonerating" and "forgiving." *Exonerating* represents the part of the process that is primarily psychological—achieving insight into the transgression and understanding or reframing the offender's actions. *Forgiving* is more action oriented. It involves the "opportunity for compensation" and "an overt act of forgiveness." The act of forgiveness typically involves an apology and a rewriting of the relationship contract, elements that are similar to other researchers' descriptions of reconciliation (Enright & Fitzgibbons, 2000; Worthington, 1998).

Importantly, Hargrave's (1994) conceptualization was developed in the context of marital therapy, where reconciliation is often the goal. However, Enright and Fitzgibbons (2000) advise counselors that forgiveness "offers compassion," but they distinguish it from reconciliation. In fact, reconciliation with a perceived offender may not be wise or desirable (McCullough et al., 2000). For example, trying to reconcile with an abusive spouse may place one in a psychologically or physically dangerous situation (Rye, Folck, Heim, Olszewski, & Traina, 2004). Moreover, conceptualizing reconciliation as a required component of forgiveness unnecessarily empowers the offender to stop the forgiveness process. Enright and Fitzgibbons (2000) grapple with this issue as they state, "Forgiveness is one person's individual choice to abandon resentment and to adopt friendlier attitudes toward a wrongdoer . . . [It] is a free choice on the part of the one wronged" (p. 41). However, as we saw in the section on religious perspectives, forgiveness is integral to healthy, full reconciliation. We consider these concepts to be distinct but closely connected.

Forgiveness and justice

Any complete treatment of forgiveness as a construct needs to explore its relationship to *justice*. Enright and the Human Development Study Group (1991) claimed that harmed individuals face a basic choice between justice and mercy. Essentially, justice is the perception that one is treated fairly or equitably within a given system of rights, responsibilities, and moral values. Forgiveness is a "merciful" response to violations of justice (Hill, Exline, & Cohen, 2005; Worthington, 2001). However, as Worthington notes, retaliation and retribution are opposing responses often used when the "goal is to reestablish justice" (p. 478).

Merciful and justice-seeking behaviors can be usefully aligned along a continuum. Acceptance, discussed above, is positioned at the mercy end of the continuum. On the opposite side are extreme justice-seeking strategies like revenge or retaliation. Forgiveness is inherently merciful but it demands recognition of wrongful behavior. We place it near the middle of the continuum, but closer to the mercy side (see Figure 1.1). As Volf (2001) posits, "Forgiveness does not stand outside

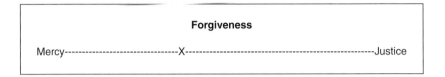

Figure 1.1   Forgiveness Blends Mercy and Justice

of justice. To the contrary, forgiveness is possible only against the back-drop of a tacit affirmation of justice. Forgiveness always entails blame." (p. 45). Consider a coworker treated poorly by a peer who unfairly "takes the credit" for a joint project. The offended party may respond in a merciful manner (e.g., choosing to communicate constructively rather than pouting or avoiding the remorseful offender). However, in the interest of justice she may insist that wrongdoing be acknowledged and the rules of the relationship be reexamined. This blending of mercy and acknowledgment may be a prerequisite to eventual reconciliation.

A Communicative Perspective

Although theologians and social scientists have portrayed forgive-ness as an interpersonal process, they have been slow to consider for-giveness as a communicative construct. Ironically, however, a form of communication with implications for *forgiveness-seeking* has been the primary concern of rhetoricians for several millennia. We refer to the study of *apologia,* perhaps the most enduring of rhetorical genres (Ware & Linkugel, 1973). In the *Rhetoric,* Aristotle (1954) foregrounds the various rhetorical devices used in public situations by offenders and illustrates that forgiveness arises from the interaction of speaker and audience. Recent high-profile examples are found in the use of strategic ambiguity in President Clinton's apology to the nation for the Monica Lewinsky affair (Simons, 2000) and the Roman Catholic Church's arguably unsuccessful apologies to the victims of sex abuses commit-ted by clergy (Dunne, 2004). In the interpersonal realm, communica-tion researchers have produced numerous studies on the means by which speakers account for failures and redress misdeeds (Cody & McLaughlin, 1988). One of these, apology, is often identified as a cru-cial element of the forgiveness process (McCullough, Worthington, & Rachal, 1997).

A communicative approach to forgiveness in personal relationships involves social interaction as well as a psychological transformation.

We see it as the primary means by which harmful conduct is interpreted and relationships renegotiated. To repeat our definition

*Forgiveness is a relational process whereby harmful conduct is acknowl-
edged by one or both partners; the harmed partner extends undeserved
mercy to the perceived transgressor; one or both partners experience a transformation from negative to positive psychological states, and the meaning of
the relationship is renegotiated, with the possibility of reconciliation.*

Three elements are critical to this definition: (1) it is relationally
based, (2) a wrong must be identified, and (3) there is a renegotiation
of the relationship's meaning. First, this definition is relationally based.
We recognize that forgiveness is both a psychological and communicative phenomenon. Forgiveness prompts relational partners to renegotiate their relationship, which may (or may not) lead to some level of
reconciliation. Other individuals may feel the need to say the words
"I forgive you" as a way of managing their own psychological health.
We recognize that reconciliation is not always an outcome of forgiveness processes. Yet, our primary focus is on *forgiveness as a central part
of relationship renegotiation.*

Second, this communicatively grounded definition emphasizes
overt recognition of harmful behavior. We recognize that reconciliation
takes multiple forms. However, from our point of view, reconciliation
efforts that fail to acknowledge wrongdoing proceed without forgiveness. Relational negotiations characterized by tolerance, acceptance, or
excuses more often lead to what some writers call false or "cheap" forgiveness (Volf, 2001). In our minds, forgiveness is merciful but at the
same time promotes relational justice and mutual respect.

Finally, our definition emphasizes that forgiveness inevitably
changes relationships. The process of redefinition unfolds over time as
partners reexamine personal and relational values, collectively remember the forgiveness episode, and reconsider their future. The negotiation
may bring about reconciliation of varying degrees, it may lead to a
stronger or weaker relationship, or it may result in relational dissolution.

2

Elements of the Forgiveness Process

❖   ❖   ❖

I had a good friend named Kevin. We were close but at times I felt he wanted more than that. I found myself putting him down, trying to defend myself so I wouldn't have to deal with him wanting a relationship. He wrote me a letter and told me that I had really hurt him. I felt so horrible! I immediately went to him and asked forgiveness. He forgave me because he still wanted us to be friends. He expressed it to me verbally. However, for a few weeks I don't believe he still emotionally forgave me. I was very happy that he did and careful to never do that again! Our relationship took awhile to rebuild because I had been destructive for so long. It was slow but there came a point when we started to grow again.

—Trang, age 23

T rang's account is in some ways typical of the forgiveness stories told by friends, family members, coworkers, and romantic partners. Forgiveness episodes are uniquely shaped by the relational histories and motives of the parties, and they often evoke emotional reactions like surprise, anger, or guilt. The parties are prompted to engage in individual soul searching and relational sense-making. As in the case of Trang and Kevin, the forgiveness process often leads to a redefinition of the relationship, but that process unfolds over time. Communication is crucial in shaping the relational outcomes of such episodes. In this case, Kevin's efforts to communicate his hurt and Trang's apparently heartfelt request for forgiveness were important factors. Kevin's gradual granting of forgiveness is also familiar. Verbal expressions of forgiveness are often preceded or followed by periods of uncertainty and emotional distress, often revealed through nonverbal behavior.

Although partly a psychological decision of individuals, forgiveness is for several reasons best conceptualized as an interpersonal and relational process. First, forgiveness episodes are triggered by a perceived relational transgression. Trang's "putdowns" were designed to create relational distance, but they were inappropriate in the context of friendship. Second, transgression events, and their consequences, are often complicated by relational expectations and blurry boundaries. Kevin wants "something more," but Trang values the friendship. Moreover, the relationship is likely embedded in a larger relationship web that includes an "audience" of friends and family members. Third, it is evident that the negotiation of forgiveness requires communicative action. Kevin's written message initiates a cycle of interaction through which the parties express emotions, make sense of their behavior, seek and grant forgiveness, and negotiate a relational future. Finally, we simply note that forgiveness episodes have significant relational consequences. As Trang suggests, the communication of forgiveness can lead to relationship recovery, or even stronger relationship bonds. However, negative outcomes, including relationship termination, are also possible.

The purpose of this chapter is to organize and synthesize research on the many factors that potentially shape the communication of forgiveness. We focus on the most important elements of the process, the ones most studied by researchers and most frequently mentioned in forgiveness narratives. Our communication perspective is grounded in the definition offered in Chapter 1.

Forgiveness is a relational process whereby harmful conduct is acknowledged by one or both partners; the harmed partner extends undeserved mercy to the perceived transgressor; one or both partners experience a transformation from negative to positive psychological states, and the mean-ing of the relationship is renegotiated, with the possibility of reconciliation.

Figure 2.1 presents a descriptive model derived in part from care-ful study of the forgiveness stories told by friends, family members, romantic partners, and coworkers. A descriptive model provides a means of organizing and simplifying a complicated process. Chapter 3 presents communication theories that help us understand how partners move through the forgiveness process. Chapter 4 provides in-depth coverage of communication behaviors and strategies.

❖   SENSITIZING CONCEPTS: COMMUNICATION
    AS AN OBSERVATIONAL LENS

Experienced ethnographers know that observers can be quickly over-whelmed by the complexity of the social situations they study. Sensitizing concepts are assumptions and categories that provide a kind of lens for the observer. Using them, researchers bring certain dimensions of com-plex situations into focus. At the same time, other dimensions fade into the background. As scholars of interpersonal and organizational commu-nication, we foreground those aspects of forgiveness that are relational, message-based, and socially negotiated. Psychological and sociological dimensions, although important, are not our *primary* concern. Instead, we use a communicative lens as we examine each component of the model.

In doing so, we first ask how partners use their communication to talk *about* forgiveness or parts of the process. For example, partners might talk to one another about what forgiveness means in their rela-tionship or about the transgressions they could not forgive. In this way, forgiveness is the object of relational communication. Second, we are curious about how communication functions as an intrinsic part of the forgiveness process, the means by which elements of the model are expressed or enacted. Consider the *transgression* component of the model. It is often the case that partners talk *about* a transgression; other times, however, an act of communication *is* the transgression. Uttering an insult, revealing confidences, or failing to share important informa-tion with your partner are all communicative transgressions. In this sense, communication is the means by which forgiveness is *enacted.*

Third, we consider the role of communication as partners *negotiate the relational meaning* of forgiveness episodes. Negotiation implies a process that unfolds over time through a series of interactions. From this point of view, an act like infidelity is a "transgression" only if the

Relational Context (e.g., family, romantic, work, friend)

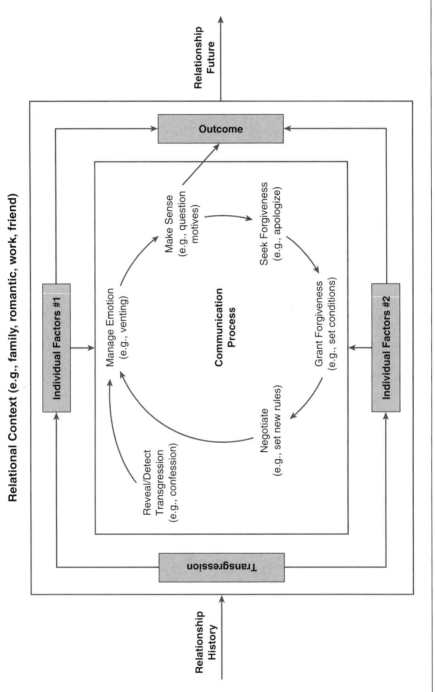

Figure 2.1   Elements of the Forgiveness Process

parties define it that way within the context of their relationship. Moreover, the meaning of the transgression—its seriousness, for example—may change as the parties discuss it, reframe it, share it with others, and jointly remember it.

Finally, we view forgiving communication as a tool in the process of *relationship recovery.* With each communicative act, the parties define their relationship and propel it forward in time. For example, by apologizing for a transgression, an offending partner makes it possible for the parties to move past issues of blame and to considerations of "where we go from here." In another example, offering conditional forgiveness to one's partner necessitates a discussion of how relational rules will be redefined. Clinicians embrace this view of communication; they are concerned with developing interventions or skills that help clients find forgiveness in their relationships.

❖ TRANSGRESSIONS AND
   TRAUMATIC RELATIONAL EVENTS

Most stories of forgiveness proceed from the description of a hurtful act, one that harms the partner or threatens the very definition of the relationship. For that reason, relational transgressions hold a central position in Figure 2.1.

When Samuel and Lisa were first married, she managed the finances. For the young couple (now in their 60s), it seemed the natural thing to do since Lisa's mother had always handled the money in her home. It seems, however, that Mom forgot to pass on her financial skills. Twice in their first two years of marriage Lisa spent the young couple into serious financial trouble. What's more, Lisa was so embarrassed by her inability to keep the books straight that both times she neglected to tell her husband until creditors were practically at the door. Even now, more than 30 years later, Lisa recalls her behavior with a strong sense of shame:

> I could cry now. Why I didn't have confidence is the worst for me. It was mostly that I was ashamed of getting into my own trouble, that I was incompetent. And so it made it look like I didn't have confidence in him.

Samuel recalls the situation vividly:

> She got us into big trouble, but I had to forgive her for not *confiding* in me, not for getting us into financial trouble. Any kind of forgiveness I had to do was to forgive her for not confiding in me.

In personal relationships, the trigger for the forgiveness process is typically a memorable, negative, and hurtful relational incident. Often communication behavior plays an integral part, as in this event. Lisa's financial mismanagement certainly harmed the couple, but it appears her deceptive communication, her unwillingness to confide in her husband, was what really triggered the forgiveness process.

Researchers have long recognized that *communicative transgressions* can be the source of harm in relationships, even as communication behavior is the means by which couples recover from damaging events. Writing more than a decade ago in a volume dedicated to the "dark side" of personal relationships (Cupach & Spitzberg, 1994), researcher Sandra Metts (1994) conceptualized transgressions as violations of relational rules. Working with data collected from several samples of college students, Metts cited such behaviors as flirting with a third party and betraying confidences as rule-breaking transgressions. Writing in the same volume, Vangelisti (1994) focused on *messages* rather than rules. In several studies, she asked undergraduates to describe "a situation in which someone said something that hurt their feelings" (p. 60). Accusations ("you are such a liar') and threats ("if I find out you are ever with that person, never come home again") were among the types of hurtful messages she reported.

Inspired in part by this earlier work, we have been asking romantic couples, both younger and older, to describe events in their relationships that created a need for forgiveness (Kelley, 1998; Kelley & Waldron, 2005; Waldron & Kelley, 2005). Rule violations as described by Metts, and hurtful messages as presented by Vangelisti, certainly trigger forgiveness episodes. However, some fail to "qualify" as forgivable acts, because they are not serious enough, are too serious to be forgiven, or the partner believes forgiveness is an inappropriate social response to the act in question (i.e., as when the act was an unintended mistake or a misunderstanding). As well, events other than rule violations and hurtful messages may trigger a forgiveness episode.

In an interview study, we asked long-term couples (married more than 30 years) to discuss behaviors or events that required them to forgive (for details, see Chapter 6). Their answers were further explored in separate interviews with each partner. A few couples (fewer than 5%) just couldn't recall anything important enough to require forgiveness. Several others could only identify what most people would call minor infractions. However, the large majority described what to them (and us) seemed to be very serious relational incidents, ones that shook the very foundations of their relationships. Most triggering events were *transgressions* clearly attributable to one or both of the partners. Other times, the trigger might be better described as a *traumatic relational experience*, usually emanating from outside the relationship (e.g., the death of a child, a layoff). Here, the connection between the incident and the forgiveness episode was usually indirect. In other words, it was the *reaction* to the event by one or both partners that created the need for forgiveness. For example, when a child dies, partners may exchange hurtful messages of guilt, loss, and blame.

Table 2.1 presents a taxonomy of the forgiveness-requiring events reported by long-term married couples. Jessica Harvey, one of our graduate students, created the taxonomy by using the constant-comparative method of qualitative data analysis. She read and reread a portion of the transcripts, developed a working set of categories, discussed them with various couples and the interviewers on our research team, then "tested" a revised taxonomy on the remainder of the transcripts. This process led her to collapse some of the categories because of redundancy, add some new ones, and adjust the definitions, until more than 90% of the incidents were accounted for (Harvey, 2004). In all, she located 75 distinct triggering events falling into 15 categories.

Traumatic Relational Experiences

Harvey (2004) conceptualized all forgiveness-requiring incidents in terms of relationship "trauma." But only several of her categories describe events that fit our definition of *traumatic relational experiences*—events attributable to forces beyond the direct control of the partners and experienced by them together. For example, her *money* category included job layoffs and financial losses due to natural disasters. *Family tragedies* included the loss of a child to illness or accident. The *in-laws/family* category included some instances of uninvited interference by extended family members. Theories of attribution (e.g., Kelley, 1971) suggest that relational partners distinguish between acts that are under the control of the partner and those that are accidental or controlled by external forces. As we have argued, forgiveness is *most* called for when harmful acts stem from the actions of one's partner. In fact, Vangelisti (1994) reported that messages were less hurtful when they were assumed to be accidental. Thus, unintended traumatic experiences normally shouldn't trigger forgiveness responses.

However, as Harvey's (2004) investigation makes clear, traumatic relational experiences are sometimes included in forgiveness narratives. In some cases, the couple has lingering doubts about culpability. Could the layoff have been avoided if the partner had worked harder? Could the car accident have been avoided with more careful driving? These

Table 2.1   Transgressions Requiring Forgiveness as Reported by
                     Long-Term Married Couples

Trauma	Frequency
Money (mismanagement, priorities)	14
Parenting	9
Health-related	7
Alcoholism/drug dependence	6
In-laws/family	6
Verbal aggression	6
Personality differences	5
Work-related	5
Infidelity	4
Anger/temper	4
Deception/lying	2
Neglect/disengagement	2
Family tragedy	2
Unilateral decisions	2
Public embarrassment	1
Total	**75**

SOURCE: Adapted from Harvey, J. (2004). *Trauma and recovery strategies across the lifespan of long-term married couples.* Phoenix: Arizona State University West. Reprinted with permission of the author.

suspicions might then lead to an exchange of accusations, triggering a cycle of forgiving communication. For Susan and Dan, a series of financial losses caused relational conflicts and a leveling of blame that eventually required forgiveness.

Dan: I started in the business in 1978 and the business went downhill. The economy went bad and I lost the business. And we put everything that I had made, fifty-some thousand dollars, into this business. And lost it all. And previous to that, we lost the house!

Susan: So I began to think he wasn't being a real successful business-
man and I started getting hard feelings about that. We had our
arguments. We've had our ups and downs.

Traumatic relational experiences can also create the emotional conditions that make partners more vulnerable. A long and serious illness
stresses a sick family member but also creates unfair burdens on the
caretaking spouse. In such cases, the burden is unintentional, but it may
lead to impatience or irritability, eventually requiring the partners to
negotiate forgiveness.

Transgression Severity

Most researchers agree that forgiveness is required after serious
breaches in relational trust, but not the minor annoyances and disap-
pointments that characterize normal relational interaction. If anything
seems sure in the growing forgiveness literature, it is that the perceived
severity of a transgression is a primary predictor of how partners approach
forgiveness (Fincham & Beach, 2002). Waldron and Kelley (2005) found
that romantic partners minimized the need for forgiveness when transgressions were considered to be relatively mild. When transgressions
were severe, they responded more cautiously, often making forgiveness conditional. John was offered forgiveness by his girlfriend for
some insulting comments, but "she said we could get back together
again only if I wasn't so critical in the future." These kinds of conditional statements are attempts to maintain a valued relationship while
simultaneously protecting against recurrences.

The importance of offense severity is established in a long line of
research studies on partner responses to social and relational transgressions (Cody & McLaughlin, 1990; Emmers-Sommer, 2003; Metts, 1994).
Truly severe offenses can raise grave doubts about the long-term trustworthiness of the partner or the psychological safety of the relationship
(Worthington & Wade, 1999). Under such conditions, communication is
daunting. The offended partner may be tempted to skip the "communication part" and simply terminate the relationship. However, romantic
partners (Waldron & Kelley, 2005) report that forgiving communication
can be helpful, even for grave transgressions, such as infidelity.

Types of Transgressions

Transgressions are deliberate and harmful acts performed by one
or more partners in a relationship. In Harvey's (2004) analysis, they

include acts of verbal aggression, expressions of anger, public embarrassments, betrayal, unilateral decision making, infidelity, and persistent drug and alcohol abuse, among other things. Although these acts appear to be quite different, experience tells us they can be "boiled down" to three fundamental problems. First, some of these behaviors convey disrespect for the partner and attack his or her identity. Behaviors such as being rude in public or making insults imply that the partner is inferior, devalued, incompetent, and undeserving of equal treatment. Drawing from the work of Goffman (1959), Afifi, Falato, and Weiner (2001) reason that these face-threatening acts are sometimes implicated in the forgiveness process.

Second, some transgressions violate what Hargrave (1994) calls the "relationship covenant." Even if they aren't expressed explicitly, certain values are "hallowed ground" when it comes to our important relationships. In most cases, these include mutual trust, loyalty, collaborative decision making, confidentiality, and honesty, among others. In romantic relationships, the list typically includes sexual exclusivity. As Metts (1994) indicates, some of these values may be encoded as informal rules and behavioral expectations. For example, "no flirting with others" is a common rule in romantic relationships. "Don't ask the boss for special favors" may apply in work settings. A young married woman told us

> While fighting one day, my husband called me stupid. I was so astounded and hurt, I simply closed the door and left. Later we talked about it and he explained his stress and the fact that he did not mean it. I forgave him, but explained that certain things simply shouldn't be said, because I could not forget. "No name calling" has become a rule in our relationship and we stand by it. It's helped us fight fairly.

Autocratic decision making is a common theme in forgiveness episodes reported by married couples. Judy and Dion (now retired) had been married for 15 years when he decided unilaterally to move the family from Pennsylvania to Mississippi (see the textbox for their story). To this day, Judy isn't sure she completely forgives him. There were plenty of things for Judy to be frustrated about: loss of friends, the complications of moving, being near in-laws. But the key transgression was this: "We didn't *share* the decision. And I think that's the biggest thing with relationships. You must share in decisions. You can't have one that just dominates."

Relational Transgressions: The Case of Judy and Dion

Dion and Judy were living a comfortable life in Fallstown, Pennsylvania, when Dion was laid off from a well-paying position at a local plant. Fallstown, a small and friendly community, was a great place to live, but not a great place to find another job.

Dion's father owned a successful construction business in Mississippi, but in the early years of their marriage the couple valued their independence. Dion had little interest in the family business. He wanted to make his own way. And to be honest, Judy just didn't get along with Dion's family. She didn't relish living in the southern part of the country.

Now, 15 years into their marriage, a job offer came from Dion's dad. With no employment prospects on the immediate horizon, Dion jumped at the chance to work in the family business. Spontaneously, he committed himself, Judy, and the kids to move to Jackson. Later that evening, with some trepidation, he shared the decision with his loving and strong-willed wife.

Judy went ballistic.

Mississippi? What about all of the friends they had made in their close-knit community? The thought of moving close to Dion's difficult family was daunting at best. What's more, how could he make this decision without consulting *her*, his wife, his partner? They always made big decisions *together*. As they both admit now, this was not a pretty marital moment. Even so, six weeks later the moving truck was packed, and our once-happy couple was on their way "home."

It took only three years before the truck was packed again and the family was on their way to a new job in a small South Carolina town. Judy and her "outlaws" just couldn't see eye to eye. Even to this day, Judy mutters about Dion's "boneheaded" behavior.

The third general type of transgression involves acts of injustice or unfairness. In work relationships, these transgressions often are perceived as abuses of power. Inequity, favoritism, and unfairness fit here as well. As Waldron (2000) noted after reviewing the reports of numerous blue- and white-collar workers, workplace transgressions are most profound when the power differential between leader and member is pronounced, when the audience includes one's peers, when the violator's public behavior conflicts with previously displayed private behavior, and when the victim believes she or he is acting in the best interests of the organization (as opposed to self-interest). Ken, a middle manager in a large bank, believed he was unjustly criticized by a senior colleague. The situation was made worse by the presence of an audience of peers and managers.

For Ken, this damaging blow to his work identity was an unforgivable violation of the informal rules that govern workplace relationships:

> I was angry—felt humiliated and betrayed. [I] felt like I had been stabbed in the back, with no way to defend myself or explain my position. [Because of the audience] . . . I probably would not have confronted the senior management person in this meeting even if time permitted . . . He forever damaged my credibility. I never trusted him again.

Messages That Hurt

In a series of studies, Vangelisti (1994;Vangelisti & Young, 2000) described hurtful messages, which take the form of accusations, lies, jokes, directives, deceptions, insults, threats, and other devaluing statements. Messages that use negative, intense, harsh language are most damaging. In fact, the use of hurtful words is commonly cited as a triggering factor in forgiveness stories. Ray admitted that in the early years of his marriage frustration with his mother-in-law was redirected to his wife.

> I wanted to have a good relationship with my wife, but . . . it didn't work out that way for a lot of years. So if things didn't go right I would say nasty things, like "you are just like your stupid mother."

Ray eventually learned to communicate more constructively, but obviously this kind of verbal transgression required him to seek forgiveness. Nonverbal behaviors like a snide tone of voice or rolling of the eyes add to the hurt.

Intentional and Unintentional Offenses

For the couples we have studied, it is *intentional* transgressions that most require forgiveness. In fact, one of the offended partner's first responses is to assess whether the act was an unintentional mistake, a "misunderstanding," or beyond the control of the offender. "He didn't mean to hurt me," one woman said about her husband's outburst of bad temper after a stressful workday. Vangelisti and Young (2000) confirmed that messages were considered more hurtful when they were intentional. (Recall that Samuel seemed relatively unconcerned about Lisa's financial mistakes.) Nonetheless, we sometimes hear that an offender "should have known better" or "should have thought about my feelings." From these comments, we conclude that pleas of ignorance may not absolve the offender from forgiveness-seeking obligations.

As indicated in this account from a young woman, some largely *unintentional* offenses can be so hurtful that forgiveness negotiations will ensue:

> A friend and I were joking about the shapes of our bodies and what we would change. We decided we could switch our bodies and then we would be happy. She asked me to switch one more thing (her thighs) and I made a funny face and said "No way!" I didn't laugh so she took it seriously and was very hurt. I could see she was hurt, so I apologized over and over. She finally said she would forgive me, but there was no contact like a handshake or a hug. I think she was still upset but wanted to drop the subject. She is no longer my friend. We never talked about our weight, diets, body shapes, or exercising again.

Enduring Patterns of Behavior

In forgiveness stories, couples sometimes relate how repeated mild transgressions can become serious. One husband described how a persistent pattern led to a major blow-up:

> And it led back to the fact that I was leaving my socks around. I mean, it's just something so stupid, minor, but you keep bringing it up and bringing it up and bringing it up and it becomes major, you know.

These simmering resentments sometimes become volatile, as Rose (in her mid-60s) related in this story about her marriage with Jim, who in the early days of their marriage was frequently more focused on his work than on her emotional needs. After repeatedly taking second place to Jim's work, Rose exploded:

> He just made me mad. Whatever difficulties he had had that day at work, he brought them home and I was cooking and I was happy. Then he said something that upset me and I just . . . I had a knife in my hand and just turned and threw it at him! He looked and went out the door, went to the store, came back in, put his beer in the refrigerator and we sat down for dinner. We didn't say very much. Then we went to bed and the next morning we got up and he says, "I'm sorry." And I says, "Okay." And that was it.

The couple looked back upon this episode rather sheepishly, assuring us that nothing like it occurred again. And whereas we certainly don't recommend expressing your feelings with cutlery, this story illustrates how problems left to fester can suddenly erupt. For Rose, the point seemed to be that her husband's obsession with his own concerns finally drove her to the brink. Jim must have recognized this, as he offered an apology (and apparently decided against pressing charges!).

The case of Rose and Jim clearly illustrates that transgressions needn't be fully intentional and they needn't be discrete events. They can unfold over long periods of time. In fact, we noticed that some transgressions were described more as bad habits or patterns of harmful behavior. Sustained periods of alcohol and drug abuse, poor temper, or habitual inconsiderateness were all provided as examples of enduring forms of behavior that triggered a cycle of forgiveness-seeking and forgiveness-granting communication.

Forgivable and Unforgivable Offenses

"That is where I draw the line. I just couldn't stay with him if he had sex with someone else. I don't see how anyone could. It's just not part of my moral code. Forget it!" These sentiments, expressed by one of our students, underscore the fact that a person's moral sensibility can make some relational transgressions seem truly unforgivable (Backman, 1985). Our student was commenting on the most frequently mentioned unforgivable offense in romantic relationships (at least in our studies): infidelity. Some older couples shared this sentiment too. Margaret (in her mid-60s) noted first, "We were brought up that you try to stay with your husband no matter what." Then she added, "But I think if Asa had wandered off or something, I would have probably been out of here. You know that?"

Some intriguing forgiveness stories come from long-term partners who managed to recover from affairs. Jan wanted to at least try to preserve her investment in a long-term relationship:

Are we willing to throw away 32 years, you know, just for a fling? I take it seriously; it crushed me. And it's probably changed me a lot, but I still don't know that I want to be alone and give up what we have, even though the marriage was on real shaky ground there for a while. So we went through a couple of years of crap. Are we going to throw away 32 years because of it? If you're not willing to work through the hard times, you're just not going to make it.

Other potentially unforgivable transgressions involved physical violence, drug abuse, and neglectful parenting. As we discuss in Chapter 5, some partners eventually forgive these offenses, but doing so typically requires tremendous effort and third-party assistance.

Mutual Offenses

We sometimes use the convenient terms "victims" and "offenders," but forgiveness theorists recognize that the responsibility for transgressions is often shared, even when one party is mostly to blame (Exline & Baumeister, 2000). Drug dependence is sometimes "enabled" by family members. Relational neglect can be a function of mutual indifference or distraction. Expressions of anger are frequently reciprocal. Hostile behavior sometimes arises from a mutual failure to address simmering differences. In Harvey's (2004) analysis, some couples described personality differences as a triggering condition for forgiveness episodes. For these couples, a mismatch on such personality features as extroversion/introversion or emotionality led to persistent conflicts and occasional blow-outs. These examples support the perspective that transgressions often arise from the interaction of the parties, not just the actions of an individual transgressor. As with the other process elements in Figure 2.1, the triggering transgression is assumed to be a communicative and relational phenomenon.

❖ RELATIONAL CONTEXT

As indicated in Figure 2.1, transgressions are interpreted and forgiving communication is practiced within a context, which includes both the type and quality of the relationship. Forgiveness is negotiated with reference to social expectations that govern various *types* of relationships. For example, forgiveness in families is different from at work because the latter may be influenced by formalized procedures for handling serious grievances. Moreover, within each type, the characteristics, shared values, and communication rules that contribute to the quality of a given relationship at the time of the forgiveness episode must be considered.

Relationship Types

Theorists have long urged researchers to pay more attention to the diversity of human relationships (Duck, 1990). Forgiveness researchers have often studied romantic relationships, with a particular emphasis on married couples undergoing counseling. Other family relationships have also received attention. The focus is often on parent-child relations (e.g., Al-Mabuk, Enright, & Cardis, 1995). However, Kelley's (1998) study of 304 narratives revealed how forgiveness was practiced in a larger variety of relationships. He asked participants (mean age = 26 years) to describe three kinds of events: (1) a time when they had been forgiven by someone else, (2) a time when they had granted forgiveness to another person, and (3) a time when the respondent "felt a need for forgiveness" from another person (p. 259). One of the foci of Kelley's subsequent report was the relational context of the forgiveness episodes. Table 2.2 summarizes his data.

Family relationships

Roughly 44% of the forgiveness episodes occurred in the context of family relationships. Parent-child encounters (26% of total narratives) were most frequently described, but sibling relationships (7%) were also mentioned. Kelley (1998) created a separate category for extended family relationships, which were mentioned in 4% of the narratives. As

Table 2.2   Relationship Types Referenced in Forgiveness Narratives

Type	*Frequency (N = 304)*	*Percentage*
Family	135	44
Spousal	24	7
Parent-child	78	26
Sibling	22	7
Extended Family	11	4
Dating	69	23
Friends	75	25
Work		
Coworker	18	6
Supervisory	11	4
Stranger/Acquaintance	7	2

SOURCE: Adapted from Kelley, D. (1998). The communication of forgiveness. *Communication Studies, 49*(3), 255–271. Reprinted with permission of Taylor & Francis. http://www.tandf .co.uk/journals.

Vangelisti (2006) noted recently, family relationships are relatively unique because of their involuntary nature, long histories, and contextual variations. In practice, members do sometimes distance themselves geographically or psychologically from their families. Nevertheless, estranged siblings may find themselves in close proximity at certain family gatherings such as weddings or anniversary celebrations. They may feel compelled to negotiate forgiveness by other members who wish to preserve the family unit. On the other hand, because termination of the relationship is an unlikely option for aggrieved family members, they are sometimes treated with more indifference than close friends.

Kelley (1998) reported that family members were less likely than expected to report relationship change as a consequence of forgiveness episodes. Current family interactions are often colored by long-held resentments and memories of past injustice. In such circumstances, forgiveness becomes a weightier matter. Forgiving a parent for years of neglect can be more difficult than forgiving a momentary bout of bad temper. Thus, in long-term family relationships, we might expect forgiveness processes to unfold over years or even decades, not over the course of a single conversation. Yet, when parents or siblings respond to a transgression in an unexpectedly forgiving manner, the episode may be particularly memorable and relationally potent. In the episode below, a persistently antagonistic pattern of communication suddenly gave way. The change stemmed from Jason's constructive approach to a difficult situation and his father's "surprisingly" forgiving response:

I sent a check to my father to cover some expenses that I had incurred. I had forgotten to record a very large check so my account was overdrawn and his check bounced. I became aware of the overdraft before he received notice of it. I explained the situation to him and what he might expect from his bank. Most important was my owning up to the mistake and preparing him for the hassle he was about to suffer at his end and my assurances that another check was on its way. Surprisingly, instead of going ballistic (his normal pattern) there were expressions of concern over my befuddled financial affairs. I took the normal and calm mode of his voice as the forgiveness I sought, and was pleased that my "doing the right thing," including the communication in advance, had quieted an expected explosion. Communication (via phone) has been on a more pleasant and amicable level since then, and I view him as being more reasonable in his reactions than in the past.

Finally, family interaction is characterized by contextual variation. Parent-child relationships are characterized by strong emotional ties and power differences. Sibling relationships can be shaped by age differences and the potential for rivalry. Relationships with extended family members can be perfunctory and distant. They can also be engaged, intrusive, or supportive. Nontraditional relationships, such as those experienced in step-families, can add layers of complexity to the forgiveness process. We would expect forgiving communication to reflect these relational variations. For example, although young children are likely to exhibit less varied repertoires of forgiveness-seeking behavior, they might be particularly motivated to seek forgiveness from a valued parent.

Romantic relationships

Romantic pairs were prominently mentioned in Kelley's (1998) narratives. Few of these involved spousal forgiveness (just 7% of the total), but this may reflect the relatively young age of the sample. Most had not been married. Kelley's data revealed that many of the forgiveness episodes occurred in the context of *dating* relationships. Theorists like Hargrave (1994) have addressed convincingly the important role of forgiveness in marriage. Forgiveness may be particularly important in romantic relationships because the relational stakes are high. For dating partners, particularly those with a short history, failure to negotiate forgiveness may lead to relationship termination. Marital ties are more resilient, particularly with the passing of time. Yet marriages involve high levels of emotional investment, trust, and interdependence and highly valued behavioral norms. For these reasons, certain transgressions (e.g., sexual infidelity) can be emotionally devastating. They create high levels of relational disruption and uncertainty. Forgiveness in such circumstances is both difficult and potentially crucial to relationship recovery (Gordon, Baucom, & Snyder, 2000).

Clinicians have brought attention to the role of forgiveness-based therapies and interventions in preserving marriage (Chapter 5). But we would argue that the practice of more "ordinary" forms of forgiveness in nontherapeutic relationships needs more attention. Because most long-term romantic relationships encounter serious challenges at one time or another, it is likely that the negotiation of forgiveness is an important relationship maintenance practice (Waldron & Kelley, 2005). Generational differences influence couples' practice of forgiveness. Couples married in recent decades may be more inclined to seek marriage therapy, which sometimes creates structured opportunities to practice forgiveness. For older couples, societal norms against divorce may discourage relationship termination.

These norms can be conceptualized as social "constraints" (O'Riordan & Yoshimura, 2005), which limit choice, but may encourage couples to weather difficult times and, in some cases, negotiate forgiveness. Sally and Jack, a couple married in the 1940s, commented on why they never divorced, despite some potent disagreements early in their marriage. Jack served as a pilot and officer during the war years. He saw many of his friends die, and the war hardened him. Sally found him to be autocratic and distant upon his return, but she felt selfish for wanting her soldier husband to be more respectful and emotionally engaged. After all, she hadn't served on the front lines. It took many years and many arguments to fully appreciate how the war had changed their relationship. Eventually, Sally learned to express her concerns. Jack apologized and gradually learned to communicate more respectfully. They never really considered divorce:

Jack: I don't know . . . divorce wasn't talked about. I mean, we just . . . we knew we weren't going to divorce over it and, um, it just hasn't really been an option. Or we don't look at it as an option in our marriage.

Sally: Our generation didn't run away from marriages in general, and marriages stayed together, particularly through those war years. It was just the way things were.

Friends

Friendships were sites for forgiveness in 25% Kelley's (1998) narratives, but its role in maintaining these important bonds has received scant attention in the literature on relationship maintenance (e.g., Dainton, Zelley, & Langan, 2003). Kelley noted that the episodes described by friends tended to result in significant relational changes. For friends, the primary motive for seeking and granting forgiveness was a desire to restore a valuable relationship. This quote from one of our student participants illustrates the common sentiment that dating relationships can be fleeting, but friendships can last forever:

I remember a situation when I dated for a short time my best friend's ex-boyfriend from a few years earlier. It was a weird situation. When my friend found out, she felt like I had violated her . . . After I stopped seeing him, we worked it out. I asked her to forgive me for stepping on her territory. She forgave me and we repaired our friendship. In fact, I think it is probably stronger now than before. I also realized that friends, unlike boyfriends, don't come and go. Nothing should stand in the way of a solid friendship.

Work relationships

Coworker relationships, cited in 6% of Kelley's (1998) narratives, are largely unexplored sites for forgiveness (but see Metts, Cupach, & Lippert, 2006). Work can be stressful for any number of reasons, but the dynamics of organizational relationships are among the most frequently cited sources of emotional distress. A report on the experiences of probation workers and prison guards illustrated this point (Waldron, 2000; Waldron & Krone, 1991). These workers toiled daily at stressful and relatively low paid jobs, working closely with potentially violent convicted criminals. Those laboring at the front lines of the justice system expect emotional abuse from these clients and developed psychological defenses against them. But, their relations with coworkers were the most frequent source of emotional pain. Painful betrayals by coworkers, abusive supervision, and blatant discrimination were among the many relational transgressions.

The work context is unique in several ways. One is the tension between the public and private realms of relational experience. In personal relationships, disagreements tend to be negotiated in private, whereas at work they may occur in front of an "audience" of coworkers or even clients. Betrayed secrets may be quickly communicated down the hallways through gossip, discussed quietly around the water cooler, or broadcast to the whole department through e-mails.

Another factor is the power differential that defines some work relationships. Waldron (2000) noted that the "emotional tyranny" associated with public humiliation of the weak by the powerful is a common theme in the relational narratives he collected from employees. Powerful people feel less obligated to seek forgiveness, whereas the less powerful may feel compelled to do so. A supervisor shared this account, which amply illustrates the theme:

An employee at work was upset at me and would not tell me why she was upset. This made me angry because I am very open and frank with my employees. After a little while I called her into a conference room and discussed why she would not disclose why she was upset with me.

Finally, workplace relationships are often governed by formal and informal rules prohibiting certain kinds of relational interaction. These may inhibit efforts to negotiate forgiveness. For legal reasons, doctors may be reluctant to seek forgiveness for medical mistakes. In other settings, displays of negative emotion may be discouraged so as not to upset customers or lower the morale of employees working on a team.

For that reason, constructive discussion of perceived transgressions may be limited. This in turn encourages employees to "stew" over problems, hold grudges, and nurture resentments. One implication is that organizations may create structures that facilitate forgiveness processes. By doing so, organizations create alternatives to vengeful responses like retaliation, disengagement, and even violence.

Stranger/acquaintance relationships

Only 2% of the narratives in Kelley's (1998) study involved strangers or acquaintances. Emotional investment in these relationships is typically low, and the consequences of relational transgressions are limited. In short, these relationships may not "matter" enough for participants to engage in the process of forgiveness, which, after all, can take considerable time and effort. Instead, rules of politeness and self-presentation (Brown & Levison, 1978; Goffman, 1959) have evolved to manage public encounters among strangers. Certain social gaffes may call for apologies ("Sorry about that") and a perfunctory dispensation ("That's ok"), but these interactions are ritualized and superficial.

Relationship Quality in Personal Relationships

Relationship quality is the second element constituting relationship context. Dindia (2003) recently provided an excellent synthesis of the many dimensions researchers consider as they study the quality and maintenance of personal relationships. First, it is worth distinguishing between global and more specific relational dimensions. In her review, Dindia suggests that we make global judgments about the quality of our relationships and our satisfaction with them. These global judgments are based on more specific assessments of trust, intimacy, commitment, and equity. Psychologist Frank Fincham and colleagues have recently studied connections between relationship quality and the practice of forgiveness (e.g., Fincham, 2000; Fincham & Beach, 2002). He reports that wounded partners forgive more freely in romantic relationships they judge to be close, committed, and satisfying. When relationship satisfaction is high, offending partners are more likely to offer apologies and are more likely to display empathy (McCullough, et al., 1997). Kelley (1998) suggests that satisfied partners may be more *motivated* to forgive. In addition, positive assessments of relationship quality lead to more benign interpretations of transgressions, which in turn foster feelings of forgiveness (Kearns & Fincham, 2005). However, an earlier study suggested that relationship quality may not be the most important consideration. In that analysis, the simple decision to forgive was a key predictor of behavior toward an offending partner, independent of marital satisfaction (Fincham, 2000).

With reference to specific relationship dimensions, McCullough et al. (2000) argue that forgiveness facilitates, and results from, relational *intimacy*. For some partners, successfully forgiving emotionally charged transgressions apparently strengthens emotional bonds in the long run, as the episode becomes part of the couple's history. In contrast, lower intimacy couples may lack experience with the kind of emotional dialogue that frequently accompanies forgiveness negotiations. Kate and her boyfriend were closer once they negotiated forgiveness and "made up":

> My boyfriend and I got in an argument because I slow danced with another guy. I didn't think it was a big deal. But, I didn't consider how he would feel. I guess the reason why I was forgiven was because he loves me. The forgiveness wasn't spontaneous. We had to argue first. Eventually he said that he wanted me to know he wasn't mad. He was just hurt and he wished I would put myself in his shoes. I think I was relieved he wasn't mad but I wanted to make clear my intentions were not bad. After we "made-up," we were closer.

Trust may be the dimension most disrupted by transgressions. Most relationships are grounded in a sense of certainty that the partners will honor relationship rules, look out for the interests of the relationship, and behave in predictable ways. Trust reduces uncertainty about the future and decreases the risk associated with intimacy. On the other hand, a history of violations makes trust problematic for a partner who has been "burned." Janice describes the feelings of distrust that followed the discovery of her husband's affair.

> It took a while (to forgive). Yeah, 'cause I couldn't trust him after that . . . Every time he went to the gym, I thought he would be calling that girl. I always had that in my mind, but it wasn't true you know. And I was playing games with him . . . It took me about six months before I could trust him again.

Relationship *commitment* is also likely to shape forgiveness responses. Commitment is an intention to persist in a relationship despite inevitable difficulties. It stems from three sources, including (1) a personal desire to remain in the relationship, (2) the moral sense that one *should* persist, and (3) structural factors that encourage persistence, such as divorce statutes or economic constraints (Johnson, 1999). In a study of forgiving and revengeful responses to hurtful relational events, O'Riordan and Yoshimura (2005) found commitment to be a significant predictor. For current romantic partners (N = 131), increased degrees of personal commitment and lower degrees of structural commitment predicted expressions of forgiveness. For past romantics, moral commitment was the significant predictor.

For Alice, both personal and moral commitment seemed to explain why she forgave her husband after he committed adultery:

> Because I loved him and to me, my whole view on marriage is commitment. And we're committed to each other, good, bad . . . whatever. And um, so even if I quote "hated him" for what he did, I still was committed to this marriage and the institution itself and we were going to get through it.

Commitment is linked to relational investment. The simple fact that partners have invested time and effort in developing and maintaining a relationship can provide the motivation for negotiating forgiveness. "She was very unhappy and it could have ended in divorce," Mark commented as he described his repeated efforts to seek forgiveness from his wife of 39 years after revealing an affair. "But we had too many years. I wasn't going to let it happen."

Equity (the relative balance of perceived costs and rewards) is a dimension of relationship quality that may influence forgiveness in personal and work relationships. Many communication scholars have explored the possibility that inequity is a source of relational dissatisfaction in various relationships and the stimulus for efforts to repair them. For example, Vogl-Bauer (2003) surveyed the literature on family relationships, finding that parents were more satisfied when relationships with their children became more equitable and siblings were more satisfied when parents treated them more equitably. Obviously, inequity is commonplace in relationships (parents invest more than children), but one function of the forgiveness process might be to manage inequity or redress inequity that exceeds tolerable thresholds. For example, parents are often forgiving of children who don't fully "carry their weight" in the household, but high levels of indolence may require a cycle of apologizing and forgiving communication.

Relationship Quality in Work Relationships

In the workplace, relevant dimensions of quality include informality, power, and justice (Waldron, 2003). Relationships with low degrees of *formality* appear more "friendlike," which leaves the parties more latitude in determining what "counts as" a transgression. Transgressions in formal relationships are more clearly task or procedure related (e.g., failing to do your part on a work team), and relational obligations tend to be more clearly defined. As mentioned previously, *power* differences change forgiveness dynamics. The effects of transgressions are multiplied when committed by powerful people, as opposed to our peers, and organizations sometimes insist that powerful people be publicly accountable for errors in judgment (even as they deny them the means to pursue forgiveness). Jake, who supervised a large construction company, agreed to transfer a coworker/friend to a more dangerous job, despite some hesitations about his lack of experience. He is bitter because his company chose to blame him rather than forgive him for his error in judgment:

> A phone call from one of my foremen told me that he [the transferred employee] had taken a serious fall that ultimately led to his death. I experienced a feeling of guilt and responsibility for making the transfer that very morning. I was at his wedding and the christening of his two children. Much confusion and fear . . . a sense of loss that I still experience to this day, 12 years after the fact. Even though it was an accident, the bureaucracy had to put the blame on someone which ultimately was me. (Waldron, 2000, p. 72)

Understandably wary of confronting powerful transgressors, employees sometimes experience fear, helplessness, or building rage at relational injustices. In fact, the need for forgiveness at work is linked closely to issues of relational justice and fairness. The interdependence inherent in many tasks makes it essential that workers do their "fair share" and offer mutual support. The potential for abuse of power in hierarchical relationships makes it necessary for low-power workers to protect one another when possible. For all these reasons, workers develop unwritten codes of relational ethics. The following account describes an apparent breach in relational ethics, a situation in which a coworker's desire for revenge was more powerful than any urge toward forgiveness:

> [My coworker] wrongly assumed that I was trying to make him look bad in front of our supervisor. He covertly tried to take revenge [by spreading rumors] but refused to talk about it. The emotional tension became so electric that I was emotionally drained just preparing for work each day. I felt traumatized and

when he refused to cease his game playing, I swore at him, which only made the situation worse. (Adapted from Waldron, 2000, p. 66)

❖ INDIVIDUAL FACTORS

Researchers have identified only a handful of individual traits and demographic variables that may influence a person's approach to seeking or granting forgiveness. In Figure 2.1, these are nested within relational context because it is presumed that the expression of individual characteristics is muted or magnified depending on contextual factors.

Individual Traits and Orientations

Researchers have argued that "willingness to forgive" is a traitlike tendency (Brown & Phillips, 2005; Hebl & Enright, 1993). Some individuals are more inclined to be forgiving than others. Chapter 6 provides information about various measures of forgiveness orientation, including those presented by Mauger, Perry, Freeman, and Grove (1992), Berry, Worthington, Parrot, O'Connor, and Wade (2001), and Rye et al. (2001). Some existing measures have been criticized for being idiosyncratic to original study conditions and lacking convincing evidence of validity (Ross, Kendall, Matters, Wrobel, & Rye, 2004).

Forgiveness has been linked only tentatively with established personality traits. For example, Ross and colleagues (2004) used the popular five-factor model (FFM) of personality in a study of 147 college students. They gauged association between forgiveness orientation and measures of neuroticism-emotional stability, extraversion-introversion, openness-closedness, agreeableness-antagonism, and conscientiousness-undirectedness. They reported only a few modest statistical relationships. For example, students who tended to be forgiving also scored positively on the dimensions of agreeableness and extraversion (warmth and positive emotions subscale). They scored negatively on the hostility component of the neuroticism.

Although researchers have reported limited success in predicting forgiveness responses from personality measures, laypersons often mention personality. Sal and Dorothy have been married more than 30 years. He told us, "Me being one of those 'fire, ready, aim' [kind of people], if she didn't forgive me each day, I'd either be dead or divorced." Dorothy responded, "I am slow to anger. Sal is quick to anger. But he is also very, very quick to say he's sorry. So the forgiveness has been easy for me because of how he handles it."

As noted in Chapter 1, forgiveness is an important element of several religious traditions. For that reason, the degree to which religion is part of a person's psychological orientation, their "religiosity," may shape their communication. In fact, Rye and colleagues (2000) argue that religious people value forgiveness more highly, and Kelley (1998) found religious beliefs to be a frequent motive for forgiveness. The role of religiosity has not been widely examined in empirical studies, but one of our graduate students, Dena Lee, found religion to be important in the accounts provided by some long-term couples. In an analysis of interview transcripts, Lee noted that religious beliefs and sacred texts were often offered as motives for forgiveness. Charles explained how he and his wife Becky are guided by their interpretation of biblical precepts:

> There's a lot in the Bible about love, but there's also a lot in the Bible about forgiveness. Without forgiveness, we don't have a Christian relationship . . . Accepting of one another, loving unconditionally, and forgiveness has just got to be part of our lives.

Situated Psychological Reactions

Psychological responses to transgressions shape the subsequent communication process. Empathy and rumination have received the most research attention. For example, McCullough et al. (1997) argued that successful forgiveness requires partners to eventually develop an empathetic response. Empathy requires a shift in focus away from one's own feelings of hurt and anger and toward the partner's perspective. Measures of empathy have successfully predicted forgiveness in studies of married partners (Paleari, Regalia, & Fincham, 2005). In contrast, the tendency to dwell on a transgression has been associated with unforgiving attitudes (Worthington & Wade, 1999). Partners who experienced this kind of rumination also reported lower levels of forgiveness in a study of 87 married couples (Kachadourian, Fincham, & Davila, 2005).

Altruism is a human quality that blends several psychosocial responses. Smith and her colleagues (2005) define altruism as a voluntary action intended to benefit others. Altruistic responses should not be confused with mere politeness or the enactment of role obligations. Smith associates altruism with concern for others and empathy. Forgiveness could be considered an instance of altruistic relational behavior. In fact, Worthington (2001) includes altruism as part of his prominent prescriptive model. Forgiveness is considered an "altruistic gift," an unselfish and generous response, which primarily benefits the offender. Chapter 5 further discusses Worthington's model.

❖ COMMUNICATION PROCESSES

Communication is the means by which partners discover transgressions, express and manage their emotional reactions, make sense of the situation they find themselves in, seek and grant forgiveness when appropriate, and (re)negotiate their relationship as they look to the future. As the central concern of this volume, and the sole topic of Chapter 4, communication practices have a prominent place in Figure 2.1. We will not discuss them in detail here. However, we argue that forgiving communication is much more than a set of discrete behaviors used to seek and grant forgiveness. Rather, it is a negotiation that unfolds through a cycle as emotions flare and cool, interpretations change, motives evolve, and new relational agreements are constructed. The process is not orderly, and it may take many years to play out. In this long-term view, communication practices include ongoing efforts to negotiate relational values, reframe memories of the forgiveness episode, and maintain relational identities.

❖ RELATIONSHIP OUTCOMES

Of the 54 long-term married couples we interviewed, nearly all identified times when the capacity to negotiate forgiveness was crucial in sustaining their relationship. Forgiveness has relational consequences. Kelley (1998) found that substantive relationship consequences were mentioned in roughly 40% of 304 narratives reported by friends, romantic partners, and family members. This estimate is probably low, given that participants were not questioned about consequences in any detail. In our studies of younger romantic partners (Kelley & Waldron, 2005; Waldron & Kelley, 2005), we asked participants to estimate the quality of their relationship immediately before a transgression, immediately after, and a third time after forgiveness was granted. Statistical tests indicated significant negative change after the transgression and significant improvement after forgiveness was communicated. One implication is that forgiveness-requiring events can be significant "turning points" (Baxter & Bullis, 1986) in personal relationships.

Table 2.3   Conceptualizing Relational Outcomes

Outcome	Sample Descriptions (paraphrased from transcripts and survey responses)
New relationship type	"We are friends now, but not dating" "It is more a friendship than a parent-child thing"
Rule change	"We don't call names anymore when we fight" "Now I always call her when I am going to be late"
Strengthening	"It was a hard time, but we talk more now than before" "If we can survive that, we can survive anything"
Weakening	"He did forgive me, but we aren't as good of friends" "I am not sure I trust him the way I used to"
Normalizing	"I could tell he forgave me when things felt normal" "We eventually went back to our familiar family pattern"
Terminating	"After that we drifted apart and eventually stopped calling" "He dumped me. For good reason."
Short-term	"Immediate shock. Confusion about what to do. Anger" "We couldn't talk about it for days"
Long-term	"I forgive him but I will never forget how it hurt" "Twenty years later, we are just now really dealing with it"

Turning points are times when negative or positive relationship change is accelerated.

Relationship consequences can be conceptualized in a variety of ways, some of which are presented in Table 2.3. Kelley (1998) conceptualized two broad relational outcomes associated with forgiving communication: relationship changing and relationship normalizing. He found several distinct types of change in forgiveness narratives.

Changes in Relationship Type

In some cases, it was the *type* of relationship that was altered. For example, a son reported that, "The typical father/son relationship we had . . . is gone and has been replaced by one where we exist more as friends" (Kelley, 1998, p. 264). In less positive cases, transgressions apparently made existing levels of intimacy unsustainable. Examples included romantic partners who became "just friends" or former coworker/friends who now "just worked together." Less common but equally painful examples involve family relationships, when parents "disown" their offspring rather than forgive. Winberg Chai, whose story is recounted in the textbox, eventually reconciled with his mother, but his experience illustrates how painful events can motivate even close family members to fundamentally redefine relationships (Chai & Chai, 2001).

In *The Girl From Purple Mountain*, Chinese scholar Winberg Chai, writing with his daughter May-lee, provides a poignant account of his mother's trials and triumphs as a highly educated Chinese woman during the years immediately prior to the Cultural Revolution (Chai & Chai, 2001). One of the first women accepted to a Chinese university, Ruth Chai was also educated at U.S. colleges before returning to China to open a school and assume a prestigious role in a male-dominated society. However, the vibrant and proud matriarch lost her school and home as the political winds changed. She became embittered by what she perceived as the treachery of her husband's family, particularly a brother whose political activities placed the whole family at great risk and caused her husband Charles to lose a high government post. Ruth was outraged at this interference, which left the family poor and politically adrift. She threatened to leave her husband unless he cut off all future contact with his family. Charles promised to do so.

Years later, after the family immigrated to the United States, Charles's brother sent word that he was dying. Facing what he feared would be an unpleasant afterlife, he sought reconciliation with his brother. Ruth Chai would have nothing of it. However, at the bidding of his father, Winberg Chai (Ruth and Charles's son) secretly traveled to Taiwan to comfort his uncle. Upon returning, Winberg confessed to his brothers, who promptly told the imposing matriarch. As Winberg later wrote, his mother was furious at his father for breaking the code of silence, for sending her first born son to visit the enemy. But she directed her fury at Winberg:

My mother wrote a long letter to me then, reminding me of the special bond she had expected to share with me, her first born son, how she had opened her heart to me throughout her life, how she had raised me like a prince, sacrificed for me, lived for me. She reminded me of the sins of her enemy, her brother-in-law. How he had allowed us to nearly starve in Chongqing without lifting a finger to help us . . . She could never forgive this act of betrayal, my mother wrote; I was no longer her son.

Changes in Relational Rules

One frequent consequence of forgiveness episodes is a decision by the partners to change the rules of interaction. Typically, the rule changes are designed to avoid future occurrences of the transgression. Rule changes may have the effect of protecting the partners, managing uncertainty about future behavior, and generally reducing relational risk. For example, a couple may pledge to explicitly address negative feelings before they fester to the point where a hostile conflict erupts. They may create new restrictions on flirting behavior to avoid misperceptions and maximize feelings of security. In families, rules may be adjusted to permit discussion of previously taboo topics. At work, procedures for addressing grievances may be instituted as a response to workplace tensions.

Friends also negotiate new procedures. Trent admitted that he was habitually late or even absent to social events planned by his friends. After one particularly frustrating incident at a car race, his friend Rick imposed a new procedure for avoiding future mishaps:

> I was supposed to meet Rick at our designated rendezvous point at 8 A.M. Needless to say, he made it there and I didn't. That evening when he got home from the races he called and wanted an explanation, quite upset with me. I explained to him what had happened the night before and apologized for not meeting him. He, being the party type himself, understood and told me that I was "forgiven, just don't let it happen again." I thanked him and assured him it would not. Since then the only thing that is different in our relationship is if we make plans, he questions me about what time and where we're going to meet to instill in my head that he wants me there at the set time.

Changes in Relationship Quality

Even when partners negotiate forgiveness, they may still experience deterioration in global or specific qualities of their relationship. Waldron and Kelley (2005) asked romantic partners to rate the degree to which their relationships had deteriorated, strengthened, or "returned to normal" as a function of the forgiveness-granting behaviors used by the offended partner. As they conceptualized it, each of these states could be experienced over the course of a single episode, although they made no assumption about the sequencing of these outcomes. They found explicit forgiveness, discussion-based approaches, and nonverbal approaches all to be modestly and positively associated with the measure of relationship strengthening. Conditional approaches to forgiveness were associated with relationship deterioration. No behavior was strongly associated with normalizing, but the authors concluded that normalizing effects may be harder to estimate because of its "fuzzier definition." For some couples, returning to normal may be a temporary stop on the way to an improved or deteriorated relationship. Kelley and Waldron (2005) examined relationship change as a function of forgiveness-seeking behaviors used by the offending partner. Change was measured by asking participants to use a rating scale, ranging from –3 (highly negative change) to +3 (highly positive change). Zero represented no change. They also computed difference scores on measures of relationship quality (satisfaction, quality, stability) and intimacy/closeness before the transgression, after the transgression, and after forgiveness was communicated. The results indicated that efforts to communicate forgiveness significantly improved relationship quality over posttransgression levels, indicating that forgiveness facilitated recovery. These results build on a previous analysis that suggested that partners who avoid forgiveness experience less positive outcomes (Fincham, Beach, & Davila, 2004). Interestingly, estimates of postforgiveness satisfaction remained somewhat lower than original relationship satisfaction levels. One explanation for this result is that for some couples, recovery from hurtful events is a continuing process of forgiveness, one that may take years to complete.

Kelley (1998) found that of those forgiveness narratives that included relationship changes, 29% reported deterioration, 26% reported strengthening, and 28% recorded a "return to normal." Our subsequent work on romantic relationships indicated that both forgiveness-granting and forgiveness-seeking strategies seem to facilitate positive, or at least less negative, relationship outcomes. Forgiving communication appeared to allow partners to release negative emotion and bitterness, while renegotiating relationship values and rules.

Relationship normalizing

When individuals describe a relationship as "returning to normal," they are typically experiencing a level of relationship comfort similar to that experienced prior to the transgression. A return to the relational routine may be a great relief, especially if partners truly feel that "all is forgiven." Normalizing may also signal that the transgression was an "abnormality," one that needn't result in change.

Long-term versus short-term outcomes

Our research results remind us that communication behavior has both short-term and long-term effects. The immediate relational effects of hurtful transgressions are obviously negative, but the long-term outcome depends on many factors, including sustained efforts to seek and grant forgiveness. The explicit communication of forgiveness may have some immediate ameliorating effects, but it is likely that forgiveness proceeds in halting steps. The relationship between forgiveness and relationship quality is reciprocal, such that changes in one may lead to changes in the other. Again, this takes time. Veteran couples tell us that the process can take decades and it may never be fully complete. In some cases, forgiveness may be granted in the short term, but in the long term the relationship may be altered. Such was the case with Shari and Sanji, who remain friends, although she sometimes wishes they were more than that:

> The story that stands out most is very close and personal, one that I think of every day of my life. I had been dating a man and was with him about a year, when out of insecurity and foolishness, I was unfaithful. We then broke up (my doing). I knew I had broken his heart. I felt so low. In our "break up" conversation he told me he forgave me. I didn't ask him for it. I was crying and Sanji told me "I understand why you did this; I'll always love you, and most of all I forgive you." I couldn't say anything, I felt even worse because he was so forgiving and selfless. We became friends, very good friends after about a year of not speaking too often. I still care (6 years later), but we're just friends.

In Lauren's case, her boyfriend apparently tried to forgive her for a dalliance, but it appears he could not sustain it. He used the memory "as a weapon" in their arguments. Eventually, the relationship was terminated.

> I was in a long-term relationship and became involved briefly with another individual. After a short affair, the relationship terminated. I told my partner about the affair, after much reflection. The relationship suffered, and I thought it might end, but I was forgiven after promising to make it up and not do it again. However, a sense of trust was lost, and we never regained a certain sense of intimacy that was present before the affair. Also, the incident was brought up time after time by my partner, almost as a weapon. The relationship deteriorated sharply, and then terminated.

❖ CONCLUSION

This chapter has reviewed key elements in our descriptive model, which portrays forgiveness as a communicative process rather than a psychological decision. In doing so, we emphasized that hurtful transgressions or traumatic relational events create the need for partners to forgive. These painful incidents are interpreted within relationships that vary in type and quality. Individual tendencies and psychological processes play a role in this process, but the behaviors used for uncovering transgressions, managing emotions, making sense, seeking forgiveness, and granting forgiveness are of primary interest to communication scholars. Forgiving communication may best be characterized by cycles of interaction rather than discrete behaviors. We will address these communicative elements of the model in Chapter 4. We argued that forgiving communication has relational consequences, including changes in the quality of relationships and the rules by which they are managed. It is clear that relationship changes and the forgiveness process itself may take many years to unfold. However, researchers and clinicians are increasingly convinced that forgiveness practices can promote positive changes in relationships. We address effective practices in Chapter 5.

3

Theorizing Forgiveness

This chapter demonstrates how theories of communication can enrich understanding of forgiveness processes. For traditional social scientists, theories are explanatory frameworks. A given theory offers a logic for understanding how complex social processes work. *Communication* theories are primarily concerned with explaining the role of symbolic behavior, including the tactics relational partners use to seek and grant forgiveness and their effects on relational outcomes. In this sense, theories do more than simply describe the "parts" of a communication process, as we did in Chapter 2. Instead, they make specific claims about how and why communication functions in human relationships. So, in Chapter 2 we simply described the elements of forgiveness episodes, such as relational history, the transgression, and communication processes. But here we consider various theoretical explanations for *why* certain kinds of forgiving communication might be used and *how* they might influence our relationships. As a case in point, identity management theories view transgressions as potential threats to the identities of the offender and the victim. Why are communication strategies more or less successful? Because they vary in the extent to which they protect the identity of the offended party (for example, by making clear that the victim is not to blame). How does forgiving communication influence relationships? From this theoretical perspective, we claim that partners who succeed in supporting mutual identity needs are likely to feel more valued, respected, and comfortable as they recover from a transgression.

For traditional social scientists, the ability to produce these kinds of "testable" claims is a crucial contribution of theory. As more studies confirm the theory's principles, researchers gain confidence in it, apply it to new situations, and seek its limitations. For example, does a theory that explains forgiveness in romantic relationships also apply to families? As confidence in a theory grows, practitioners and clinicians may use the theory to solve practical problems. Marriage counselors may use forgiveness-related theory to design therapies, and human resource professionals may use it in their efforts to mediate workplace grievances.

Only a small portion of what we know about forgiveness comes from this "theory-testing" paradigm. In fact, theory development has been relatively neglected, even as practitioners propose innovative therapies and interventions (e.g., Hargrave, 1994). Given the pressing need for therapists to assist persons who have experienced hurt in their relationships, the focus on intervention is understandable and desirable. But new theorizing is needed to prompt alternative conceptualizations of forgiveness, encourage new kinds of intervention, and generate claims that can be rigorously evaluated.

As is the case with so many complex social processes, our understanding of forgiveness would be quite limited if we relied solely on the traditional theory-testing paradigm. In fact, much of our insight comes from researchers who operate from a different set of assumptions. From the *interpretative* perspective, a primary purpose of theory is to enrich our understanding of how people experience social life. A good theory provides a language, sometimes one radically different from our existing assumptions, which allows us to reimagine communication in a manner grounded in the lived experiences and interpretations of those we study. New language may liberate researchers (and the rest of us) from dominant but limited assumptions, including the scientific assumptions about the predictability of human behavior.

Guided by the philosophy of Mikhail Bakhtin (1981), interpretative communication scholar Lesley Baxter and various colleagues offer dialectical theory as one alternative language to traditional ways of thinking about communication in personal relationships (e.g., Baxter & Montgomery, 1996). Traditional views emphasize that relationships progress systematically from low levels of intimacy (acquaintances) to higher levels (romantics). Communication functions to move relationships through the stages and then stabilize the relationship at a given point of development, to maintain *stasis.* In contrast, from the dialectical point of view, relationships are always in flux. Partners use communication to manage a series of "contradictory motivations" that arise *inevitably* when the needs and values of two or more individuals are merged in a relationship. For example, most romantic partners express a motivation to be emotionally close to their partners. They use communication (e.g., self-disclosures) to move the relationship toward intimacy. But the same partners may be motivated to create emotional distance when they feel vulnerable or emotionally exhausted. Again, discourse is the means by which partners manage these contradicting desires, for example by changing the topic to something lighthearted to avoid a "heart-to-heart" talk.

It is quite possible, in fact likely, that multiple theories are "right" in explaining forgiveness behavior. Both of the theoretical positions mentioned thus far, identity management and dialectical, as well as other frameworks, can be useful in understanding the communication of forgiveness. Because forgiveness processes are complex, a given theory will focus on some factors while deemphasizing others. In this chapter, we apply three existing theoretical frameworks that highlight *communicative* aspects of forgiveness and use them to generate research questions for students and scholars. These three have been particularly *useful* in helping us understand our interview data and self-reported forgiveness narratives. We then turn our attention to the task of developing a new theory of forgiving communication, one indebted to existing approaches but responsive to our research findings over the years. We call this a *Negotiated Morality Theory* (NMT) of forgiveness.

❖ DIALECTICAL THEORY

Dialectical theory has been useful in generating a rich understanding of how meaning is created in human relationships. We have found it particularly helpful in understanding the complex and often conflicting discourses that develop around forgiveness episodes.

Theoretical Principles

According to Baxter's (2003) recounting of the dialectical framework's development from its roots in the philosophical work of Bakhtin (1981), its central themes are contradiction and dialogue. *Contradiction* emerges from the merging of two or more individual identities and the inevitable co-occurrence of relational phenomena that are opposites, such as closedness/openness, interdependence/autonomy, or novelty/predictability. Relationships are in constant flux, as partners give voice to these contradictory but essential qualities (Baxter & Montgomery,

1996). A related dialectical construct is the "unity of opposites," the idea that relationships are the loci for the integration or coexistence of these opposing relational forces. Baxter (2003) notes that unique dialectical contradictions should emerge as new relational contexts and practices are studied closely. Forgiveness may be one such practice, involving at its core a fundamental contradiction between a partner's legitimate right to seek revenge and other conflicting motivations, such as the desire to preserve a loving relationship.

For theorists such as Baxter who study *relational* dialectics, contradictions are not found in the minds of individuals; rather, they are located in the discourse that expresses and manages contradiction. Discourse is the means by which individual and relational identities are conceived and enacted. For that reason, we consider the theory to be a communicative framework, one well suited to understanding the processes by which persons *negotiate* forgiveness. As a practical matter, partners manage contradictions by engaging in concrete conversational practices such as negotiating time apart, enacting familiar rituals (such as talking over dinner every night), or increasing the intimacy of self-disclosures. Yet, as Baxter and West (2003) note in reference to the study of similarities within couples, "understudied is dyadic meaning-making in which parties come to perceive their similarity and the sense that they jointly make of their commonalities and differences" (p. 493).

Baxter and colleagues (Baxter & Montgomery, 1996; Baxter & West, 2003) discuss multiple communicative methods of managing dialectical tensions, several of which are paraphrased here. One approach is to separate or *sequence* the opposing concepts, so each is expressed at different points in time or in different contexts. For example, partners can manage the tension between autonomy and interdependence by sharing some decision-making responsibilities (e.g., childcare, family budgeting) and entrusting others to individual members (home maintenance decisions, managing in-law relationships).

Another approach is to simply *embrace* one dimension while actively suppressing the other. This can be observed when an employee chooses to remain silent rather than express bad news to a supervisor as protection against a "blame-the-messenger" response. A third approach requires a creative *integration* of the opposites, expressing both simultaneously. In this sense, families may gain predictability through rituals such as talking at the dinner table every day and novelty by assuring that conversation includes a range of topics and dinner guests. Finally, couples may *reframe* an apparent contradiction by redefining it. For example, parents and teenagers sometimes experience tensions around decision-making autonomy when considering college choices. Does the child decide for himself or herself? How much influence should the parents seek? Rather than label this a struggle between autonomy and interdependence, the family members might reframe it as a "period of growth" in the parent-child relationship. This kind of reframing moves the discussion away from issues of control and toward discussion of maturity, mutual learning, and change.

Application to Forgiveness

The process by which persons negotiate forgiveness of a serious transgression is a potentially rich example of the dyadic meaning-making referenced by Baxter and West (2003). Forgiveness is a process that raises any number of contradictions. In our research, understanding dialectics has been useful to us and our students, as we pored over the tapes and transcripts, looking for a language to capture what is a complex, "fuzzy," and still-open process of relational sense-making. Here are some of the primary dialectical tensions expressed as romantic partners, coworkers, and families discuss their reactions to the most trying events in their relationships.

Mercy versus justice

Perhaps the most fundamental dialectical tension involves mercy and justice. In many accounts, forgiveness is complicated by a motivation to "let go" of hostile feelings on one hand and the desire to seek retribution on the other. This tension is enacted in expressions of compassion, empathy, and acceptance *and/or* hostility, resentment, and verbal aggression. Some wounded partners mutually embrace *vengeance* in the aftermath of a transgression. One young woman described an angry episode with her then-boyfriend: "We hurt each other so bad, that we never recovered." She ended up dating one of his friends as a kind of revenge. As she said, "It was kind of stupid, but I did it to get back at him." The boyfriend responded by "spreading nasty rumors about me." The former partners still don't talk. Other couples describe the "silent treatment" as the preferred response to a transgression. For them, extended silence is a form of punishment, and it also precludes the possibility of forgiveness negotiations.

In contrast, some couples actively suppress their desire for revenge by embracing *mercy*. Some of our older couples use phrases such as "just get over it" when describing their reactions to transgressions. They may express compassion and understanding, even as they contemplate the possibility of vengeance. One of our middle-aged students described interactions with her husband: "I know he gets moody when my mother visits. But I have realized that she can be a real pain. I just cut him some slack, even though I want to smack him." Some choose a merciful response because of expediency or efficiency. "It's not worth fighting when you have been together this long," said one husband of 47 years. "You just end up hurting each other and not solving the problem." He recommended "just letting it go."

The mercy/justice dialectic can be more complicated, as indicated by the words of Justin, a young man who is "trying" to forgive his parents even as he continues to "throw the situation in their faces":

> Last Christmas I went to visit my dad, who lives in another state for the holidays. While I was gone, my mom and stepdad took my car without permission and got into an accident. It supposedly was not their fault. I went crazy when I found out. I was not as mad that the car was wrecked but furious that they took the car without asking. I did not forgive them until about a month later because they did not want to take responsibility for their actions. They broke down one day and said how sorry they were and I forgave them. I have a tendency to throw the situation in their faces because they were so *wrong*. In a way I do not think I can completely forgive them, but I'm trying.

This situation highlights the highly contextualized nature of forgiveness, which for Justin may be complicated by his youth and a strained relationship with his stepfather. Yet, we see in this account a struggle to unify his desires to express mercy and restore justice.

When asked, most people initially agree that forgiveness is a merciful response to a transgression. However, the theme of relational justice looms large in many forgiveness narratives, including Justin's. He seems unable to *completely* forgive because his mother and stepfather "were so wrong" and were reluctant "to take responsibility for their actions." For Justin, the desire to show mercy (forgive) is impeded by his sense that relational justice has yet to prevail. In his mind at least, the parents have failed to sufficiently acknowledge their lack of respect for him and his property. By framing the situation as one of injustice, Justin creates a rationale for enacting partial forgiveness while retaining his right to seek vengeance. A mere apology, especially a delayed one, is insufficient acknowledgment of wrongdoing and undeserving of complete forgiveness. Apparently in Justin's mind, for justice to be fully served, forgiveness (if only partial) must be supplemented by continued reminders of the wrongdoing. Although complicated by any number of relational factors, Justin's account illustrates that justice can be a pivotal concept as families, friends, and lovers weigh the competing impulses of forgiveness and revenge. It also demonstrates that dialectical theory allows apparently opposite concepts, such as mercy and justice, to be co-present in human relationships.

We have argued elsewhere that relational justice and mercy are both important components of the forgiveness process (Kelley & Waldron, 2006). The sufficient *acknowledgment* of wrongdoing is a necessary part of reasserting relational justice. As a communication process, forgiveness expresses, changes, or reinforces the moral order of our relationships. It is this process of recognizing injustice that allows one to act mercifully by forgiving. In some cases, offenders are forgiven unconditionally. Admitting wrongdoing, taking responsibility for transgressions, is often enough to assure our partners that commonly agreed-on values will be respected in the future—that "justice will prevail." Other times, forgiveness is offered with conditions—a kind of "probationary response," which allows the offending partner a period of time to demonstrate "good behavior." When these processes are deemed unlikely to succeed or when partners subscribe to extreme standards of justice (e.g., "an eye for an eye"), they seek justice through retribution or simply terminate the relationship.

Remembering versus forgetting

Couples frequently verbalize tension between remembering and forgetting relational transgressions. Of course, partners are motivated to recall positive shared experiences as a means of reinforcing their bond and generating positive emotions. Remembering unpleasant experiences is also necessary if mistakes of the past are to be avoided in the present. At the same time, partners may wish to forget or suppress negative experiences and the emotions that accompany them. *Intentional forgetting* of the past may be necessary if partners are to remain focused on the relational present. This tension between remembering and forgetting appears frequently in discourse about forgiveness, as indicated by the often-invoked phrase "forgive and forget."

Some of the long-term married couples we interviewed embraced the forgetting side of this dialectical tension, as indicated by such statements as "You just forget about it," "Put it in the past," and literally "Forgive and forget." For these couples, the conversation is firmly focused on present practices and future plans. Discussion of hurtful past events is censored by topic changes ("Let's not relive that disaster!"). Clichéd speech and ritualistic conversation create distance from the emotional trauma of the past. This is a kind of active forgetting as expressed in phrases such as "No use kicking a dead horse," "You can't hold a grudge," and "We've moved on." By embracing the forgetting side of the contradiction, these couples indicate that forgiveness was complete or not worth continued communicative effort.

Other couples manage this dialectic with what might be called a *forgive and remember* approach. Mike, married to Darlene for 36 years, had three different times steered his family into deep financial trouble with bad investment decisions and ill-fated businesses. During the early years, Darlene entrusted financial decisions to Mike. Out of pride or unrealistic optimism, he hid the problems from Darlene. Mike was always convinced that things would "turn around soon." However, the couple indicated that their past financial difficulties are now a frequent topic of discussion. Mike says they need to relive the past so he doesn't "hurt us again." Darlene realized that she needed to provide "reality checks" for Mike's well-intended but sometimes unrealistic financial schemes. She has forgiven her husband and is proud that their marriage survived very trying times. She believes they are now more honest and emotionally close. Mike and Darlene forgive but don't forget.

Forgiveness discourse is sometimes used to integrate the processes of remembering and forgetting. Ray recalled an incident in which he got into an altercation with some teenage "punks," publicly embarrassing himself and his wife Doris, who had to bail him out of their small town jail. Today he recalls the incident to illustrate his stubbornness and insensitivity as a young husband (he described himself as a "jerk"). Ray valorizes his wife, whom he said could have left him over the incident, but stood by his side. In this way, Ray recalls the past as a way of affirming his wife's forgiving nature, then and now.

But Ray and Doris also reveal how individual memories are both merged and disentangled via ongoing forgiveness discourse. As they talked, it became evident that Doris remembered the event well, but interpreted it differently. She is still emotionally upset by the memory of the embarrassing incident, and only recently (16 years later) had she fully shared with Ray the resentment she harbored. As it turns out, Ray may have overestimated his wife's willingness to forgive him those many years ago. Even as our interview progressed, the couple came to a new understanding of the event. It may be only now that Doris has fully "let go" of the resentment she felt toward her husband. In that sense, the forgiveness has been a lengthy relational process of forgetting *and* remembering.

Partners sometimes express marked ambivalence about forgiving and forgetting. Recall Judy and Dion from Chapter 2, the couple that quarreled over a move to Alabama. "I don't think I've *ever* forgiven him," Judy commented. "You know, I've *forgotten* about it." She still doesn't understand why Dion made the relocation decision without her. "I will probably always kind of hold that against him. I don't know that I can really fully forgive." Yet, "it's like, now, we just kind of *kid* about it. So maybe in my heart I *have* forgiven." Judy's comments also remind us that contradiction between cognition and emotion appears in the dialogues of many long-term couples.

Heart versus mind

Serious transgressions elicit intense emotional responses, including shock, anger, and fear. In their discourse, couples often contrast these emotions with their cognitive/intellectual reactions. They identify tensions between "heart" and "head." Frequently the emotional dimension is given more credence. Thus, an apology "from the heart" may have deeper significance than simply saying "I am sorry." The expression of emotion seems to "authenticate" the apology and signal that the offender "really means it."

In contrast, after her husband's affair, Sally described an intellectual *decision* to communicate forgiveness before she *felt* forgiving:

Therapists say you don't have to forgive in the beginning; you have to work at it. Well, I learned you could forgive in the beginning. Even if you just mouth it in your heart. Because there is something to saying, "I forgive you . . ." And then you start building on that.

As Sally indicates, using forgiveness discourse, saying "I forgive you" or similar words, is one way to manage the dialectic of heart and mind. For her, these words initiated a process that would eventually allow her emotions to catch up to her intellectual commitments. This conversational move may exploit the inherent ambiguity of the forgiveness concept. Someone in Sally's position may be signaling a decision to forgo revenge and a commitment (or at least an openness) to rehabilitate the relationship. At the same time, she withholds comment on her emotions, which remain unsettled. Sally wondered out loud if she would ever *really* love her husband again. Yet, she initiated what turned out to be an extended emotional journey that continues to this day, through which she has gradually come to feel loving toward her once-unfaithful husband.

For one of our anonymous survey respondents, this emotional journey never really began. He described being terribly embarrassed by a coworker in the presence of peers. When the coworker apologized, "I said I forgave him. But we no longer work with each other and, deep down, I never *really* forgave him." In this case, the communication of (false) forgiveness may simply relieve relational awkwardness. In work relationships, role requirements may prescribe such pseudo-forgiveness

("Don't worry about it"). Aware of these expectations, our respondent manages the heart/mind dialectic by creating the expected appearance of equanimity and hiding his "deep down" feelings. If the relationship had persisted, communicative opportunities for integrating cognitive and emotional dimensions of forgiveness eventually may have presented themselves. Perhaps the offended employee would have admitted his continued hard feelings. Or, the offender may have offered a heartfelt apology and pledged to rectify the situation. However, in this instance, forgiveness discourse simply functioned as a delaying tactic until the relationship could be terminated.

In another example, Betty described forgiveness as a kind of ongoing struggle between heart and mind as she and her husband recovered from an affair. Betty knew things were better when she could curtail her obsessive thinking and start feeling again:

> I would say in the past month, we've made giant strides. Or *I've* made giant strides. I don't know if he's felt it as I have, but my mind doesn't dwell on it all the time and I can truly love him again. And um, I really want it to work, not just an act of my will but really in my heart. You know?

For Betty, the early stages of forgiveness apparently required considerable cognitive effort, an "act of will" as she describes it. The emergence of positive emotions seems to signal an important turning point, where heart and mind are aligned.

Trust versus risk

Transgressions degrade trust. Forgiveness is sometimes described as a process of rebuilding trust while reducing the risk of future harm. Karla doesn't know if she and her previously unfaithful husband will ever experience 100% trust because she is "afraid to be vulnerable." At the same time, she wants "a real marriage," one that presumably includes high levels of trust and safety:

> I'm still working through the forgiveness . . . and I think I'm getting there. I know we're going to stay married. There's no question in my mind and I know we're going to have a good marriage. And I don't know if there'll be 100% trust ever again. I don't know. Right now, I don't feel trust. But, I think you can forgive and still have to . . . hopefully we can get to that point again. You know, I'm afraid to be vulnerable, but at the same time, I don't want

a marriage where we're just going through the motions so that we stayed married. I want a marriage, I mean a real marriage.

As we discuss in Chapter 4, partners sometimes "hedge their bets" by offering conditional forgiveness. They manage the trust/risk dialectic by offering forgiveness with qualifications designed to protect themselves and reduce relational risk. This approach is evident in discourse of the type "I will forgive you but don't ever do that to me again" or the institution of new rules: "From now on, you call me if you are going to be late more than 10 minutes." Increased monitoring of the offender's compliance with relational rules may gradually lead to the conclusion that he or she can be trusted again.

As Lisa and her husband recovered from recurring financial crises, she realized that she had undermined trust by seeking safety. She wanted to protect herself and her husband from bad financial news and avoid the conflicts that they experienced over money. "I didn't discuss it. It was silly on my part, but I was trying to protect him." By hiding their financial problems, Lisa bought temporary safety at the cost of trust. A new communication practice emerged from their efforts to negotiate forgiveness. Lisa learned to initiate discussion as soon as she saw financial problems starting. As she said, "I got a little more mature. I learned to say, 'wait a minute, before I get to that point, let's discuss this . . . and see if I can't diffuse it before it gets out of hand.'" For his part, Samuel agreed to encourage such discussions and not overreact when Lisa brought up bad news. These communication practices enhanced trust and reduced the relational risk associated with financial discussions.

Questions Raised by Dialectical Theory

The primary issues raised by dialectical theory concern types of dialectics and the means by which they are managed (see Table 3.1 for other questions). As Baxter (2003) notes, the dialectics identified in earlier work, such as autonomy/interdependence, were not exhaustive. New contradictions emerge as people participate in different kinds of relationships and confront different relational circumstances. We have identified several that emerge as couples discuss transgressions and forgiveness. But students and researchers should question whether new dialectics emerge in such discourse. From our experience, several possibilities emerge. For example, there may be inherent tensions between concepts such as *exoneration and blame* or *mercy and punishment*. Relationships are characterized by obligation and altruism. Are these potentially oppositional forces expressed in forgiveness discourse? How?

Table 3.1   Dialectical Theory: Questions for Students and Researchers

1. What other dialectics emerge in discussions about forgiveness? Consider such possibilities as exoneration/blame or obligation/altruism.

2. How is forgiveness practiced differently in nonromantic relationships? What factors make forgiveness different in family and extended family relationships?

3. What about work relationships? Are certain kinds of organizational cultures experienced as more forgiving? Which communication practices and organizational values would help employees negotiate forgiveness rather than enact vengeance?

4. What forms of discourse allow opposing forces to coexist as the forgiveness process proceeds? Consider such conversational devices as hedges, delays, questions, reasons, self-disclosures, recollections, and humorous comments. How is nonverbal behavior incorporated in these forms?

5. How are religious and secular approaches to forgiveness similar and different? What kinds of language reveal these differences?

As we discussed in Chapter 1, the notion of forgiveness has both secular and religious roots. Some couples find motivation to repair damaged relationships in religious teachings about the sacredness of marriage and the forgiving nature of God. Others derive motivation from secular sources, such as the power of romantic love or the need to preserve family ties. At the same time, religious sanctions make some acts (e.g., infidelity) seem unforgivable and some secular practices (e.g., adversarial divorce proceedings) discourage forgiving behavior. Students and scholars should examine the role of forgiving discourse in light of the *secular/sacred* dynamic.

Dialectical theory assumes that contradiction arises inevitably from merging of individual identities and motivations in the context of a relationship. Yet, most of the work to date has been limited to dyadic personal relationships (Baxter, 2003). What kinds of dialectics emerge in the discourse of families as they collectively recover from transgressions committed by one or more members? One of our long-married couples told us that the bride's parents refused to attend the wedding because of religious differences with the groom's family. Later, the parents regretted the decision and sought to rebuild ties with the young couple. How is forgiveness negotiated in such situations? Organizations are characterized by formal and informal relational networks, and define such factors as power, quality of communication, and geographic distance. How is forgiveness interpreted, negotiated, and communicated across a network? How do the mission and culture of an organization create or manage contradictions in forgiveness practices? Thus far, only a handful of researchers have considered forgiveness in work contexts (Aquino, Grover, Goldman, & Folger, 2003; Bradfield & Aquino, 1999; Metts et al., 2006).

Finally, the role of speech behavior in expressing dialectics of forgiveness requires study in more detail. We have seen that participants use communication *tactics* to manage oppositional forces, for example by offering conditional forgiveness to build trust and protect against additional hurt. However, by looking more closely and simultaneously at the verbal and nonverbal dimensions of forgiveness dialogue, we appreciate the subtleties of this process. Consider this exchange between two friends:

Friend #1:   Listen, I really am sorry. I had *no idea* you would be so hurt when I told about your break-up with Eric.

Friend #2:   No, it's OK. It's just that I *trusted* you to keep it secret. I am not ready to talk to others about it yet.

These utterances enact forgiveness quite differently, depending on the elements emphasized by the speakers. Friend #1 emphasizes that she had *no idea.* She may be saying that although she is sorry for the hurt that was experienced, the situation was accidental, and thus not really requiring of forgiveness. In fact, she may be implying that her friend is being unreasonably extreme in her sensitivity. Friend #2 chooses not to emphasize her releasing of the friend, as she might have by saying "No, *really,* it's *ok.*" Instead she emphasizes the violation of trust. Presumably, future exchanges will address this relational issue before forgiveness is fully granted.

❖ UNCERTAINTY MANAGEMENT FRAMEWORKS

Uncertainty has been a central construct in communication theory since the introduction of uncertainty reduction theory in the 1970s (Berger & Calabrese, 1975). This early work hypothesized that relational partners were motivated to reduce uncertainty so they could make informed choices about potential mates and predict reactions to communication behaviors. Questions, self-disclosures, and consultations with third parties are among the communication tools used to reduce uncertainty and increase social knowledge (Berger & Kellermann, 1994). In subsequent decades, scholars have offered a host of alternative theories, including most recently problematic integration theory (Babrow, 2001), uncertainty management theory (Brashers, 2001), and the theory of motivated information management (Afifi & Weiner, 2004). The new formulations have addressed limitations of the earlier work, including (1) recognition that uncertainty is an inevitable and sometimes positive condition rather than simply a negative motivator of communication behavior, (2) increased interest in how uncertainty is managed and sustained through communication, and (3) acknowledgment of the role played by information *providers* as well as seekers.

In this section, we draw most heavily on the theory of motivated information management (Afifi & Weiner, 2004) because it is recent, compatible with most other uncertainty-related frameworks, and useful in discussing some aspects of forgiveness negotiations.

Theoretical Principles

The theory assumes that information management proceeds through stages of *interpretation, evaluation,* and *decision.* As indicated in Figure 3.1, the process starts when a discrepancy between desired and experienced levels of uncertainty is detected and interpreted. This discrepancy may trigger anxiety, although as others have noted (e.g., Brashers, 2001), elevated levels of uncertainty can be perceived positively. Uncertainty may alleviate boredom and create the possibility for novelty in an otherwise predictable relationship. In a chronically troubled relationship, increased uncertainty about the future may be a hopeful sign that the relationship could improve rather than continue along a certain path toward dissolution. In either case, the communicators may feel motivated to increase or decrease the size of the discrepancy.

During the evaluation stage, communicators consider the potential *outcomes* of information management behaviors. What are the likely costs and benefits of seeking information? Is the information obtained likely to be worth the effort expended? Will it be negative or positive in nature? For example, is the process of "checking up" with third parties on the sexual fidelity of one's mate worth the damaged relational trust potentially wrought by such inquiries?

Efficacy is also considered during the evaluation stage. Do the communicators possess the competencies needed to decrease or increase uncertainty? For example, can they be tactful enough to extract delicate information from a reluctant source? Are they capable of withholding

Information Seeker

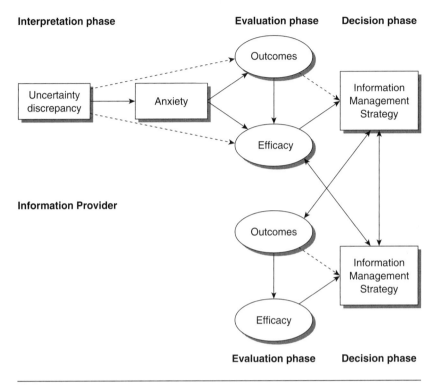

Figure 3.1 The Information Management Process as Proposed in the Theory of Motivated Information Management

SOURCE: From Afifi, W. A., & Weiner, J. L. (2004). Toward a theory of motivated information management. *Communication Theory, 14,* 167–190. Figure 1 reprinted with permission of Blackwell Publishing.

information when questioned aggressively? According to Afifi and Weiner (2004), the information seeker's ability to *cope* with negative information and the likelihood that a source can provide the needed information are other efficacy factors. Ultimately, the third stage (decision) involves the selection of an information management strategy that is responsive to these interpretation and evaluation factors.

Application to Forgiveness

The construct of uncertainty has received some attention from forgiveness researchers. An indirect example comes from a study reported by Emmers and Canary (1996), who adapted uncertainty reduction theory (Berger & Calebrese, 1975) to study the relationship-repair tactics young couples use. They theorized that transgressions in romantic relationships heightened uncertainty and that efforts to repair romantic relationships could be conceptualized as uncertainty management tactics. Although not a primary focus of this research, "forgiveness" emerged in participant reports as one means of managing the uncertainty associated with broken relationships. We see this in our own research when participants describe forgiveness as a means of bringing closure to an argument or reducing relational doubt. However, as indicated in the example below, the relationship between forgiveness and uncertainty is not always straightforward.

Shana worked as an assistant youth minister in a large church, but her relationship with the youth minister (Y.M.) was complicated because the pair had dated briefly in the past. Y.M. had "trouble letting go" of his feelings for Shana. Over time she grew weary and resentful of his "inappropriate comments." These frustrations were a contributing factor in her decision to leave the job. Shana explains what happened about one month later:

> Y.M. set a date to have lunch with me and we talked. At this time he apologized and explained that he felt responsible for my leaving. Because I hadn't given it much thought at the time, I told him, "No problem. No, you weren't the cause." But after doing some soul searching and trying to address the roots of some of my anger, I realize he did owe me an apology. At the time of the lunch I forgave him but not with much thought. For him this settled it. He felt better knowing that I forgave him. But now I feel like I need to forgive him *again.* Because I hadn't really come to terms for why I was forgiving him then. I still have doubts about him—and our relationship has not grown or gotten stronger.

By offering superficial forgiveness, Shana relieved her boss of uncertainty. For him, the matter was "settled." But for Shana, this forgiveness episode prolonged uncertainty and maybe even increased it. She still has "doubts about him" and needs to "forgive him again" now that she has sifted through the reasons for her anger. Perhaps this second interaction will bring clarity and closure to her relationship with Y.M.

Severe transgressions heighten relational uncertainty. They raise questions about the partner's motives and the degree of concordance in partner expectations (Kelley & Waldron, 2005). This uncertainty complicates predictions about the future of the relationship, so the offended party may monitor communication more closely, looking for clues. The sincerity of an apology may be gauged carefully for sincerity; ambivalence may signal to the victim that a "repeat performance" is possible. The result may be continued efforts to reduce uncertainty ("How do I *know* this won't happen again?"). In contrast, offers of conditional forgiveness (e.g., "I will forgive you, but only if you promise to do [not do] X") may add predictability to the relationship. One form of forgiveness-seeking discourse, the set of behaviors we previously labeled "explanations," seems particularly well suited to information management (Waldron & Kelley, 2005). Explanations provide information about the circumstances surrounding a transgression; they are frequently provided in response to requests from the wounded party. Request-explanation sequences are part of the "sense-making" step of the forgiveness process (see Chapter 4; see also Gordon et al., 2000).

We see other forgiveness-related applications of Afifi and Weiner's (2004) theory of motivated information management. The theory posits that larger discrepancies yield more motivated information seeking. In fact, as we noted in Chapter 2, severe transgressions do seem to result in heightened communicative activity. Consistent with Weick's seminal (1969) observations on organizational sense-making, we would expect more "cycles" of sense-making communication to follow serious transgressions. The theory leads to more subtle predictions as well, because it acknowledges two additional factors: (1) the importance of managing/ reducing uncertainty and (2) the communicative effort required in the process. A given transgression (e.g., sexual infidelity) will create considerable uncertainty about the offender's motives and the circumstances surrounding the offense. Nonetheless, reducing this uncertainty may be unimportant if the victimized partner believes that infidelity is an unforgivable offense under *any* circumstance. Too, the costs of managing this uncertainty (hours of counseling, emotional pain, awkward discussions with mutual friends) may outweigh the perceived benefits. In such cases, severe transgressions may lead *directly* to relationship termination, with no real effort to manage uncertainty or explore possibilities for forgiveness. Alternatively, partners may view infidelity as potentially forgivable under certain circumstances. In response, they may use communication that sustains uncertainty about the future of the relationship in the hope that continued discussion will reveal mitigating factors and possible paths to reconciliation.

The uncertainty management framework is also useful in prompting us to think more concretely about the forms of communication used during forgiveness negotiations. Afifi and Weiner (2004) discuss three strategies. The first, *seeking relevant information*, corresponds to the transgression detection/presentation strategies discussed in Chapter 4, including questioning the offender, consulting third parties, hinting, and self-disclosure. *Avoiding relevant information* is a second strategy, one that might reveal itself when partners use delay, deception, editing, and diversion tactics (e.g., humor) when communicating about transgressions. A third strategy is *cognitive appraisal*, or what we earlier called *reframing*. Here the partners redefine uncertainty. In the case of forgiveness episodes, we have heard partners describe their now-uncertain future as a "new journey," a "test of faith," and "throwing out the rule book and starting over."

Questions Raised by Uncertainty Management Theories

As with any conceptual framework, uncertainty management approaches direct our attention to only selected aspects of the communication process. They underplay other potentially important elements, such as the role of individual and relational identity in shaping reactions to transgressions. Nonetheless, we are convinced that forgiveness is in part a process in which people manage uncertainty about their shared expectations, values, and relational plans. This approach yields a rich set of research and discussion questions, some of which are presented in Table 3.2. Perhaps most important are those that address our assumption that uncertainty "drives" the production of some forgiveness-seeking and -granting behavior. Do partners report higher levels of relational uncertainty after transgressions, as we assume? If so, what are they uncertain *about*? Is it the intent of the violator, circumstances surrounding the transgression, the victim's values related to the act, responsibility for the transgression, or perceptions of third parties who witness the act? How do forgiveness negotiations vary in light of these different objects of uncertainty? For example, if third-party perceptions are at issue, an unfaithful spouse may offer explanations not just to the victimized partner but also to family members and mutual friends.

From the theory of motivated information management (Afifi & Weiner, 2004), we also draw questions about efficacy. Which forgiveness-seeking behaviors reduce uncertainty most effectively? Is uncertainty management behavior associated with more forgiving partner responses? Is the ability of a wounded partner to predict a reoccurrence of the transgression important in the decision to forgive? To reconcile? Do partners feel confident that they can make such predictions based on current behavior (e.g., forgiveness-seeking behaviors)? If so, what verbal and nonverbal cues do they use?

Table 3.2   Uncertainty Management Theories: Questions for Students
                   and Researchers

---

1. Do transgressions raise levels of uncertainty?

2. Does the amount of uncertainty predict forgiveness behavior?

3. Does the amount of uncertainty predict the outcome of forgiveness
    processes?

4. Which forgiveness-seeking behaviors function to reduce or increase
    uncertainty?

5. Which forgiveness-granting behaviors function to reduce or increase
    uncertainty?

6. Does the object of the uncertainty alter the communicative response?

7. How do couples manage this uncertainty?

8. Is the ability of a wounded partner to predict a reoccurrence of the
    transgression important in shaping forgiving communication?

9. Do wounded partners predict the future on the basis of forgiveness-
    seeking behaviors?

10. What verbal and nonverbal behaviors increase confidence in such
    predictions?

11. What uncertainty management patterns develop under conditions of
    sustained uncertainty?

❖ IDENTITY MANAGEMENT THEORIES

This theoretical approach links forgiveness to the face-management
activities of relational partners (e.g., Afifi et al., 2001). Central to the
seminal work of sociologist Erving Goffman (1955, 1959), "face" refers
to the identity we create and sustain through our social interactions. For
Goffman, face is not merely a dispassionate public performance. People
value their self-perceptions as competent, compassionate, humorous,
and so forth. They count on others to show support through displays
of deference or by laughing appropriately at jokes. In this way, face
management is a cooperative social process, not merely an individual
production. We feel defensive when our face is ignored, threatened,
or attacked. These *face-threatening acts* require a response, from either
the offenders who must make amends (e.g., through apology) or the
offended parties who reassert their desirable qualities or mount a coun-
terattack. Goffman further observed that social actors feel *out of face*, that
is, embarrassed and out-of-sorts, when their behavior is revealed to be

inconsistent with their public identity, as when an apparently honest person is caught in a deception, a calm person loses his or her temper, or an otherwise savvy person is snared by a practical joke.

Identity management theories are clearly communicative in that face is presented, sustained, and threatened through symbolic action. This approach has spawned countless studies of the communicative acts that threaten or protect face, a good deal of which can be traced to the writings of Brown and Levinson (1978). These linguists proposed *politeness theory* as an extension of Goffman's work. They refined the face concept by arguing that it included positive and negative dimensions. *Positive* face refers to the need for approval—our desire that others accept and reinforce our self-definition. *Negative* face is our desire to be unimpeded in self-presentation. According to Brown and Levinson, social actors require autonomy if they are to create their own identities; acts that restrict that autonomy are face threatening. For example, closed questions ("Yes or no?") and threats ("Do what I say or you will be punished.") limit response options to those created by the interrogator.

Theoretical Principles

Forgiving communication can be conceptualized as a process of managing self-presentation in the presence of face-threatening relational transgressions. For example, when discovered, the act of adultery threatens the reputation of the adulterer. As well, a victim of adultery may feel embarrassment, shame, or anger in part because his or her positive face (e.g., I am a valued and exclusive mate) is threatened. Recall that Lisa (introduced in Chapter 2) interpreted her financial missteps in face-management terms: "It was mostly that I was ashamed of getting into my own trouble—that I was incompetent." To sustain her image as a competent spouse, she avoided discussing the problem with her husband.

Researchers adopting this theoretical perspective describe the behaviors that mitigate or redress face threats. For example, a private confession and earnest request for forgiveness would be less face-threatening to the victim of adultery than an approach that implied shared blame. In fact, Afifi and colleagues (2001) found that such forgiveness-seeking behavior could have ameliorating effects on the partner's perceptions of the affair (but perhaps not on relational outcomes). Cindy recalled a face-threatening incident in high school, when "four of my girl friends came over to my house and told me that they didn't want to be friends anymore." She was hurt and angry and the girls "all exchanged words." Over time however, "one-by-one, all of them made an attempt to be chummy with me." The girls didn't apologize outright but they were "meek and careful with what they said at first." These girls were using what Brown and Levinson (1978) call "tact." They avoided calling attention to their own face-threatening rejection of Cindy. At the same time, they allowed her to signal whether she would again accept them as friends.

Unlike Cindy's friends, most social actors feel pressure to *account for* inappropriate behavior. *Account-making* is the communicative process by which social failures are managed between actors (Antaki, 1994; Cody & McLaughlin, 1988). The accounting process begins with the experience of a failure event, which could be a transgression (excessive speeding by a driver) or an omission (failing to remember a spouse's birthday). The offender is then asked to account for this failure (by a judge or the neglected spouse). Accounts take a variety of forms, including excuses ("The speed limit sign was too small to read."), justifications ("Driving slower would have caused traffic congestion."), and concessions ("Sorry. I was wrong to forget your birthday."). The offender then evaluates the credibility of the account and decides how to proceed. Some research has evaluated the effectiveness of various kinds of accounts in such settings as traffic court (Cody & McLaughlin, 1988). In general, the research suggests that excuses are relatively ineffective in such settings, perhaps because they attempt to side-step the system of rules and laws that regulate human conduct. Judges (and other evaluators) have a vested interest in making sure these rules are upheld. Accounts that explicitly acknowledge violations and pledge compliance are sometimes treated more sympathetically.

Application to Forgiveness

It can be fruitful to conceive forgiveness as a process of managing identity. Clearly, the relational transgressions that trigger the forgiveness process can be conceptualized as potentially face-threatening acts. We can see that the employee who chooses to "go over the head" of a supervisor questions that person's authority and competence (threat to positive face) while potentially risking some aspects of their own identity (e.g., as a loyal subordinate). Parents who make threats are attempting to restrict the autonomy of their children (threat to negative face). From this point of view, a primary task of forgiving communication may be the restoration of face for both parties. Forgiveness-seeking tactics discussed in Chapter 4, such as "explicit acknowledgement" and "compensation," may function to mitigate face threat. In the first instance, the offender makes clear that he or she, not the victim, is at fault. This move affirms the victim's identity as an innocent party. In the second case, reparations are offered to "make up for" for the identity loss.

Afifi et al. (2001) argued for the link between identity management and forgiveness in an article on infidelity in young romantic pairs. The authors studied how the "method of discovery" shaped partners' reactions to infidelity and their perceptions of relational damage. Was it best to learn about a partner's infidelity through a direct confession, reports from a third party, accidental discovery, or though some other method? The authors reasoned that prospects for forgiveness and possible reconciliation would be lessened when identity threats to the "innocent" partner were maximized. For example, any suggestion that blame for the affair was shared would add to the already substantial face threat inherent in infidelity. As well, discovery through third parties should be more face-threatening than private confession. The task of face restoration is more onerous when multiple parties witness the face threat. As might be expected, responses to infidelity were uniformly negative, as most romantic relationships were seriously damaged. However, the authors found some evidence that face-protective discovery methods may have mitigated the damage.

The account-making literature provides fertile ground for forgiveness research. The nature of the account offered by the transgressor may advance or impede progress toward forgiveness. For example, Metts (1994) argues that acknowledging the harm caused by one's behavior (and offering an apology) potentially transforms the emotional tone of an encounter. When the offender takes responsibility, it is easier for the victimized party to release feelings of hostility and contemplate reconciliation (see Enright et al., 1991). In contrast are discourses that minimize the offense, defend it, or avoid it. Victims are more likely to reject these, and the relationship may trend toward increased conflict (Schonbach & Kleibaumhuter, 1990). In presenting his forgiveness model, Hargrave (1994) suggested that apology, one kind of account, is a necessary prelude to relationship renegotiation. In fact, the relationship between apology and forgiveness has been well established (McCullough et al., 1997). All of this research supports the idea that forgiveness is fostered by communication that helps the partners sustain valued aspects of their identities despite the occurrence of serious transgressions.

Questions Raised by Identity Management Theories

Identity management theories raise unexplored questions about the forgiveness processes. Table 3.3 lists some of these. We wonder if (and how) identity protection functions as a *motivator* for forgiving communication. Does the desire for identity affirmation motivate individuals to seek or grant forgiveness? Consider the otherwise honest person who confesses to telling a lie and is forgiven by a friend. Is the granting of forgiveness essential to restoring the offender's sense of an honest self? Does the forgiveness-granter find identity gratification as well, by appearing to be compassionate, reasonable, or generous? If so, forgiveness episodes should be studied more closely as social sites for the production and reinforcement of individual identities.

If we assume that forgiveness transactions have the potential to threaten and restore identity, then we should ask what kinds of communication behaviors serve this purpose. What kinds of forgiveness-seeking behaviors are most responsive to identity concerns? What about forgiveness-granting behaviors? Several of the behaviors discussed in Chapter 4, such as hinting (about a transgression) and offering assurance (when granting forgiveness), seem well suited to ward off threats to identity or to reaffirm it.

In addition to examining identities of *individuals,* researchers should examine the role of forgiveness in forging *relational* identity. The fact that partners have forgiven past transgressions (or chosen not to) may be an important element in their shared identity ("the kind of couple we are"). Forgiveness may be implicit in some couples' definition of "real" marriage (Waldron & Kelley, 2005), particularly if they practice marriage within the definitions of some Christian churches.

Table 3.3   Identity Management Theories: Questions for Students and Researchers

1. Is the need to protect identity a motivator for forgiveness seeking and forgiveness granting?
2. What kinds of behaviors function to manage identity during forgiveness episodes?
3. How does forgiveness shape relational identity?
4. How is forgiveness referenced in relational narratives?
5. Is forgiveness a core element in the definition of marriage for some couples? Does this influence their use of forgiveness behaviors?
6. For what goals do people use "strategic forgiveness"? What forms does it take? What are the effects of this kind of communication on granters and receivers?

Analysis of individual and jointly told relational narratives may reveal the role of forgiveness in the construction of couple identity.

Another set of questions concerns the *strategic* use of forgiving communication for identity management purposes. Strategic forgiveness, the kind Shana initially practiced in the earlier example, divorces the verbal act of granting forgiveness from the more complicated and comprehensive process described throughout this book. In our view, genuine forgiveness is characterized by efforts to acknowledge harm, release hostility, and forgo retaliation. In contrast, strategic forgiveness is directed to the relatively narrow, but often noble, goal of assuaging identity concerns. Some examples from our data include a young woman who verbally forgave her neglectful father because "he needed it to feel better about himself." Others describe forgiving "out of pity" for the offender or to help the offender "clear his conscience." Forgiving communication may be used to meet a duty or role obligation. One daughter told us that she was "ordered to apologize" by her mother, who then "forgave her" for an insulting comment. Presumably, this kind of coerced forgiveness reinforces parental identity, but fails to address the underlying relational issues. Students and researchers may find it useful to identify other examples of "forced forgiveness." What identity management functions does it serve? Presumably these kinds of behavior allow partners to finesse problematic situations at least for the short term. Do they have long-term positive or negative effects on relationships? What are the emotional implications for the forgiver?

❖   TOWARD A NEGOTIATED MORALITY THEORY
     (NMT) OF FORGIVENESS

The theories we have reviewed thus far provide useful and very different ways of thinking about the communication of forgiveness. They all demonstrate how aspects of the forgiveness process might be *enacted* through communication, as partners negotiate contradictions, manage uncertainties, and protect identities. In proposing the beginnings of a new communicative theory of forgiveness, we are indebted to all three (and many others). Yet we find that existing communicative theories overlook some elements of the "lived experience" of forgiveness, at least as articulated so richly by participants in our interview and questionnaire studies. Perhaps most neglected are the issues that most *energize* forgiveness episodes and make them *matter* so much. At its core, forgiveness is fundamentally about issues of *morality*— questions of right and wrong, relational justice, and human dignity.

Morality and forgiveness have been linked in psychological (Enright et al., 1992) and theological treatments of forgiveness (Kirkup, 1993). NMT draws attention to the means by which moral standards are expressed, questioned, reinforced, and reevaluated as forgiveness is negotiated.

Theoretical Principles

We start with some core assumptions and principles (see Table 3.4). First, we assume that *human relationships are interpreted with reference to a system of implicit or explicit values.* Values are the standards that define conduct as right or wrong, better or worse, just or unjust, respectful or disrespectful. Examples include honesty, respect for free choice (over coercion), equity, and loyalty. We don't mean that values are always conceived as simple bipolar constructs, although some persons may experience them that way. They are often complicated, conflicting, and subject to reinterpretation as relational circumstances change. As a case in point, honesty can be conceived along a right/wrong continuum, with some behavior being judged "too honest" or "not honest enough." Honesty may be in tension with other values (as when value of honest criticism conflicts with the value of loyalty to one's partner). Dishonest behavior may be reinterpreted, as when deception is rationalized as a "just a white lie." Drawing from dialectical theory, we assume that forgiveness discourse enacts the tensions that inevitably emerge as the value systems of individuals and are merged with those of work groups, families, friends, and romantic partners.

Second, we assume that *values are derived from three sources.* (1) *Community* values are the normative standards shared by large social groups, including subcultures, religious groups, and organizations. Members are socialized to the importance of education, elders, marriage and other community values. (2) *Personal* values are based on individual decisions to accept, modify, reject, or replace social values. Personal values are inherent to the identity of an individual. They define the person *across* relationships and situations. An individual may decide, for example, that he or she will be forgiving, honest, or deserving of respect regardless of the relationship context or situation. (3) *Relational* values define family, romantic, friend, coworker, and other close relationships. They are negotiated implicitly or explicitly and may concern such factors as openness of communication, privacy, sexual fidelity, or equality in decision making. Relational values are shared (at least in part) by those participating in a relationship. They are negotiated, not merely inherited through

Table 3.4   Theoretical Assumptions of the Negotiated Morality Theory
(NMT) of Forgiveness

1. Human relationships are interpreted with reference to a system of implicit or explicit values.

2. Forgiveness-related values are derived from community, personal, and relational sources.

3. The desire to preserve moral codes motivates forgiving (and unforgiving) behavior.

4. Values that are socially sanctioned, individually internalized, and relationally shared are most motivating of forgiving and unforgiving behavior.

5. Values with long relational histories are more motivating than those with short histories.

6. Behavior that threatens important values provokes emotional responses in those with a vested interest in maintaining those values.

7. The processes of forgiving communication are a primary means by which moral codes are expressed, negotiated, and restored in human relationships.

8. The process of forgiveness influences the quality of post-transgression relationships, including the extent to which it is experienced as trustworthy, intimate, and just.

SOURCE: From Afifi, W. A., & Weiner, J. L. (2004). Toward a theory of motivated information management. *Communication Theory, 14,* 167–190. Figure reprinted with permission of Blackwell Publishing.

community membership. When key values cease to be shared, relationships are redefined and, sometimes, ended. In keeping with early versions of uncertainty management theory (e.g., Berger & Calabrese, 1975), we assume that relationship partners integrate their social and personal values as part of a larger process of developing idiosyncratic relational understandings. In this sense, relationships are primary sites for the negotiation of moral codes.

Third, we assume that *the desire to preserve moral codes is what motivates forgiving (and unforgiving) behavior.* Value importance, the degree to which persons are *committed to* or *invested in* values, also stems from multiple sources. Social values shape acceptance in a culture or an organization; they are important because they lead to rewards or negative sanctions. For example, positive evaluations at work may depend in part on acceptance of an organization's core values, such as respect for authority. Personal values are important because they are linked to identity, dignity, and, ultimately, ego. They define who we are and how we expect to be treated by others. As Goffman (1955) did with his notion of face, we assume that individuals feel emotionally invested in their personal values and are motivated to display, affirm, and protect them in their interactions with others. Finally, relational values are important because they provide predictability, assurance, safety, and a shared identity. For example, a daughter's acceptance of a family's values related to marriage and children may help her parents predict the future of the relationship ("She is likely to marry. We are likely to be grandparents to her children."). A tardy employee who apologizes to a supervisor offers assurance that shared values regarding timeliness are respected. Romantic partners find emotional safety and reduced risk when they negotiate shared commitments to values such as sexual fidelity or fiscal responsibility. Moreover, relational identities can be nested in protective and beneficial social structures—a reason some gay couples desire the relational identity associated with marriage.

Fourth, we further assume that values vary in importance. *Those which are socially sanctioned, individually internalized, and relationally shared are considered more important* than those which are endorsed at just one or two of these levels. Thus, a person who belongs to a church that values traditional marriage, identifies himself or herself in terms of traditional gender roles, and negotiates traditional ways of relating with a spouse, will weight this value more heavily than a person who belongs to the same church but chooses not to internalize this value or practice it in romantic relationship. Fifth, we assume *that history is associated with importance:* values that have been held for long periods of time are more important than those with short histories.

A sixth principle is that because values are important, *behavior that threatens important values provokes emotional responses in those with a vested interest in maintaining those values.* Forgiveness is most challenging and most called for when highly important values are involved in this inconsistency. Inconsistency takes multiple forms. Individuals can behave in a manner inconsistent with their personal values, as when a normally honest child lies to a parent. On discovery of the lie, the child may feel guilt or shame (his or her identity as an honest person is called into question), the parent may feel threatened (his or her identity as a good parent is less assured), and both may experience uncertainty about the relationship's future given that a shared value (trustworthiness) has been violated. In addition, consistent with Goffman (1955) and Brown and Levinson (1978), certain behaviors performed by others may be interpreted as direct attacks on values. This is the case when a worker questions a peer's task competence or a parent accuses a child of selfishness.

The seventh principle is this: *The processes of forgiving communication (e.g., forgiveness seeking) are a primary means by which moral codes are expressed and negotiated in human relationships.* We discuss the moral functions of forgiving communication below.

Finally, we propose that *the extent to which values are successfully negotiated through forgiveness can determine the quality of post-transgression relationships, including the extent to which the relationship is experienced as trustworthy, intimate, and just.*

Moral Functions of Forgiveness Negotiations

Earlier, we described forgiveness as a negotiation enacted through the communication processes of transgression presentation/detection, emotion management, sense-making, forgiveness-seeking, forgiveness-granting, and relationship negotiation. Each of these processes is enacted through the symbolic behavior of multiple parties, such as members of a work team, family, or romantic relationship. This relational focus is central to our Negotiated Morality Theory of forgiveness, in that relationships are assumed to be the sites where value inconsistencies are "worked out." As noted in Table 3.5, episodes of forgiving communication serve a number of moral functions in personal and work relationships.

Table 3.5   Moral Functions of Forgiving Communication

1. Defining moral standards
2. Establishing accountability
3. Engaging moral tensions
4. Restoring relational justice through atonement
5. Hope: (Re)imagining a moral future
6. Honoring the self
7. Redirecting hostility
8. Increasing safety and certainty
9. Finding closure
10. Possible reconciliation

Defining moral standards

Forgiveness episodes typically begin when an important moral assumption has been called into question. When a young student confesses cheating on an exam, the behaviors of the student and the teacher assert and reinforce a moral standard. They make moral *meaning*. Has a wrong been committed? The teacher might use a sense-making question ("Did you *know* you were cheating when you asked Molly for the answer?") to determine if the student intentionally broke the standard. Fully informed, intentional cheating may be "more wrong" than unintentional cheating. If the cheating was intentional, she may decide that conditional forgiveness is the best way to clarify the standard ("I am glad you told me about this. During recess, why don't you write about why cheating is wrong, so it won't happen again."). In addition to clarifying the standard, the teacher implicitly communicates conditional forgiveness ("It is OK if you don't do it again.") and simultaneously praises the child for enacting another value (honestly admitting mistakes).

Consider another example, this time from the workplace. A worker accuses a team leader of favoritism in the distribution of work tasks. The accusation has the effect of highlighting a presumed value (equitable treatment). The team leader's response may clarify the underlying value. For example, the leader may indicate that task assignments are based on seniority—those with the longest tenure are allowed to choose tasks first. Alternatively, the team leader may offer to discuss the task assignment process, only to discover that the employee has in fact been treated wrongly given the equity standards of their community.

In some cases, the applicable moral standards may be easily determined. In others, the parties may *disagree* about the standards or one party may choose to *deny* them. In an example of the latter, former President Bill Clinton famously held that his intimate relations with White House intern Monica Lewinsky did not count as an extramarital affair, because the pair never engaged in sexual intercourse. Most of the public, and his spouse, disagreed. In yet another variation, the relevant relational standards may be *unarticulated* or ambiguous. In such cases, a goal of forgiveness negotiations may be to reduce uncertainty about the shared standards. For example, teenaged couples frequently report negative incidents in which one partner initiates sexual behavior considered off-limits by the other. Part of the forgiveness process would involve clarifying sexual values and the degree to which they are truly shared.

Establishing accountability

Another moral task is to determine responsibility for wrongful acts. Communication is the means by which responsibility is claimed, denied, or shared. Accountability can be communicated straightforwardly. Jan reported (discussed in Chapter 4) that her unfaithful husband admitted to being "100% wrong." However, establishing accountability can also be a contentious and protracted process. Jill (also discussed in Chapter 4) reported that her boyfriend failed to recognize the seriousness of his drunken behavior. She chose not to accept his "insincere" apology and waited several days until he accepted full responsibility for his actions. Of course, many relational transgressions involve shared responsibility to some degree. In such cases, forgiveness is characterized by behavior sequences such as mutual confessions or joint pledges of forgiveness.

Engaging moral tensions

Almost inevitably, forgiveness situations involve multiple values, some of which are brought into a state of contradiction or tension. In the workplace situation above, the values of equity and seniority are in tension. Team member and leader may acknowledge that both values define their relationship. Drawing in part from Baxter's evolving discussion of relational dialectics (Baxter, 2003), we conceptualize forgiving communication as a primary means by which these tensions are engaged and managed. Several approaches are obvious in our data.

First, communication can be used to *prioritize* values. One version of this involves context shifting—a process of determining whether social, relational, or personal values receive primacy in a given forgiveness episode. When one partner commits adultery, a couple may be forced to discuss how their shared value commitments ("Sexual infidelity is unforgivable in this marriage.") should be weighed against the values of the communities to which they belong. For example, Marta, a Mexican American woman, told us that she was bothered by her husband's womanizing earlier in their marriage. However, she cited her church and her own mother as sources for her motivation to forgive Alejandro when he asked for it. (Her mother told her that men become more domesticated as they age.) In her talks with Alejandro, Marta prioritized longevity of marriage over his sexual fidelity, explaining that she could forgive his infidelity only if he pledged to remain an otherwise responsible husband. As we sat in their living room, Alejandro recounted his early transgressions with regret and tenderly described her repeated willingness to forgive him until he "learned the error of my ways."

In contrast to Marta, others might choose personal values over relational and cultural values as they practice forgiveness. For example, one's personal commitment to relational fidelity may trump relational commitments to marriage or religious dictates. In such instances, forgiveness discourse may be a matter of affirming that wrongdoing has occurred and seeking apology as a way to affirm one's personal dignity. An apology may be accepted and forgiveness may be granted, but the relationship may be terminated to protect the self from future violations.

Personal commitments are sometimes prioritized over community commitments. Mason is a young homosexual who believes that gay people should have the right to marry. He rejects his church's teaching on homosexuality because it conflicts with his sense that all human beings, including himself, were created equal under God. Mason had a blow-up with his father over this issue, after his father criticized his "gay lifestyle." He insisted that his father apologize and called him a "bigot." After the pair cooled down, a discussion of values ensued. Mason explained that denying his identity was out of the question and that his relationship with his father (and his church) would always be strained if he were asked to do so. It took several years of uncomfortable family gatherings before Mason's father came to prioritize his relationship with Mason over this particular religious teaching. He eventually apologized to his son. Mason had negotiated a kind of uneasy peace with his father long before the apology, but it was only then that he really "let go of the anger I felt toward him."

Values in tension are sometimes *reframed*, as Kelley (1998) suggested in his article on the communication of forgiveness. Reframing can be accomplished by invoking a superordinate value that allows the conflicting values to coexist in relative harmony. In the preceding leader-member example, the tension between equity and seniority may be resolved by invoking the value of fairness. Perhaps they can agree that the member has been wronged according to the standard of fairness. After all, employees have not been treated the same. Yet the leader has been wrongly accused, in the sense that the seniority system is fair. Those who have invested the most time receive the most benefit. In this case, the forgiveness negotiation proceeds from a mutual recognition of violated values and (perhaps) mutual efforts to seek forgiveness through apology ("Sorry, I should not have accused you of unfairness.") and explanation ("I should have let you know about the seniority rule."). In each of these statements, the use of the word "should" is recognition of the moral code.

Finally, we should note that the commitment to forgiveness as a community, personal, and relational value is itself an important factor in values negotiation. Psychologists have long considered forgiveness to be a motivating construct (e.g., Hargrave, 1994) more than a communication process. People who are committed to forgiveness as a core value are presumed to be more likely to seek and grant forgiveness.

Restoring relational justice through atonement

Justice is the sense that people are treated fairly and that a shared set of moral values will prevail. As we view it, forgiving communication is an informal means of deriving justice in personal relationships. Atonement is the making of amends for violations of relational justice. One option is to offer restitution by offering compensation for losses, as when a teenager offers to pay for repairs after damaging the family car. Self-criticism is a form of atonement ("I really don't deserve to keep my job after that bone-headed mistake."). Requests for, and pledges of, improved behavior may be enough to make amends ("I promise to never hurt you again."), as are sustained efforts to comply with relational standards. We notice that parent-child discourse reveals positive responses to such atonement efforts ("I appreciate how you have been working on calling me if you are going to be late."). Accepting punishment may also function as atonement ("I don't blame you for giving me the silent treatment."), as are efforts to "do penance."

In Catholic theology, penance involves repetitive, ritualistic behavior performed as a way to prompt thinking about an offense, purify the soul, and make amends with God. "Say ten 'Hail Marys,'" was the instruction a priest delivered to one of us (Vince) in his youth, an instruction he received all too often! Penance rituals may be seen in informal forgiveness discourse. A parent may tell a misbehaving child "go to your room and think about what you have done," and a teacher requires a tardy student to write "I will not be late" repeatedly on the blackboard.

Whereas penance is a type of compensation for harm done to the moral order, other approaches to atonement are closer to purification rituals. These erase the stain of hurtful behavior, often by removing the offender from the community and requiring a kind of sacrifice.

In the highly popular fictional novel *The Da Vinci Code*, author Dan Brown (2003) concocts a shocking, if historically suspect, account of a group of religious zealots who commit heinous crimes in the name of God. A central character retreats to his isolated lodgings to engage in self-flagellation, harming himself with a kind of whip before and after his evil deeds. The infliction of pain apparently atones for the pain he causes others and God.

Sacrifice may have atoning effects in interpersonal relationships as well. As one spouse told us about her abusive husband, "He had to give up the booze if he wanted to prove himself worthy of a wife and kids. He had a choice to make, and he did." She forgave him once he began regularly attending AA meetings and she was certain he had given up his favorite drug. In the work setting, the stain of bad behavior may be (partially) removed by atonement, when a misbehaving employee accepts leave without pay or an insensitive supervisor assents to diversity training.

Hope: (Re)imagining a hopeful future

By restoring the partners' shared understanding of relational morality, forgiving communication creates hope for the future. Confidence in relational rules can be rebuilt. Accountability is reestablished. Defensiveness, guilt, and the desire for revenge may recede. Feelings of fairness and equity may return. When forgiveness has run its course, key questions raised by the transgression will be largely resolved. Who is at fault? What did they do wrong? How can things be made right? What does the future hold for this relationship? The upset and uncertainty created by transgressions are placed more firmly in the past and the groundwork for the relational future is laid. Ultimately, forgiveness makes it possible for wounded people to imagine a future in which their individual dignity is honored and relational justice prevails (even if justice comes to be defined by an altered set of relational values). Given these positive prospects, feelings of hostility and the desire for revenge may be replaced by hope and even positive regard for those who have participated in this trying process.

Honoring the self

The forgiveness process calls attention to core values of the self and insists that these values be respected. Behavior disrespectful of core values, whether committed by the self or another, must be acknowledged and rectified before forgiveness can proceed. Thus, we would expect that forgiveness ultimately leads to an invigorated understanding of one's values and a renewed respect for self.

Redirecting hostility

The forgiveness process can provide a mechanism for persons to express negative emotion rather than retaining it or ruminating over its causes. As we conceive of the process, communication expresses and acknowledges the intense emotion that inevitably follows a transgression. Emotion is "released" in the sense that it no longer serves a purpose

Table 3.6   Selected Research Questions Raised by NMT

1. Forgiveness discourse: How are moral standards invoked? Infractions identified? Injustices claimed? Community, personal, and relational standards balanced?

2. Do cultural or religious differences influence the quality of moral discourse in forgiveness episodes? Do they make people more or less forgiving?

3. Does forgiveness spur changes in relational values or is value maintenance a more common outcome? Under what relational conditions is value transformation more likely?

4. Are such practices as self-criticism, offers of restitution, pledges of improved behavior, and penance expected by wounded partners? Perceived positively?

5. Which kinds of moral discourse lead to a restored sense of relational trust, fairness, or intimacy? Which do not? Why?

6. Should certain acts (e.g., physical abuse) remain unforgiven by the larger collective (families, organizations, societies) even when individual victims are forgiving?

7. What are the moral implications when victims (e.g., the parents of a murdered child) offer forgiveness to a perpetrator who is unrepentant or deceased?

8. Can entities (e.g., the Catholic church) request forgiveness for the immoral behavior of individual members (e.g., abusive priests?). Does doing so facilitate or impede the moral functions of forgiving communication?

once it is legitimized. Forgiveness is an alternative to the conflict that might be driven by unregulated emotion and long-held grudges.

Increasing certainty and safety

The forgiveness process may yield new relational rules or moral guidelines that make the future of the relationship more predictable and safe.

Finding closure

We have established that forgiveness can take a very long time. But the granting of forgiveness, especially the explicit kind, clearly signals a commitment to put the transgression in the past. The communicative energy expended on such moral tasks as establishing accountability now becomes available for investment in other activities, such as planning for the future.

Possible reconciliation

As we have noted, forgiveness is not the same as reconciliation. One might release hostile feelings and the desire for revenge but decide not to reconcile with the offender for any number of reasons, including protecting the self from further harm. However, we believe that the negotiation of forgiveness, the restoration of a mutually acceptable moral code, is a prerequisite for full reconciliation.

Questions Raised by NMT

We end this chapter with a brief discussion of the questions raised by our Negotiated Morality Theory of forgiveness. Table 3.6 summarizes some of these. We start with questions about discourse. How are moral concerns manifested in forgiveness discourse? Aside from the examples presented in this chapter, the nature of forgiveness discourse is rarely shared in the research literature. In forgiveness episodes, how do partners invoke moral standards? Call attention to moral infractions? Claim relational justice? Balance community, personal, and relational standards? Next, individual differences come to mind. Do cultural or religious differences influence the quality of moral discourse in forgiveness episodes? Do they make people more or less forgiving? We also wonder about the transformational effects of forgiveness episodes. Do they spur changes in relational values, or is value maintenance a more common outcome? Under what relational conditions is value transformation more likely? The connection between values-related discourse and relational outcomes is another rich area of inquiry. Are such practices as self-criticism, offers of restitution, pledges of improved behavior, and penance perceived positively? Do they in fact lead to a restored sense of relational trust, fairness, or intimacy? Finally, we call attention to situations in which the practice of forgiveness in the short term may be morally damaging in the long run. Should certain acts (e.g., physical abuse) not be forgiven by the larger collective (families, organizations, societies) even when individual victims are forgiving? What does it mean for our shared moral code when victims (e.g., the parents of a murdered child) offer forgiveness to a perpetrator who is unrepentant or deceased? Can entities (e.g., the Catholic Church) request forgiveness for the immoral behavior of individual members (e.g., abusive priests?). Does doing so facilitate or impede the moral functions of forgiving communication?

4

Communicating Forgiveness

My sister and I had a party when we were in high school. Our parents were out of town, so we saw it as a prime opportunity. We had been planning it for a couple of weeks. Everyone knew about it. Well, over a hundred people showed up! Anyway, it turned out that a chair caught on fire, someone stole our Dustbuster (don't ask!), and some tile in the family room was broken. Needless to say, when my parents got home the %x#@ hit the fan!

Of course, my sister and I cried and told them it wasn't supposed to be that big. We told them how sorry we were and that it would never happen again. They were really mad at us (understandable), but they forgave us. They said they understood we were young and things are going to happen, but it didn't excuse what we had done. They pointed out all the repercussions that could have come along with our stupidity. Considering what we had done, it was pretty good of

them to forgive us. That was eight years ago. Now we laugh
about it. We told them that we actually planned the party—
our relationship is still great.

—Jen, age 25

In several ways Jen's story illustrates how forgiveness is negotiated through complex sequences of nonverbal and verbal communication. Jen and her sister cried. Then, they presented a mitigating explanation— the party simply got bigger than expected. Next, the siblings offered an apology and a promise of improved behavior. The parents displayed anger initially but also expressed understanding and offered to forgive the girls. They communicated the reasons for their anger and used the forgiveness episode as a "teachable moment." It took years, but the sisters finally offered a full confession. The episode is now collectively reconstructed by family members and reinterpreted as a humorous incident. In fact, recollection of the parents' forgiving response seems to reinforce what the girls consider to be "a great relationship."

For the most part, communication researchers have ignored forgiveness, even as they have developed rich programs of research on other dimensions of relationship repair and maintenance (see the comprehensive volume edited by Canary & Dainton, 2003). Early studies of relationship repair tactics barely mentioned forgiveness (Dindia & Baxter, 1987). A later study indicated that young couples described "forgiveness" as one means of recovering from a negative relational event (Emmers & Canary, 1996). More recently, Metts et al. (2006) contributed a chapter conceptualizing the nature of forgiveness in the workplace. The communication behaviors that enact forgiveness in personal relationships have been the subject of only a handful of empirical studies (Kelley, 1998; Kelley & Waldron, 2005). Ironically, research psychologists and clinicians have been for some time issuing calls for more research on interpersonal dimensions of forgiveness (Exline & Baumeister, 2000; Worthington, 2005b). They have argued that "constructive" communication should be central in cultivation of marital forgiveness (Fincham & Beach, 2002).

Stimulating the increased interest in communication is theorizing by psychologists such as Gordon and associates (2000), who posit that forgiveness episodes proceed through several interpersonal processes. First, the emotional impact of the offense is expressed, interpreted, and managed. Second, the partners engage in sense-making, a process of determining the causes, motives, and relational implications of the offense. Third, having progressed through the first two tasks, partners can plan a revised relational future. We use their work as a starting place for our own communicative approach.

❖ THE FORGIVENESS EPISODE: SIX COMMUNICATION PROCESSES

As we have noted elsewhere (Waldron, Kelley, & Harvey, in press), at least six communication processes are integral to the negotiation of forgiveness: (1) revealing and detecting transgressions, (2) managing emotions, (3) sense-making, (4) seeking forgiveness, (5) granting forgiveness, and (6) negotiating the relationship. Figure 4.1 depicts the six processes of forgiving communication as embedded in the *current episode*. This episode is embedded in the unfolding history of a relationship. It is a process that moves through time, shaped in part by memories of *past* communication practices. For example, communicative reactions to a partner's insult may vary depending on the past history of such transgressions. Repeated past violations may lead to a less forgiving response in the present. As well, the partners construct their communication with reference to the relational *future.* If they imagine a long-term relationship, partners may take steps now to renegotiate communication rules meant to minimize the risk of a stormy or unpleasant future together. The new arrangements will be tested and monitored during what we call the *transitional* period. As indicated in the figure, relational failures during this later period may reactivate the forgiveness episode, launching another cycle of relationship negotiation, emotion management, and so on.

The *initial episode* varies in length, from minutes to years, but it begins with a transgression and ends when forgiveness has been granted (at least tentatively). The current episode is defined by cycles of interaction that repeat until the six processes are satisfactorily completed. Furthermore, communication across all six processes is *multidimensional.* It is verbal and nonverbal, intended and unintended, individual and relational, and/or explicit and implicit. Nonverbal cues include touching, crying, or hugging. Sometimes these displays are spontaneous and unintended (unexpected tears); other times they are mindful (the use of eye contact to communicate sincerity). Forgiveness episode include verbal messages such as "I'm sorry," "You really hurt me," or "Never do that again!" Some communication practices are jointly produced through the interactions of the partners rather than "owned" by any individual. For example, the process of discovering a transgression may evolve through a series of observations ("We haven't been that close

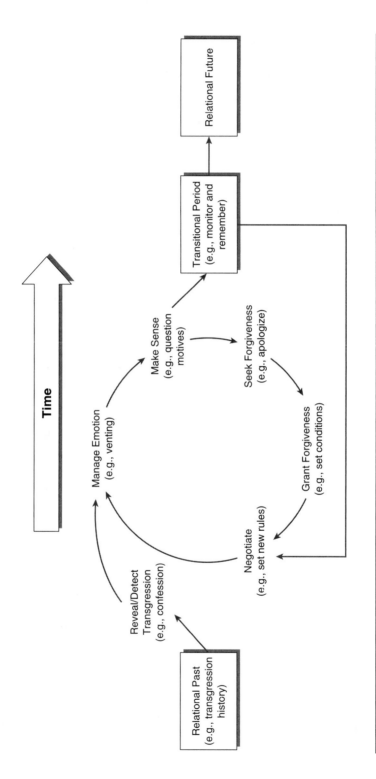

Figure 4.1 The Forgiveness Episode

lately."), questions ("Has something been bothering you?"), and partial revelations ("I haven't been completely up-front about something."). Forgiving communication can be explicit. In Jen's story, the sisters asked for and the parents granted forgiveness. Of course, some aspects of forgiveness are implicit. For example, the sisters may have displayed their "best behavior" after the incident—an indirect way of showing that they were remorseful and worthy of forgiveness. The simple act of "returning to normal" is often cited as indirect evidence of forgiveness.

Managing relational transition is our label for the period after forgiveness is granted but before the future of the relationship is determined. As we mentioned in Chapter 1, forgiveness sometimes leads to reconciliation, although that is only one of several possibilities. Whatever the ultimate outcome, transitional communication allows the relationship to remain intact as new practices are enacted, practiced, and monitored. Transitional communication may help the partnership "return to normal," or it may be the period during which pledges of improved communication are incorporated into daily routines. In less fortunate circumstances, transitional periods are characterized by gradual relational deterioration. Partners realize that they have not "truly" forgiven, or despite forgiving, they no longer desire the relationship. On the basis of our interviews with long-term romantic couples, this transitional period can be lengthy, even unending, as partners make adjustments based on new understandings of past episodes.

For us, the communication of forgiveness is a collective process of redressing harm that also can be "invitational" (Foss & Griffin, 1995) in that it creates the conditions for dialogue and change. Forgiving communication is not just another "relationship repair tactic." It is instead a symbolic process closely linked to issues of relational morality, justice, and meaning. It is a means by which we enact, negotiate, or reinforce the values and rules that define relationships and communities. Serious relational transgressions inevitably cause emotional pain and relational damage. However, we believe that the ultimate meanings and relational consequences of hurtful acts are shaped by the six communication processes we address in this chapter.

❖ REVEALING AND DETECTING TRANSGRESSIONS

At times, transgressions are explicit and obvious. Hurtful words and abusive behaviors speak for themselves. At other times, relational transgressions occur "off-stage," or outside the awareness of the victimized partner. Wayward partners use communication behaviors to reveal such transgressions. Alternatively, violations are detected through the inquiries of a suspicious partner or because the hurtful act is "forced to the surface" through abnormal patterns of interaction. Yet another possibility is that the transgression will be presented by a third party. Table 4.1 presents various methods of revealing and detecting transgressions. All of these processes can be intentional, as when guilt drives the offender to offer an explicit confession. But revelations can also be unintentional. An offhand reference or communicative blunder may inadvertently reveal that a deception has been perpetrated. In any case, research suggests that the *method of discovery* shapes a partner's reactions to hurtful events (Afifi et al., 2001). We would argue that the communication behaviors used to reveal or detect the offense may minimize or exacerbate the relational damage it creates.

Revealing Transgressions

Transgressions are revealed by offenders through confessions, hints, third-party interventions, and communicative blunders.

Table 4.1   Presenting and Detecting Transitions

Category	Variations/Examples
Presenting Transactions	
Confessions	"honest"; guilt-driven; revenge-seeking; preemptive; corrective; written; self-protective
Hints/indirectness	Invoke third-party perspective; nonverbal signs, silence, enlist friends
Third-party reports	Have a friend reveal the transgression; "squealing"
Blunders	"letting it slip"; accidental revelations
Detecting Transgressions	
Probing questions	"So, why do you look so miserable?"
Requesting explanations	"Why did you show up late last night?"
Offering observations	"I noticed you have been avoiding me lately."
Consulting third parties	"Do you think she is cheating on me?" "Have you noticed anything?"
Self-discovery	"I saw her with another guy."

Confessions

Confessions are communicative acts of admission. They reveal that a transgression has been committed and typically acknowledge guilt. By itself, a confession is not an explicit request for forgiveness, although confession frequently initiates a forgiveness episode. For many, an *honest confession* is a prerequisite for forgiveness, an act that makes forgiveness a possibility, if not a reality. In the reports we have collected, an honest confession is one that strikes a tone of emotional authenticity. It is initiated by the perpetrator without coercion, and he or she makes no attempt to diffuse his or her responsibility. After many years of marriage, Jan discovered that her husband had participated in an extramarital relationship. Recovery from that unwelcome event has been difficult, but Jan refers to her husband's straightforward confession as a reason for her belief that the relationship could eventually be repaired. "He never justified himself ever when he confessed to me. It wasn't, 'Well if you hadn't been such a horrible person to live with.' He said, 'I was 100% wrong.' And I think that probably helped."

Confessions both express and reinforce a sense of relational morality. They are frequently driven by guilt or sometimes fear. Jasmine told this story:

> I was in a long-time relationship in which I began to feel unhappy. I was not in love anymore. I began to hang out with my friends more and go out like my "single" friends did. I really wasn't thinking about my boyfriend and how to end it. I was scared. Instead, I met someone else and had a "moderate" romance. Nothing too drastic. When my feelings of guilt surfaced I confessed to my extracurricular love life. I really didn't expect forgiveness, nor deserve it.

As Jasmine's account indicates, it is quite possible to confess without intending to seek forgiveness. Jasmine was not sure forgiveness was "deserved" in her case. Of course, forgiveness is an act *defined* by a willingness to pardon others even when they don't deserve it. But Jasmine may have felt undeserving because her confession was motivated by a fear of being discovered or a growing sense of guilt rather than concern for her partner. *We would argue that confession and forgiveness are linked by a spirit of concern for the partner and a sense of relational goodwill.* Otherwise, confession is simply a notification of bad behavior.

Confessions take a variety of additional forms, not all of them constructive. The offender may confess as a way to rub "salt into the wound" or even seek revenge. One of our students wrote that she revealed the sexual details of an affair to her boyfriend so he would understand "what he was missing" by ignoring her so much. Confessors sometimes claim that the hurtful act was performed for some "larger cause" more important than the immediate relational needs of the partners. For example, one of the authors was attending a high-school basketball game and overheard the following conversation between two teenage girls:

A: I really haven't seen you too much lately.

B: No kidding! What's up with you, girl?

A: I've been hanging more with Katie and her crowd. The ones that do the theater stuff, you know? I hate to tell you this, but people think you have gotten kind of mean. Like maybe you're mad all of the time or somethin'. You're gonna hear it anyway, but I told 'em that too. I think you might need to treat your friends better.

Girl A admits to criticizing her friend behind her back, and she knew Girl B would "hear it anyway" through the grapevine. Her admission prepares her friend for hurtful comments. In this sense, her behavior is a *preemptive* confession. This brief interchange reveals the dyadic nature of confession and its complex relationship to forgiveness. At the same time that Girl A is engaging in potential damage control, she is laying the groundwork for Girl B to see the error of her ways. Her final statement was uttered with a sense of both concern and foreboding. Indeed the whole interchange may function as a warning to Girl B to change her ways or face social ostracism from their shared social network. Confessions of the type, "You may hate me for saying this, but . . ." often serve a corrective function in addition to alerting the victim to the violation. In this case, Girl A seems to think that Girl B shares responsibility for the situation. Interestingly, Girl A's confession prompted Girl B to confess herself. "I guess I *have been* bitchy lately," she commented. "I said some bad things about you but I didn't really mean it, you know? It wasn't really me talking . . . just some bad stuff I have been goin' through."

Confessions, then, are a form of *self-disclosure* that can trigger a cycle of forgiving communication. In the example above, the response was a reciprocating confession. However, as Jasmine knew, disclosures also can reveal highly damaging information about the self, information that may have been carefully concealed from the partner. The effects can be devastating because the confession calls into question the assumed identities of the partners and upsets the agreements that form the very foundation of their relationship.

Transgressors sometimes choose *written confessions*. This approach allows for more detailed and thoughtful presentation of the offense and has the added advantage of avoiding immediate confrontation. Judee and Jeff had been dating for about 12 months when he left for a year's study in Europe. During that time, she "hooked up" one night with one of Jeff's former roommates. Judee reported that the encounter was "nothing really sexual" but she felt Jeff needed to know, partly because his friends had observed the situation and were likely to tell him. She chose to write him a letter because she wanted to "get all of the details out." Judee was afraid he would "blow up" and she would "just cry" if they talked on the phone. A written message might prompt a more measured response from Jeff. As was the case with Judee and Jeff, written confessions are often followed by extended discussion of the relational infraction. They are a short-term strategy for managing the emotional fallout and relational uncertainty that stems from a transgression.

Hints and indirectness

In the conversation reported above, a hint was used to start the process of confessing. Girl A, who has been avoiding B after talking behind her back, merely notes, "I haven't seen you too much lately." An alternative would be to comment more directly on the transgression: "You may have heard that I said you were mean." This direct approach unequivocally identifies both the act and the perpetrator. Using the language of politeness theory (Brown & Levinson, 1978), hinting and other indirect forms of speech are responsive to the face concerns of conversational partners. Indirect speech has the double advantage of preserving the autonomy of the offended partner while allowing the parties to minimize identity damage. By hinting ("You may have noticed I have been withdrawn lately.") the offender creates an opportunity for the partner to pursue the subject or avoid it. If the decision is to pursue ("I *have* noticed that. Is something wrong?"), presentation of the transgression is easier ("OK. Well, I thought you might want to know. I wasn't completely honest with you the other day when I told you . . ."). Politeness theory implies that offended partners should prefer autonomy-enhancing confessions because it allows them more control of their self-presentation. The response to a transgression may be more controlled, less emotional, and less embarrassing if the aggrieved partner "sees it coming" and chooses when and how to hear about it.

Indirect confessions manage hurt or embarrassment. Wagoner and Waldron (1999) examined the communication strategies used by supervisors at United Parcel Service to deliver bad news, including confessions of mistakes and misdeeds. In some cases, the supervisor hinted at problems as a way to "test the waters." The employee's initial reactions were observed, and the supervisor made adjustments in the presentation to soften the blow, minimize self-blame, or make the nature of the offense more explicit. By using indirectness initially, the speaker preserves the option of delaying the confession ("Let's talk about this at our next meeting") or denying its importance ("It's not a big deal"). Indirect approaches may identify the problem while (at least temporarily) leaving the source of the problem open for negotiation. One indirect strategy is to invoke the perspective of third parties, as in the following exchange between married parents:

Father: The kids say I have been kind of cranky lately.

Mother: Oh, the *kids* say that? I am wondering what you think.

Father: Well, I guess they are right. I have been pretty short-tempered and I know you have taken the brunt of it.

Mother: I would have to agree with your analysis.

Confessions can also be initiated indirectly through patterns of nonverbal behavior. Guilty partners may use periods of silence, superficial talk, or facial expressions to elicit inquiries like "What's wrong?" These inquiries create the conversational conditions that spawn confessions. Finally, indirect confessions are sometimes made through third parties, as when a friend is enlisted to convey the bad news. Still another variation, *self-protective confession,* is described by Risa (see textbox), a 34-year-old woman whose abusive mother admitted her transgressions after years of denial.

Risa's Mother: A Case Study in Indirect Confession

I was raised in a rigid traditional Italian Catholic household. The men ruled. I have an older sister and younger brother. I was labeled the black sheep and adopted the role of punching bag early on in my life. My mother, frustrated by her low power, hit me often out of sheer frustration, beginning when I was just a toddler. My grandmother threatened to tell her son (my father) of this abuse, but never did. The hair pulling, slapping, shoving, lasted until we moved across the country. My grandmother was 3,000 miles away. My mom came after me one afternoon. I held my ground and forcefully told her if she ever hit me again, I'd hit her back. I don't remember any physical abuse after that.

My mother never asked for forgiveness [back then] because she denied ever abusing me. It wasn't called abuse! Just crappy parenting, I guess.

> I have always stayed close to my parents. God only knows why. One morning a few years ago, out of the blue my mother turned white as a ghost after attending her ritualistic church service. She said "Oh my God! I never confessed to the priest how I treated you as a child!"
>
> Several times in the past few years she has told me in the presence of mutual friends that she feared I would "get even" for the abuse when she is old and frail! I feel physically ill when she says that to me in the presence of others.
>
> I forgave my mother years ago, realizing she was ill-equipped to be a good parent. She protected us from other evils of the world, child molestation, etc. I believe she did the best she could. She was a frustrated lady and still is.

Risa's mother failed to confess directly to her daughter. Instead she disguised her confession with indirection ("I never confessed to the priest . . .") and expressed a fear of retaliation in the "presence of mutual friends." She may have feared retaliation, but more likely she chose indirect confession because she feared rejection or felt shame over her past behavior.

Third-party reports

Transgressions can be devastating when they are revealed by a third party rather than the offending partner. Afifi and colleagues (2001) studied how reactions to infidelity varied as a function of discovery method, arguing that discovery through a third party should be more face-threatening than being told directly. This claim may extend to other kinds of offenses as well. Third-party reports magnify the hurt because the transgression most assuredly has an audience. Public embarrassment is added to the other negative emotions the victim experiences. As we noted in Chapter 2, the partner's failure to confess the offense calls into question relational assumptions of trust and openness. These themes were revealed in a story told by Evan, who lied to his girlfriend Shana:

> The lie was about another girl named Hayley, an ex-girlfriend of mine. One night out of the blue she called me at my home, about a wedding that a mutual friend would soon be having. Even though Hayley called for the first time in two years and we were barely friends, I knew that just my speaking to her would make Shana jealous. A few days later she asked if I had spoken with Hayley. I felt no need to hurt Shana by telling her of Hayley's brief call. She soon found out from the bride-to-be that Hayley was coming to the wedding and had learned the wedding date from

me! Shana confronted me with this and I then told the truth. Shana was very hurt. After this incident, I think she has a harder time trusting me.

Blunders

The communicative work required to manage a relationship is increased when a partner attempts to hide a transgression. In some cases, the offense is revealed by mistake or oversight. Elliot's girlfriend, who eventually became his wife, unintentionally revealed that she was "somewhat seeing" another guy. It took some time for the couple to recover, because Elliot had to forgive not only the secret dating, but also the fact that she had only revealed it to him by mistake:

> My wife and I, before we were married, were seeing each other. It was not a serious relationship, but it was developing into one. I found out, by catching her in a lie, that she was also somewhat seeing another guy. I was mad and did not talk to her for six months. Then, one day she called me and asked me to meet her for lunch. She apologized, and told me the other relationship was nothing and she was waiting for the right time to call me. Our relationship is great now, but I do occasionally bring it up to tease her.

Detecting Transgressions

Probing questions

When offenders decline to freely confess transgressions, they may be detected through the communicative efforts of their partners. Suspicious partners may prompt confessions by asking probing questions. Cal was the manger of a retail store when a blunder left him in a difficult spot with his boss:

> One morning I was in my store getting ready to open. I was so engulfed in work that I lost track of time. The store opened at 10 a.m. and at about 10:15 the phone rang and it was my District Manager. She asked me why my store wasn't open. In a panic I lied and said it was. But she knew it wasn't because she was at a pay phone across the hall from my store! I was mortified and she was extremely upset.

In this example, Cal's manager questioned him about something about which she already knew the truth. In this way, she allowed him the opportunity to confess. She may have been testing his fidelity and trustworthiness as well. Baxter and Wilmot (1984) described how individuals create "secret tests" in personal relationships by creating situations where the partner has the opportunity to demonstrate their commitment to the union. Evidently the manager in this situation was doing something similar. When Cal panicked and lied, he created a double transgression. Needless to say, this behavior put Cal in a difficult situation, one requiring what might be called "industrial strength" forgiveness.

Requesting an explanation is another means of eliciting a confession. In another forgiveness story, Allen admitted feeling guilty because he failed to meet a friend as scheduled for an evening at the races. Allen describes how he was "called on it . . . That evening, when he [Allen's friend] got home from the races, he called and wanted an explanation. He was quite upset. I explained to him what had happened." In this way, explanation is a dyadic, interactive communication practice. Allen confessed his misbehavior because his friend prompted him to do so.

Offering observations

Another detection strategy is to offer relational observations, particularly when the partner's behavior varies from baseline expectations. In the "ex-girlfriend" scenario reported earlier in this section, Shana might have observed to Evan, "I notice you have been spending a lot of time talking with Hayley." Observations of this type might prompt a confession. Or Shana may have *consulted third parties,* by asking a friend something like, "Have you noticed Evan spending a lot of time with Hayley?" All of these approaches are clearly communicative, in that discourse is constructed with the purpose of discovering a transgression. However, transgressions are sometime discovered through simple observation and unmediated firsthand experience. This kind of *self-discovery* can be shocking, as in the case of a young woman who observed her father's relational betrayal:

I had to forgive one of the most significant people in my life. It was my father. I had overheard a conversation on the phone with a woman who was not my mother. It was obvious it was an affair. I had walked into the kitchen and had tears built up in my eyes. He knew I was upset and hung up the phone immediately. I loved my dad but all I thought about was my mother. He kind of broke down and explained what was going on and why this woman was of significance. I pretty much knew my parents didn't have a traditional healthy marriage. I just couldn't stomach the idea of someone else.

❖ MANAGING EMOTIONS

Only truly hurtful transgressions call for forgiveness. With the hurt comes emotion. In fact, an early and integral part of most forgiveness episodes is the expression of emotion, often in raw form. However, the processes of eliciting, fabricating, masking, listening to, acknowledging, affirming, and deflecting emotions can be equally important in relationships (see Planalp, 1999 for an extended discussion). For many theorists (e.g., McCullough et al., 2000), the lessening of negative emotions toward the offender is a defining feature of forgiveness. Feelings of shock, anger, humiliation, and indignation are often expressed upon the discovery of a transgression. Guilt, regret, grief, and bitterness may be experienced as the episode progresses. For other writers, forgiveness involves more than the simple reduction of negative emotion; they consider positive feelings toward the offender to be the best indicator (e.g., Enright & Coyle, 1998; North, 1987). Positive affective states might include compassion, mercy, or love. Along these lines, Metts (1994) suggested that acknowledging and apologizing for relational hurt can have an emotionally transformative effect, making it more likely that positive feelings of affection can be restored. If such claims are correct, forgiveness episodes should be characterized by communication that elicits, expresses, and legitimizes the emotional experiences of the parties. Of course, extreme emotion may yield avoidant, defensive, or destructive discourse.

The means by which communication is used to manage emotion in relationships have been explored by us elsewhere (Waldron, 1994, 2000). Here we will review only the most prominent themes reported in forgiveness narratives.

Emotional Venting

Communication is a means by which emotions are vented. The offended party typically experiences a profound emotional response, which must be expressed and heard by the listener if forgiveness is to be negotiated. For example, during her teen years, Shalomar developed a pattern of treating her mother disrespectfully, creating nonproductive communication episodes. As she revealed, "We yelled and screamed strongly and I ended up slamming the front door and leaving for the night." The next day, having gotten it "off our chests," Shalomar and her mother addressed the underlying relational problem.

Venting can be positive as well. In the following example, emotional expression is a collective activity in which partners share mutual feelings of anger, fear, regret, or grief. Riley "cheated" on her boyfriend by going on a date with another man. After she confessed, she remembers "looking at him knowing how hurt he must be. I was hurt also—it was awful." They vented their painful emotions together as they tried to recover their relationship. "We both just cried over the whole thing—it was really very emotional."

Eliciting Emotion

Communication is used to elicit emotion, especially during the early stages of the forgiveness process. For example, an offended partner may want assurance that the offender feels guilty. One student wrote about her mother, "She wanted to make sure I knew it was wrong. She said I should feel guilty for embarrassing my sister in front of her boyfriend." In contrast, Harvey admired his wife of almost 50 years for taking a different approach. "She'll almost always accept part of the responsibility and that helps. She almost never guilted me." Offenders sometimes try to elicit sympathetic responses by sharing the depth of their regret or the reasons for their conduct. After her boyfriend responded coolly to her apology for an affair, one student "cried and told him I deeply missed him. I didn't want my stupidity to ruin things for us." Sometimes an increase in the intensity or seriousness of an emotional response is the goal. One of our students (Jill) described how her boyfriend said he was "sorry" for a drinking incident that upset her. She found his apology to be superficial, so she refused to accept it for several days, until he finally offered a revised, "heartfelt" version.

Emotional Cooling, Calming, and Editing

As in Jill's narrative, requesting or insisting on a *"cooling off"* period is a common communicative response to serious transgressions. The request may simply "buy time" so emotion can dissipate rather than be expressed in words that might be regretted later. Jill's message to her boyfriend seemed to function differently. She wanted him to ponder the seriousness of the situation and better appreciate the legitimacy of her emotional reaction. *"Calming down"* is another prominent theme in forgiveness narratives. Of course, the passing of time facilitates calming. But "remaining calm" is an important communicative act in itself. Calmness, or composure, is particularly prominent in for-giveness stories told about parents or supervisors, at least in those sto-ries with happy endings. Power differences and role expectations make it possible for bosses or parents to "blow up" at employees or children with limited relational consequences. Those who unexpectedly remain calm are described favorably. Matt (age 18) was forgiven by his very disappointed parents after being jailed briefly for underage beer drink-ing. "I don't think I was shocked that they forgave me but was more shocked at their initial reaction to it all—very calm!? I felt lucky to have them as parents. Our relationship was more open after that situation."

Emotional editing is an alternate method for managing "heat of the moment" responses to transgressions. "I wanted to scream at him for embarrassing me in front of my friends," wrote one student, "but I just shut down and told him I didn't appreciate what he said." Emotional editing seemed to be the lesson learned by another couple who sur-vived a nasty argument spurred by jealousy. "We have been doing well since the incident . . . We communicate better now because we are both able to talk about everything and know when to terminate a subject that is minor but might lead to negative emotions."

❖ MAKING SENSE

I was in a relationship with someone who went on a vacation with some friends. I found out that he wasn't so loyal to me on this trip. I forgave him but it wasn't until years later after our relationship was over . . . I wanted to forgive him because we have the same circle of friends . . . and it was ridiculous to still have that incident prevent us from being friends. During our fighting period he was seeking my forgiveness, but I could not give it to him. Years later it was more of an offering by me to finally officially tell him how I felt. I told him I could somewhat understand what happened under the circumstances (he was drunk with his buddies—still no excuse). He thanked me for finally coming to terms with it and again apologized. After I forgave him we could talk with each other again. We became friends all over again and we can be civil with each other.

—Gina, age 26.

Transgressions create uncertainties in relationships. Partners need to know *why* a transgression occurred and what it means for the rela-tionship. Gary was atypically cross with his boss one day. After he expressed his sorrow for being rude, she told him "never to do it again."

But she also "wondered *why* I did it . . . She is concerned and she told me that I can talk to her if I have problems." Gary's boss needed to know if his behavior signaled disrespect for her or her role. Was he just having a bad day or maybe going through hard times outside of work? Was the transgression a harbinger of things to come or just an anomaly?

Exploring Motives and "Real Meanings"

As discussed in Chapter 2, the severity of a transgression varies with the presumed intention of the offending partner. Partners seek and offer evidence about *why* the act was committed, whether it was *intended,* and whether it is likely to repeat itself. Years later Gina can only "somewhat understand" her former boyfriend's philandering, although she may have been convinced that it wasn't intended to hurt her. But by initiating a new round of sense-making communication she has developed a more nuanced view of the offender and the reasons for his behavior.

In deciding if and how to forgive, a wounded partner may reevaluate the character of the offender and assess the psychological safety of the relationship. Gina chose to end her romantic relationship rather than risk another occurrence. To help in this evaluation, accounts may be requested and offered, questions asked, and assurances and promises exchanged (Kelley & Waldron, 2005). In the narratives we studied, the objective of this communication was sometimes described as discovering the "real meaning" of the transgression, as indicated in statements such as "I wanted him to know that I didn't really *mean* to hurt him," "I told her the other relationship *meant* nothing to me compared to what we had together," and "when he knew I was *really* feeling sorry, he forgave me."

Motives are often obvious in forgiveness episodes, but sometimes they must be uncovered through interaction. Kelley's (1998) study uncovered a variety of motives for seeking forgiveness (see Table 4.2 for types and definitions). One of these was simply to promote *well-being*. The well-being was sometimes personal, to relieve feelings of guilt or let go of burdensome grudges. Other times the motive was more *altruistic,* directed at the partner's well-being. For example, one of our students was injured in a car accident due to her friend's driving mistake. She blamed her friend's carelessness, and the relationship never recovered. Nevertheless, she felt motivated to help remove the burden of her friend's guilt. "I saw her one day and gave her a hug before she said a word. I told her to forget about it."

In Kelley's (1998) narratives, another primary motive for both seekers and grantors of forgiveness was *relationship restoration*, a desire to

Table 4.2   Motives for Forgiveness

Category	Examples
Promote Well-Being	Wanting to release burdens; letting go of guilt or a grudge
Altruistic	"Let him off the hook"; "Help him move on"
Relationship Restoration	"Wanted to be friends again"; "get back to normal"
Love	"He forgave because he loves me"; "We love each other"
Selfish	"He did it so he could feel better"; wanted to look good
Moral Obligation	"It was right to forgive him"; religious reasons
Family Obligation	Keeping peace in the family; "Mom told me to"
Partner Communication	Apologies; expressions of regret; claims of responsibility

reclaim friendship, closeness, or trust. Gina was motivated to ease some of the awkwardness in her friendship network and restore civility to her relationship with her former boyfriend. Given these motives, she was able to recontextualize his drunken behavior and redefine its relational significance. Kelley describes this as a *reframing* process, which motivates forgiveness. In another example, Doris reframed her husband's insulting comments as just an "incident":

> He realized he shouldn't have said what he said, and it made me upset, and we just start again. It was just the fact of knowing that we loved each other. It was just an incident. It had nothing to do with our overall relationship.

For Doris, the incident was minor when reconsidered in light of the loving relationship she and her husband have enjoyed for more than 30 years.

Sherry (age 22) may have preferred that her boyfriend forgive her out of *love*. Her boyfriend wanted to restore their relationship after initially deciding to break up with her, but his motives appeared mixed: "I think I was forgiven because he decided that he wants me back for

himself. He could not handle the fact that I was going out to bars."
In Kelley's (1998) study, only 10% of narratives described love as the
primary motivation for forgiveness. However, forgiveness is frequently
motivated by *obligation.* In some cases, religious or moral obligations
provide motivation. In other cases, familial obligations are the opera-
tive motive as when parents feel compelled to forgive the mistakes of
their children. Family members sometimes seek forgiveness out of an
obligation to "keep the peace." Louisa corrected a niece's poor man-
ners at a family gathering, which greatly offended her brother-in-law:

> I wrote my brother-in-law a letter of apology and then called him a
> few days later to again say I was sorry for the misunderstanding and
> would like to put it behind us. He said, "OK" I still don't think I did
> anything to make such a big deal out of, but I apologized to keep the
> family peace. My relationship is OK with my brother-in-law now.

Kelley (1998) reported that the most commonly cited motivation
(24% of narratives) involved the forgiveness-seeking communication of
the offender. Such behaviors as apologizing, expressing remorse, and
taking responsibility were often cited. The next section addresses these
and other forgiveness-seeking tactics.

❖ SEEKING FORGIVENESS

When we ask participants in our studies why they seek forgiveness, they
often write or talk about their moral values. Having made serious relational mistakes, they seek forgiveness because they think it is the "right
thing to do," given the moral codes that define their relationships.
Forgiveness-seeking communication is a way of enacting this moral
code, of *performing moral values.* Forgiveness-seeking can be a kind of
atonement, a way of signaling a renewed commitment to values shared
by a community, family, or relationship. It may involve some form of
reparation, an offer to compensate those who have been harmed.
Together, atonement and reparation may signal a desire to restore *harmony.* The traditional Navajo people of the American Southwest embody
this search for harmony (Reid, 2000). Their faith encourages Navajos to
conduct their relationships in a manner that keeps them aligned with
spiritual forces that shaped their land and their culture (see textbox).
When individual behaviors are inconsistent with spiritual values, individual and collective rituals are performed as a means of atonement.

In Search of Harmony

Journalist Betty Reid (2000), a member of the Navajo nation, poignantly describes the search for harmony in a personal essay about the death of her father from Parkinson's disease. She wonders if his death was in part due to her own breaking of the codes of spiritual harmony.

The wind whipped our faces as we left my father's grave on a ridge known to my family as "the place where the dirt roads go uphill." This view belonged to my late father, Willie Reed Sr., for 69 years. He herded sheep, roamed the cliffs, and prayed to the Holy People. Now it cradles his body. He died February 28, 1994. It seemed as if the dust storm erased my dad's life from Bodaway, where he grew up a shepherd, a yei-bi-chei dancer, a migrant worker, a railroad worker, and a construction worker.

Like most Navajos, I straddle two worlds, modern and traditional. I follow the Earth-based traditional faith of Hozho, a state of beauty and harmony. Yet Christianity has seeped into the daily lives of my extended Navajo family.

My father introduced me to the Holy People, their philosophy and religion. He told me my goal is to live in a state of Hozho—a concept that embodied beauty, stability, and order within my life.

Embedded in Navajo philosophy is a laundry list of "don'ts" and taboos to respect. If one adheres to them, Hozho is achieved. Among the Navajo rules are: avoid contact with dead bodies, don't stare straight into a person's eye, never drive away from a coyote that crosses your path without sprinkling corn pollen in his tracks, and never say harsh words because they have the power to kill.

With the power of two religions on my side, how could my father die? I conjured up reasons:

Maybe I asked too much of the Christian God when I crammed for college finals and escaped with a B instead of an F. I figured the Presbyterian God understood college. How was I to explain English 101 to the Holy People?

Maybe God was punishing me for holding on to my Navajo beliefs.

Or maybe the Holy People were punishing me because I didn't cover my eyes quickly when I went to a bloody shooting scene while on the police beat for The Phoenix Gazette *before my father's death. I had the radio reporter describe the scene to me while I blocked the sight with a notebook.*

Or maybe it was my chosen profession. I write for newspapers and through the power of written words, have stung plenty of Navajo and non-Indian politicians.

Recriminations and remembrances filled my thoughts as my siblings and I sat at the table in my aunt's hogan and planned my dad's funeral.

After considerable acrimony about whether to practice a traditional Navajo or Christian ceremony, Betty and her family decide on a traditional burial (with some Christian prayers) to achieve harmony for her father's spirit as well as the family. Her father was buried without a coffin on a rock ledge near his home. For Betty, the ceremony is an enactment of her commitment to her father's values, perhaps a means of atonement for her embracing a nontraditional life, a way for her family to reestablish spiritual harmony.

SOURCE: From Reid, B. The way to harmony. *The Arizona Republic*. July 5, 1998. Reprinted with permission.

Although Betty Reid obviously is not responsible for her father's death, this traumatic event forced her to reflect on strongly held values and take actions that helped her address moral tensions in herself and in her family. Forgiveness-seeking communication can be conceptualized this way, as a practice that involves self-evaluation after a transgression, atonement, and, typically, collective efforts designed to "set things right."

Forgiveness-Seeking Tactics

Kelley (1998) identified more than 20 different tactics used by romantic partners, family members, friends, and coworkers to indicate that they "needed or wanted forgiveness." The main types are presented in Table 4.3, which also presents forgiveness-granting tactics. Offering an apology was one of the more familiar approaches. Other tactics were common. For example, offending partners used humor to help the victim "get over it," ingratiated themselves to get back on the partner's "good side," and promised better behavior (e.g., "overlook this one mistake and I won't ever do it again"). Some simply requested forgiveness, whereas others offered detailed explanations for their poor behavior. Transgressors offered compensation in the form of gifts, initiated familiar rituals ("let me take you out to lunch so we can talk it over"), or simply let time pass until the hurt receded and normal interaction could resume. Nonverbal displays of emotion, such as crying and looks of shame, were also described as forms of forgiveness-seeking communication.

In categorizing these behaviors, Kelley (1998) distinguished between "direct" and "indirect" approaches. Those using the former verbally acknowledged that they had committed a wrongful act. Indirect approaches were either implicit or nonverbal. This two-category system was expanded when Kelley and Waldron (2005) used quantitative techniques to analyze statistical patterns in survey rankings of the original 20 behaviors. In that study, 187 survey respondents indicated the extent to which they had used a given behavior to seek forgiveness in a romantic relationship. However, we know that

Table 4.3   Forgiveness-Seeking and Forgiveness-Granting Behaviors
(adapted from Kelley & Waldron, 2005)

Strategy	Examples
Forgiveness-seeking strategies	
1. Explicit acknowledgement	Apology; remorse
2. Nonverbal assurance	Eye contact; hugs
3. Compensation	Gifts; repeated efforts
4. Explanation	Reasons; discuss offense
5. Humor	Joking; humoring
Forgiveness-granting strategies	
1. Explicit	"I forgive you"
2. Conditional	"I forgive you, but only if . . ."
3. Nonverbal displays	Facial expressions; touch
4. Discussion	Talking about the offense
5. Minimize	"No big deal"; "don't worry"

complex interactive behavior is not adequately captured in a survey question, and we know it is not limited to romantic pairs. So we also draw on interviews and other qualitative data to present a richer and more nuanced depiction of forgiveness-seeking communication.

Explicit acknowledgment

The most frequently cited type of behavior in the statistical analysis involved explicit acknowledgement of a wrongful act. This category includes apologies, expressions of remorse or sorrow, and direct requests for forgiveness. Some of these behaviors have received attention in the literature. For example, apologies are considered "concessions" in the research on account-making (Cody & McLaughlin, 1990). However, this cluster of behaviors involves more than an individual's decision to confess. In particular, direct requests for forgiveness illustrate the transactional nature of the process (see Fincham & Beach, 2002; Hargrave, 1994). Requests pass control of the interaction to the partner, a move that makes forgiveness a collective activity.

Expressions of regret are embedded in the expectations and interaction patterns of some long-term couples. Ben, who has been married to Sue for some 51 years, told us emphatically:

If you're sorry for something, you say you're sorry. And if you forgive someone, you say, "I forgive you." And then there's a lot of hugging and that kind of stuff. It's kind of a spontaneous thing when we realize that it's necessary.

In work settings, being sorry signals respect for more formal relational expectations and may be necessary to social survival. Gary knew he needed to say he was "really sorry" after being rude to his boss, who, fortunately, was very understanding:

A few months ago, I was on the phone with my boss. At the end of the conversation I was snotty and said, "Thanks for your help," and hung up on her. Of course I realized that I had just put my job in jeopardy. After I got over that, I began to feel guilty because she didn't deserve that. She is also a nice person and my acquaintance—not just a boss. I was mad at myself for possibly upsetting her. I saw her the next day. I approached her and said, "I'm really sorry about being snotty and hanging up on you."

Apology is the most familiar form of explicit acknowledgement and an important element of many forgiveness narratives. Apology requires the offender to put aside pride and admit to wrongful behavior, as in this story told by Joanie, a 37-year-old former New Yorker:

I had agreed to a second date with a gentleman I'd met at a friend's wedding. I got a call that took me out-of-state for three days. Since I didn't have his phone number and didn't think to call my friend (whose wedding we met at), I stood him up. When I returned, he'd left a frustrated note for me which included his phone number. Since I had so little invested in the relationship, I wasn't going to call and explain (pride!). A friend from work convinced me to at least give it a try. I called him at work, explained what happened and apologized for standing him up. He was very kind, made another date with me and never mentioned the incident again. I was thankful he forgave me. It was a part of the foundation our relationship was built on. We've been happily married for eight years.

Joanie's story reveals that requesting forgiveness can be a collective activity, a communicative act emerging from the larger social network. After all, it was a friend who prompted Joanie to "give it a try." It also illustrates that apologizing and other forms of explicit acknowledgment are a kind of relational *truth-telling*. Forgiveness-seeking communication often involves "coming clean" with an unequivocal display of honesty. Her honesty and her husband's acceptance of it may be the reason this forgiveness episode is part of the "foundation" that underlies an eight-year marriage. In a different context, a teenager whose outraged parents eventually forgave him for underage drinking emphasized truth telling: "We talked about it and the *only* way I was forgiven was because I told them the truth about what happened. I obviously wanted forgiveness."

Nonverbal assurance includes behaviors such as eye contact and giving hugs. It was second in frequency of use in the Kelley and Waldron (2005) study. In interviews, people told us they could tell by "the look in his eyes" or "the way she hugged me" that an offender was sorry (and thus deserving of forgiveness). Behaviors such as eye contact and hugs can suggest that the offender is "truly" repentant or honestly committed to making amends. Nonverbal displays of emotion are often taken as signs of repentance. Lauren damaged her father's car after using it without permission. "I cried because I felt so awfully bad about the whole situation," she wrote. Her father responded with a hug, telling Lauren that bumpers could be replaced but she could not.

As a group, these nonverbal behaviors may convey emotional authenticity. As linguists E. D. Scobie and G. E. Scobie (1998) have observed, cultural norms dictate that forgiveness be offered only after sincere expressions of apology and remorse. When combined with explicit acknowledgment, nonverbal assurances likely convey an honest concern for the partner's well-being. Assurances may sooth emotional distress by communicating empathy, increasing confidence in the character of the offender, and creating the impression that the transgression is unlikely to be repeated. They may bring a particularly welcome sense of clarity given that transgressions create relational uncertainty (Emmers & Canary, 1996). In fact, the communication of assurance is one communication tool used by romantics and friends to maintain relationships (Canary & Stafford, 1992).

Explanation

Explanation was the third most common approach used by forgiveness seekers in Kelley and Waldron's (2005) study. The role of communication in explaining social failures has long been studied by communication researchers (e.g., Cody & McLaughlin, 1990). In this "account-making" literature, excuses are often identified as a form of explanation. Excuses deny responsibility, so we exclude them from our discussion of forgiveness-seeking, which starts with the assumption that a wrong has been committed and admitted. However, other forms of explanation are cited frequently in forgiveness narratives. Offenders invite the partner to "sit down and talk about it" or "discuss the matter" or "hear my side of the story." They detail the circumstances, motives, or reasons surrounding the infraction. This kind of information may be crucial in deciding whether forgiveness is warranted and whether the relationship can be mended (Gordon et al., 2000). Explanation may help the offender save face but it also helps the wounded partner interpret the transgression and assess its seriousness.

Explanatory communication is often interactive, not just one partner offering an account. In fact, one of the items included on Kelley and Waldron's (2005) survey is "we discussed the matter." This kind of communication can be "invitational" in nature, creating the conditions for dialogue and opening up possibilities for new understandings of the situation and the partners (Foss & Griffin, 1995). Even when partners disagree about key issues, forgiveness negotiations may be mutual efforts to elicit constructive argument (see Mallin & Anderson, 2000, on eliciting constructive debate). It may be that explanation and discussion are preliminary moves in forgiveness negotiations. The information generated may help partners decide whether explicit requests for forgiveness are called for and likely to be accepted.

Listening behavior may be important in this process. Diane was shocked when Jeremy described one of her ideas as "stupid" in front of friends over dinner. She stormed out of the restaurant, feeling hurt and angry. When Jeremy initially said he was "sorry," she didn't accept his apology, feeling he didn't truly understand why she was outraged. But as she explained her reactions, "He waited long enough and was caring and listening to what I had to say. I could see he really was sorry."

Compensation

The forgiveness-seeking tactics we labeled "compensation" involve investment of resources by the offender or a willingness to abide by the partner's wishes in exchange for forgiveness. Communication scholars have used equity theory to explain how relationships are preserved (Canary & Stafford, 1992). Compensatory behaviors may function to restore equity. Recognizing that they have damaged the partner and the relationship, offenders may tender gifts, such as flowers, or offer to take the partner out for lunch. After initiating a terrible argument with her sister, Jana offered to "take her out for ice cream" to "make up for" her rudeness. Other offenders describe being "extra nice" or on their "best behavior" as forgiveness-seeking cues. Repeated apologies are offered. In each of these cases, the forgiveness seeker invests "extra" communicative effort.

In fact, a certain amount of groveling may be required of the offender as compensation for pain or embarrassment. In interviews and narratives, offenders frequently describe *"begging for forgiveness."* Begging implies that the offender is unworthy of forgiveness. It elevates the status of the wounded partner. The sacrifice of one's dignity may be symbolic compensation for having degraded the partner and the relationship. In this way, offenders grant their partners considerable autonomy in determining their fate.

Compensation is sometimes part of an if/then bargain ("If you forgive me, then I will never do it again."). Often this involves a promise of improved behavior in the future as compensation for the bad behavior of the past. After her parents expressed worry and disappointment when she returned later than expected from a date, Claire "promised to always remember to call home." Chad was forgiven for a workplace transgression only after "some serious talking and promise making on my part." Audra's boyfriend forgave her for flirting with another boy, "but it took me saying that I would never do this to him again. I would not talk to that guy again." In the ratings reported by Kelley and Waldron (2005), compensation was used relatively infrequently. It also appeared to be less successful in promoting positive relational outcomes.

Humor

Forgiveness-seekers sometimes try to lighten the mood of the wounded partner, hoping that a new emotional perspective will make them more forgiving. This approach is used infrequently, probably because forgiveness episodes are generally so serious (Kelley & Waldron, 2005). Humor is not expected of forgiveness seekers, so its use may surprise the receiver and prompt a redefinition of the situation. Self-deprecating humor in particular may signal that the offender is now willing to take responsibility. Beth used a combination of humor and compensation as she sought forgiveness from her long-time friend and roommate for forgetting a birthday:

> After not talking for two days, I came home from work one day with a funny belated birthday card for her and a gift certificate to her favorite restaurant. We were both relieved because we knew that our friendship would go back to the way it was. We went to dinner and in a joking manner, I expressed to her how sorry I was and how selfish I was being since I was so wrapped up in my own life. She realized that was my way of expressing how sorry I was.

In Beth's case, the humorous card was met with "relief." It nudged the pair out of a stalemate and back to familiar patterns of friendship. Beth expressed regret in a joking manner by mocking her own selfishness. Although it worked for Beth, humor can also have less positive relationship outcomes (Kelley & Waldron, 2005). Inappropriate humor conveys a lack of appreciation for the pain experienced by the partner. It can be perceived as an attempt to divert attention away from the transgression. Forgiveness-seekers using humor may be sharply reminded that "this is no joking matter" or their behavior is "not funny."

❖ GRANTING FORGIVENESS

> ### "Like a weight had been lifted off of my shoulders"
>
> This situation is something I'm not very proud of but it fits this study to a T. As a senior in high school I was Mr. Jock and pretty popular at school. I was dating a sweetheart of a girl and she was a junior on the cheer squad. Well, prom rolled around and you know how everyone expects everyone to get "lucky" that night. Without going into too much graphic detail, we did **not** have sex that night. But, me being the immature guy I was, I asked her to *tell* people we had sex if she was asked about it. We ended up breaking up that summer and she was devastated. Every time I thought about her I would think about the horrible situation I put her in just because I was worried about my reputation. This went on for three years. I then ran into her at a high-school basketball game. I took that opportunity to get her new phone number and told her I wanted to talk to her about some things. After I got enough nerve, I called her about a week later and apologized through tears and asked her if she could ever forgive me. She did and after that was over, had a great 2 hour conversation with each other. I am so glad that I did that, it was like a weight had been lifted of off my shoulders.
>
> —Nathan, age 23

Nathan's description illustrates the powerful effects that the act of granting forgiveness can have on both individuals and relationships. His burden is lifted because of his former girlfriend's graceful response. The story also illustrates that forgiveness-granting is ultimately a transactional process, one that requires multiple parties. It took Nathan several years to apologize, but by taking advantage of the opportunity, he made it possible for his former girlfriend to express her forgiveness verbally.

Forgiveness-Granting Tactics

In a survey-based study, we analyzed 20 different behaviors romantic partners use to grant forgiveness (Waldron & Kelley, 2005). The behavioral items were culled from the forgiveness narratives collected by Kelley (1998). We used factor analysis techniques to identify the predominant categories of behavior, ultimately settling on five distinct approaches (see Table 4.3). The quotes presented below are largely drawn from data partially reported by Waldron and Kelley (2005) in the *Journal of Social and Personal Relationships*.

Nonverbal display

This category included nonverbal actions that were interpreted to be forgiving, such as embraces or certain facial expressions. One respondent described a nonverbal approach: "I forgave the other person not necessarily in words but in actions. I did not harbor ill will. I tried to show acceptance and love in my interactions with her." Another forgiver used nonverbal signs of affection rather than words: "I never said 'I forgive you.' I let him know by starting to act affectionate and loving toward him again." Other responses included, "I gave her a hug and comforted her," and, "I didn't act mad anymore. I tried to speak with normalcy."

A young woman wrote this on one of our surveys:

> I was dating someone for 2 years and I cheated on him. He forgave me for this. I remember looking at him, knowing how hurt he must be. I was hurt also. It was awful. He took a while to forgive me and understand it all. When you know someone so well, a certain look in the eyes can tell it all. I knew he forgave me when he cracked a smile.

Conditional

Forgiveness is granted conditionally when it is linked to a change in the offender's behavior. One respondent told us, "I said, 'Don't let it happen again and you're forgiven.'" Another participant used the classic conditional term *if*: "I forgave him with conditions of our relationship. I said to him, 'I'll forgive you if you promise to do things differently—to trust me and believe what I say.'" Conditional forgiveness is common, particularly when partners have been badly hurt and want protection. By meeting conditions, offending partners show they are worthy of being trusted again. However, Waldron and Kelley (2005) found that conditional forgiveness is often related to eventual relationship deterioration. The "strings attached" approach can lead to feelings of manipulation, as Julie reported:

> I once made a left hand turn in front of an oncoming motorcycle. The guy rolled over the front of my car and hit the curb. It was my fault. This guy forgave me while he lay stitched up in a hospital bed. At first I was amazed someone could be so forgiving! I thought this guy must be one in a million. He kept worrying about my feelings and saying things like, "Please don't worry about me. I'll be fine." Before he left the hospital he started saying things like, "I'll forgive you if you'll go to dinner with me." At that point I wondered if he really wanted to use me instead of forgive me. If he had not hit on me, the relationship would have gotten stronger.

Minimizing

Minimizers communicate forgiveness by redefining the seriousness of the offense. In general, minimization approaches appear to deny the feelings and rights of the wounded party. Sample messages included "I just said that the offense was no big deal and blew it off," "I made them understand that it was not so important to make a fuss about," and "I said she need not worry." Waldron and Kelley (2005) noted that this approach was sometimes used even when wounded partners reported significant levels of relational damage and personal hurt. They speculated that minimization was used to avoid confrontation or bury negative emotion, so the relationship could be maintained. In some instances, the perceived magnitude of the offense had been diminished through explanation and discussion.

Discussion

Discussion strategies are similar to the explanatory approach to forgiveness-seeking. The forgiver indicates an openness to dialogue ("We talked it out. We looked at both sides."). Discussion-based approaches are oriented to increase understanding of both partners and the reasons for the problems. A woman responded this way to a boyfriend who was unfaithful: "I told him I understood why he felt he might have to prove to himself that he was attractive to another woman and that I felt that we could move past this if we understood *why* it had happened." Another purpose is to help the offender understand the effects of the transgression. "We talked about what happened.

I let him know how disappointed I was in him and how hurt I felt. He asked me to forgive him." Forgiveness episodes often prompt the partners to reflect on and negotiate the status of their relationship. "We simply discussed the issues and nature of our relationship." Problem-solving is another theme. "She called me and we talked about the problem and resolved it."

Harold and Sophie have been using discussion-based approaches for more than 40 years:

Sophie: I will take him [and say], "I need to talk to you, now when can we sit down and discuss this?" And we make a little appointment because he may be going somewhere and need to go, and so we'll have this discussion. But we don't raise our voices.

Harold: One thing that helps us significantly, I think, is when she has something that involves me, she is considerate enough to me to say that. You know, "Let's sit down and talk about this," or she'll say, "Sometime today we need to sit down and talk."

Explicit

Included among the 20 behavioral responses Waldron and Kelley (2005) analyzed was an item describing explicit forgiveness: "I told them I forgave them." The item exhibited interesting statistical properties in that it highly correlated with both the nonverbal display and discussion categories but not with items describing conditional and minimizing communication. The utterance "I forgive you" and its close variations may have considerable force in relationships (Scobie & Scobie, 1998). It is the kind of speech act that conveys an unconditional pardon. As suggested above, it was often used in conjunction with other approaches. One participant wrote, "I told him, 'OK. I forgive you.' Then I gave him a big hug and a kiss."

Explicit forgiveness communicates a sense of finality. It may be the strongest way to indicate that things are "OK" and the offense is put firmly in the past. Because it is generically recognized as a way of pardoning others, we think participants sometimes reported explicit utterances such as "I forgive you" when they could not remember the verbal and nonverbal details of their forgiveness-granting communication. Other times, they may have refrained from using the words "I forgive you" in order to save face for their partner.

Alternative Approaches

In many (but not all) of the examples presented thus far, we have emphasized the communication behaviors of individuals. However, because forgiveness is sometimes an ongoing negotiation embedded in a complex social system, we know it is simplistic to describe only the discrete "tactics" of individuals. In fact, our interviews have revealed several approaches that are better thought of as collective and interactive.

Requesting intervention

Third parties can be instrumental in prompting forgiveness. In some cases, third parties intervene of their own volition. Other times their help is requested. Lindy wrote that she had been in a protracted conflict with her sister, who was bitter over Lindy's comments about a boyfriend:

> My sister never forgave me, until a year later. I finally had my mom intervene and she gave a very dramatic speech in which we both cried our eyes away and my sister forgave me. Ever since then, we've been on good terms.

Dahlia's husband was abusive when he drank. She forgave him only when he took her threat seriously and sought outside help for his alcohol problem:

> I said, "I can listen to you from today until tomorrow and it's not going to change anything. And you have to get some help," and he was resistant. Finally, I said, "Either you get some help or I'm going to, you know, get out of here." His decision to seek help set in motion a process that resulted in forgiveness and ultimately saved the marriage.

Returning to normal

Forgiveness is sometimes implied, but not expressed. In forgiveness narratives, this is described with sentences such as, "He never said it, but I just knew he had forgiven me." More often, partners recognize their relationship as "returning to normal." In Tessa's household, forgiveness is rarely requested explicitly. Instead, you know you are forgiven when the silent treatment ends. She wrote:

> I got into a huge fight with my father and didn't talk to him for about 2 weeks. I said some nasty things to him . . . I would see

both of my parents but only talk and acknowledge my mother. My father didn't notice me for those entire 2 weeks. It was the silent treatment. Anyways, he wanted me to apologize for what I said. I should have, because what I said was wrong . . . I guess he got sick of the silent treatment and he walked over and picked me up and gave me a big hug. Told me I was a super kid. No other words were exchanged. I didn't even hug him back because he basically just picked me up in a fun way. Our relationship was back to normal within minutes after the hug.

This happens in our family about every 6 months and always resolves the same way (fight, silent treatment, hug, normal).

Relational rituals

A variation on the *return to normal* theme is the resumption of relational rituals. Forgiveness is sought or granted when one of the partners suggests that a familiar pattern be resumed. Mindy and her sister went out for ice cream, a familiar ritual for the sisters, and a sign that they were friends again. She "made the suggestion to go out for ice-cream. After I forgave her, our relationship went back to normal. We are friends again. We laugh, giggle, and joke with each other (until the next crisis)."

Habits of forgiveness

In our interviews with long-term couples, it appeared that forgiving communication could become a habit fundamentally embedded in their patterns of interaction. Phyllis and Charlie have been married 51 years. Phyllis assumes that forgiveness will be needed and granted on a regular basis if two people are to live together for a very long time. It is a habit that keeps her marriage together, like holding hands in church:

Sometimes it happens where you know, you might wake up in the morning, you're not feeling well, or whatever. You might say something cross and you don't mean to. And yet we always make it a point to apologize, ask for forgiveness. And, uh, we go on from there. We don't let that go without being forgiving of one another. And we also, I guess, we touch a lot. Always have. We hold hands a lot when we walk. We hold hands when we're in church.

Interaction sequences

It is obvious from many of our examples that forgiving communication occurs as coordinated sequences and combinations of behavior, not single actions. Often a wounded partner chooses not to say "that's ok" until the offender apologizes. We noted that explicit acknowledgments and nonverbal assurances often occur together to take responsibility for a wrongful act and to reduce uncertainty about the relational future. Reciprocity may be particularly powerful in creating the conditions for mutual forgiveness. Jack, married more than 30 years to Amanda, is the type of person who for various reasons (the way he was raised, stereotypes about masculinity, vulnerability) finds it difficult to say "I'm sorry" first. In this marriage, his wife always starts the forgiveness sequences:

> She was always quicker to come back and say, "I'm sorry," even though she was right. Then when she did, I'd say, "No, I'm sorry." It was easier for me to say that once she had come back and done it. Otherwise I wouldn't. I was stubborn or something. I just wouldn't give in.

Using time

A factor not fully acknowledged thus far is the communicative use of *time* (but see McCullough, Fincham, & Tsang, 2003; Worthington et al., 2000). By allowing time to pass, communicators let emotions build, wounds fester, or hurt diminish. Remaining silent for long periods of time can communicate how seriously one takes an offense or how well one is listening. The passing of time can increase the burden of guilt and thus the motivation to seek forgiveness. In the next section, we address the role of time more explicitly by contemplating the communication that defines the period after forgiveness is initially granted. We assume that this can be a time of relationship redefinition. The forgiveness negotiation continues as partners reconcile or choose not to, experience a stronger relationship or a weaker one, and resume old communication patterns or experiment with new ones.

❖ RELATIONSHIP NEGOTIATION AND TRANSITION

We consider the *negotiation* and *transitional* elements in Figure 4.1 together, because they involve similar communicative practices. Forgiveness may prompt partners to negotiate new rules and values (or they may simply recommit to existing ones). During the transition period, new rules are "pilot tested" as the partners determine what their future holds. Will they fully reconcile? Deintensify their bond? Terminate the relationship? As the figure suggests, monitoring of new practices and/or recollections of the painful episode may prompt the partners to restart the forgiveness cycle. In the forgiveness narratives we have collected, several communication practices are common in the "aftermath" of the initial episode. These are ongoing processes that serve as a "bridge" from the tumultuous period that defines the early stages of forgiveness to a more stable time in the relational future.

Rescripting Relational Rules

During the negotiation and transitional period, partners often propose and practice new relational agreements. Communication scholar Sandra Metts (1994) explained that the response to relational transgressions is often a relegislation or reaffirmation of relational rules. Similarly, Hargrave (1994) argued that partners may renegotiate the "relationship covenant," or set of values and agreements that bind partners (e.g., sexual fidelity). As time passes, compliance may increase feelings of stability and psychological safety. During the transitional period, rule compliance may gradually restore trust (Kelley & Waldron, 2005). Meta-communicative behavior, the messages partners use to comment on their own patterns of communication, may be important as they experiment with and evaluate new behavior patterns (Dindia & Baxter, 1987).

Editing and Monitoring

Partners may be particularly careful to edit and monitor their behavior during the transitional period. They may go out of their way to avoid repeating past mistakes so they don't create new problems in a relationship that may be vulnerable. They may be hyperconsiderate and attentive. Kirsten explained that she now thinks of her boyfriend's feelings before she does anything "major":

> I went to Hawaii 2 years ago without calling my boyfriend the entire time I was there. I came home with a real bad attitude, thinking I could do better than him. It hit me about a week later how wrong I was to treat him that way. I apologized to him over and over. I was very grateful that he forgave me. I think back to it all the time. I was a jerk. Very selfish. I have changed a lot since then. I think of him and his feelings before I do anything major. We are closer now and treat each other with more respect.

Second Courtships

Romantic couples sometimes describe a process of "starting over again." After a serious transgression, especially infidelity, the partner may need to be "won back." The unfaithful partner may need to provide evidence that he or she "deserves" the relationship. This may involve a kind of second courtship. In one of our interviews, Roland and Shelley, a couple married for four decades, described how a combination of monitoring and renewed courtship allowed her to trust him again:

Shelley: And Roland, do you remember those ways that you know, you tried to win me back, to establish trust again? For a while I did [distrust him], you know. Just questioning everything he did. You know, "Why would I believe you *now*?"

Roland: I would make sure she knew where I was at. I'd call her. I would do things for her. I think we started courting again, in a sense, you know.

Shelley: Uh huh. He started courting me again, in a way.

Roland: And I'd do special things for her. I'd bring her flowers and stuff like that.

Collective Remembering

Parties to a forgiveness episode may jointly recollect it. Shelley's question to Roland prompted him to reconstruct an important part of their past. Collective remembering keeps mistakes from the past salient in the present, reminding us of "lessons learned." Memories of traumatic or hurtful experiences help couples keep current challenges in perspective. "We have survived worse," older couples tell us about their current difficulties. Family or friendship bonds may be strengthened through recollection of difficult times that were weathered "together." Episodes that were once painful may be recalled with humor. (Recall the example of teenage sisters who threw a party while their parents were out of town, and now recall their parents' reaction as evidence of a great relationship.)

Mutual Planning

Forgiveness researchers have identified planning (or replanning) the relational future as an essential component of relationship recovery

(Gordon et al., 2000). This kind of communication is evidenced when partners discuss goals, plan trips, or otherwise imagine a future together. As Kelley (1998) has argued, forgiveness provides *hope* to couples who have experienced distress. Mutual planning may be a way to maintain hope while the parties rebuild the foundations of their relationship. From a dialectical perspective, mutual planning is way of creating a spirit of interdependence and connectedness after a period of separateness or emotional distance.

❖ CONCLUDING THOUGHTS

In this chapter, we claimed that communication plays an important role in nearly every step of the forgiveness process. The process itself was described as episodic but nested within the longer history of a given relationship. We argued that the negotiation of forgiveness is linked to individual, relational, and community values. Forgiving communication is constructed by individuals, but it is also enacted in patterns of interaction and even stimulated by third parties. Forgiving communication is a complex blend of nonverbal and verbal behavior, some of it intentional and some not. In the messages they use and the meanings they create, partners negotiate forgiveness at a given point in time. However, communication processes continue to be important as the relationship evolves and the partners reinterpret the episode.

We have generally avoided prescriptions. We have not discussed "competent" communication or linked various approaches with relationship success. After all, the social science literature on our topic is relatively young, communication is complex, and each relationship is unique. Nevertheless, there is reason to believe that forgiving communication can have beneficial effects on relationships and individuals. Some approaches do appear to "work" better than others, and it is possible to articulate some of the "steps" involved in achieving forgiveness in relationships. Therefore, Chapter 5 is designed to provide readers with practical guidance based on the research that has accumulated thus far.

5

Practicing Forgiveness

My boyfriend called me up one Saturday night after being out with his friends. He had been drinking, and wanted me to come over. I kept saying "no," and he was getting mad. At one point he hung up on me and never called back, so I just went to bed. The next day he called and acted as if nothing was wrong. I explained to him I was upset with him and why I was upset. He said "sorry," and would I forgive him. The situation did not appear to be very serious to him. I also did not believe his apology was very sincere. He just wanted the argument to be over. I told him I needed a couple days to think about this. A few days later he called and was asking again for my forgiveness. I explained to him my reasons once again for being upset, and finally accepted his apology. Our relationship has suffered greatly because of this particular night.

—Jill, age 23

Based on Jill's account, her boyfriend is not very accomplished in the art of seeking forgiveness. His failure to appreciate the relational significance of his boorish behavior, the failure to acknowledge wrongdoing, the apparently insincere apology—in Jill's mind these communicative shortcomings put the relationship at risk. For her part, Jill responds with delaying tactics. She gives her boyfriend a chance to reframe his behavior. Later she reinforces the reasons for her outrage before finally accepting what was (presumably) a more convincing apology. We can only speculate about the long-term consequences of this episode, but the pair's prospects seem to have dimmed in part because forgiveness was practiced ineffectively.

The communication of forgiveness is often associated with concrete relational consequences, as it was by Jill. For that reason, this chapter takes a practical turn. Having reviewed a broad spectrum of research and theory in earlier chapters, we now turn our attention to the question of effectiveness. What communication practices are likely to promote positive outcomes for individuals and relationships? Does the forgiveness literature yield any sensible advice, any defensible prescriptions, or any practical wisdom that might be helpful as we practice forgiveness in our own relationships? To put it simply, what works? And, just as importantly, what doesn't?

We approach this chapter somewhat gingerly. Researchers are often loath to offer prescriptions, because we know that each forgiveness episode is shaped by so many unique factors, including the relational history of the parties, their individual communication skills, and cultural differences, among others. No generic "rulebook" can guide us through the complex maze of forgiveness interactions. No set of simple instructions can relieve us of the responsibility for creating our own communication, responding to the circumstances and meanings that arise in a given situation. Nonetheless, it would be disingenuous of us to simply "pass" on the opportunity to help readers apply forgiveness research to their own relationships. After all, some of the most intriguing writing on forgiveness comes from therapists and applied researchers who are developing and testing interventions that will be of use to people who are recovering from relational trauma. Moreover, in our own research, we have often asked the parties relating a transgression to reflect on the communication behaviors that helped them forgive and move on. In short, the forgiveness literature has evolved to the point where we feel confident in offering our own cautious synthesis of how forgiveness might be practiced effectively.

We proceed with these caveats in mind. First, as we noted in Chapter 1, we are primarily interested in the practice of "ordinary" forgiveness, the kind that inevitably arises from the interactions of families, friends, and romantic partners. Our focus is on nontherapeutic relationships and settings, not clinical interventions. Second, we have not studied, and our conclusions do not apply to, those who have survived incest, serious crime, domestic violence, and other forms of abuse. The process of recovery from these extremely serious transgressions is well beyond the scope of this book. Third, although we address forgiveness at the psychological and communicative levels, the latter continues to receive more attention in this chapter. Fourth, we continue to conceptualize forgiveness and reconciliation as separate but related processes. But in this chapter we orient more of our material to those who are seeking to *both* forgive and reconcile. Finally, our intent in this chapter is to help relational partners think more deeply about the processes and practices available to them in forgiveness situations, not to endorse one particular approach.

We begin with a brief discussion of *why* people forgive, with a focus on motivations and goals. Then we review the prominent prescriptive models proposed by psychologists such as Robert Enright and Everett Worthington. These models focus primarily on individual processes. We then turn to the communicative tasks proposed in Chapter 4, with the intent of blending psychological and communicative approaches. Along the way, we present data from our own studies linking communication tactics with relational outcomes and share lessons learned from our interviews with long-term couples. Finally, we consider the role of forgiveness in promoting reconciliation, drawing heavily from the work of Hargrave (1994).

❖ FIVE REASONS TO FORGIVE

Perhaps the first step in practicing forgiveness is developing the motivation to forgive. As we discussed in Chapter 1, forgiveness has been associated with a variety of benefits, including relationship repair, improved mental health after a distressing event, and even some physiological measures of health. In other words, in addition to moral imperatives or altruistic tendencies, there are several good reasons to forgive (Witvliet, 2001; Witvliet, Ludwig, & Vander Laan, 2001; Worthington & Scherer, 2004).

1. Forgiveness May Repair Broken Relationships

For some time, scholars have argued that the practice of forgiveness increases the chances of positive relational outcomes after a serious transgression (Hargrave, 1994). Forgiveness may "restore the peace" in families, friendship networks, and work teams. Much of the evidence for this claim comes from the literature on marriage. In a recent review, Fincham, Hall, and Beach (2005) suggested that forgiveness was correlated with "relationship and life satisfaction, intimacy, attributions, and affect, and . . . it predicts psychological aggression, marital conflict, and behavior toward the spouse after a transgression" (p. 208).

We also found that forgiveness can have positive relational consequences in romantic relationships. Kelley (1998) found that 72% of respondents reported that forgiveness episodes resulted in relationship changes. Among those experiencing change, relationship strengthening (26%) was nearly as likely as relationship weakening (29%). Another 28% reported that the episode resulted in a change of status or revised relational rules. Rusbult, Hannon, Stocker, and Finkel (2005) argue that posttransgression relational quality and dyadic adjustment are both affected by the forgiveness processes. According to these authors, positive outcomes are more likely if the offended party relinquishes hurt feelings, makes positive attributions about the transgression, and extends forgiveness. The offender can initiate reconciliation by apologizing, making amends, and pledging not to repeat the transgression.

In short, forgiveness seems to *matter* in personal relationships.

2. Forgiveness May Restore Individual Well-Being

In Kelley's (1998) study of narratives, the restoration of personal well-being was a common reason for forgiving. Holding on to the bitterness and anger that accompany *unforgiveness* (Worthington, 2001) appears to erode feelings of mental and even physical well-being. One of Kelley's respondents wrote:

> Then I began to realize that this anger was not only torturing him, but myself as well. It was eating me up inside and making me more of an angry person. Why should I suffer for what he has done? So I wrote him . . .

Reflecting an altruistic impulse, some of Kelley's (1998) respondents forgave out of concern for the offender's well-being. Offenders often experience severe guilt and pain until they are forgiven.

3. Forgiveness Can Be an Expression of Continued Love and Commitment

When asked why they forgive, many people describe forgiveness an expression of *love* for the offender. "I forgave him because I loved him so deeply," said one young woman. For some people, forgiving seems to be an intrinsic part of loving. For others, the key word is *commitment*. Remaining committed to a friendship or marriage means finding a way to forgive, to "take the good with the bad."

4. Forgiveness Recognizes Conciliatory Behavior

Kelley (1998) described individuals being influenced to forgive when an offending party expressed conciliatory behavior, such as apologizing, taking responsibility for his or her actions, or showing remorse for the damage caused by his or her actions. In essence, the goal of forgiving in these situations becomes, in part, the desire to reciprocate conciliatory actions. Reciprocated behavior is a sign that the parties are working cooperatively to develop understanding and move past the transgression.

5. Forgiveness Can Restore Relational Justice

As we suggested with our *Negotiated Morality Theory* in Chapter 3, forgiveness is a means by which parties acknowledge violations of relationship values and potentially recommit themselves to a shared moral framework. Thus, the desire to restore justice and fairness in the relationship is sometimes cited as a reason for seeking or granting forgiveness.

❖ THE DARK SIDE OF FORGIVENESS

In addition to the motives just listed, forgiveness can be initiated for a variety of unhealthy reasons. Apparent acts of forgiveness can actually be verbally aggressive behaviors designed to exploit the offended partner's position of control. Said in a *nasty* tone, the following response to an apology is designed to hurt: "I understand that you're just doing the best that you can and that you're just not as psychologically healthy as I am right now." Likewise, conditional forgiveness can be used in a controlling manner: "I'll forgive you on the one condition that you promise to always (or never!) . . ." As is discussed later in this chapter, there are good reasons to set boundaries when renegotiating the relationship. However, Waldron and Kelley (2005) found that conditional forgiveness is often related to relationship deterioration.

Individuals who forgive too readily may be maintaining an unhealthy codependent relationship with a repeat offender. Low self-esteem and/or low relational power may discourage them from fully confronting wrongdoing. Forgiveness is potentially harmful because the goal is to maintain the relationship at the price of continuing unhealthy patterns of behavior. Of course, we argue that these approaches are merely a kind of pseudo-forgiveness. They resemble acceptance or tolerance more than they do genuine forgiveness.

❖ PRESCRIPTIVE MODELS OF FORGIVENESS

This section examines prescriptive approaches to forgiving. We focus on two prominent models that have been used in clinical settings and made available to the broader public through accessible publication. In both cases, research suggests they are potentially effective in helping people forgive (see Wade, Worthington, & Meyer, 2005). Both models are psychological in nature, focused on the cognitive and emotional steps in the forgiveness process. After reviewing them briefly, we integrate these psychological models with our own communicative approach. Table 5.1 presents a summary of the key steps in each framework. Our approach differs in that it focuses on seven tasks that the partners must accomplish jointly. These tasks correspond to the communicative processes described in Chapter 4, Figure 4.1.

The Enright Process Model

Enright and the Human Development Group (1991) developed a process model of forgiveness that occurs in 20 units organized around four phases. During the *uncovering phase,* the offended party recognizes the pain he or she is experiencing because of the transgression, and examines how this injustice has affected him or her. Commenting on this part of the process, Malcolm, Warwar, and Greenberg (2005) emphasize the emotional work that must be accomplished before forgiveness can proceed. Enright (2001) recommends full acknowledgment of the anger and negative emotion. In the *decision phase*, the injured party assesses whether forgiveness is a viable option given the nature of the transgression and the value of the relationship. Interestingly, one may make the decision to forgive in this stage even if the individual

Table 5.1   Practicing Forgiveness: Three Prescriptive Models

Enright et al. (1991, 1992)	Worthington (1998, 2001)	Waldron & Kelley
Four Phases	*Five Steps*	*Seven Tasks*
Uncovering	Recall hurt	Confront transgression
Decision	Empathize	
Work	Give a gift	Manage emotion
Outcome	Public commitment	Make sense
	Hold on	Seek/invite forgiveness
		Grant/accept forgiveness
		(Re)Negotiate rules/values
		Monitor transition

does not yet *feel* forgiving (Freedman, Enright, & Knutson, 2005). Enright (2001) emphasizes committing to the path of forgiveness. This commitment often stems from the realization that vengeful strategies are not working to the advantage of the victim or the relationship.

The third phase, *work,* is characterized by conscious reframing. Similar to the cognitive process described in Kelley's (1998) forgiveness narratives, reframing allows the injured party to recontextualize the offense and feel empathy and compassion for the offender. In the Enright model, reframing is the critical step, because it leads to "acceptance and absorption of the pain and is seen as the heart of forgiveness" (Enright, Freedman, & Rique, 1998; Freedman et al., 2005, p. 395). The psychological "work" requires gaining perspective, developing understanding, and reclaiming positive thoughts, feelings, and behaviors. This shift culminates in an act of mercy. This may be expressed as a tangible gift, such as a card or object that symbolizes healing, or it can be less concrete, such as an expression of continued love. The *outcome phase* represents the experience of healing and psychological health. Elsewhere, this is referred to as the *deepening phase* (Enright & Fitzgibbons, 2000). For Enright, this phase is a release from an emotional prison. The wounded partner finds meaning in the traumatic experience. Examples might include a renewed appreciation for one's capacity to survive trying circumstances, the recognition that all humans are capable of mistakes, or a sense that preserving important relationships is more important than gaining vengeance.

After years of applying this framework, Enright (2001) has offered several observations to keep in mind. He reminds us that not everyone forgives in the same fashion or at the same speed. In addition, individuals may find themselves mired in one of the phases before eventually moving on. Finally, he noted that emotional healing can be a very long process. We would add several of our own observations. First, it may be that the forgiveness process involves loops and cycles, rather than straightforward phases. For example, the decision to forgive may trigger a new round of "uncovering" as emotions such as fear (of a repeated violation) replace anger and resentment. Second, it seems very likely that the phases might occur out of sequence. The decision to forgive may be made before emotions are really dealt with, out of a cognitive commitment to the relationship. Third, we would emphasize that progress through the stages is often a joint accomplishment, propelled by the communication of both partners. For example, emotional states may be addressed more readily when the partner listens respectfully to emotional expressions.

The Worthington Pyramid Model

Worthington (1998, 2001) proposed a pyramid model of forgiveness grounded in research on empathy (McCullough & Worthington, 1995; McCullough et al., 1997). The *Pyramid Model to Reach Forgiveness* included five steps: (1) recall the hurt, (2) empathize, (3) the altruistic gift of forgiveness, (4) commit publicly to forgive, and (5) hold on to forgiveness. *Recall the hurt* emphasizes remembering the transgression as objectively as possible. This is to be done in a supportive environment, often with the help of a therapist. The objective is to confront the reality of the transgression while keeping one's emotional responses in check. The next step, and perhaps key element of the Pyramid Model, is to *empathize.* Empathy involves perspective taking and (re)humanizing the offender. Worthington describes a process of seeing things from the offender's perspective and feeling the offender's feelings. The offender becomes a "person" as well as the object of anger.

Step three is the *altruistic gift of forgiveness,* which involves a three-part process. First, the offended parties contemplate their own past transgressions. Second, they concentrate on the feelings they had when forgiven (e.g., gratitude). According to Worthington, awareness of one's own guilt and gratitude creates a heightened state of arousal that can trigger a desire to forgive. In therapy, a facilitator might capitalize on this state by inviting the client to forgive, as follows: "You can see that the person needs your forgiveness. You can see what a gift it is to have received forgiveness yourself. Would you like to give him (or her) a gift of forgiveness?" (Worthington, 1998, p. 125).

The fourth step, *commit publicly to forgive*, helps the forgiver persevere when doubts arise. The commitment can be expressed to friends, shared in therapy, or written in journals. When the forgiver's resolve diminishes, public commitments provide reminders of the original motives behind the decision to forgive. According to Worthington (2001), these reminders potentially replace the natural desire to ruminate and dwell on negative emotions, with a more constructive process characterized by less pronounced emotion, empathy, sympathy, love, and compassion (Worthington, 2001).

The final step, *hold on to forgiveness*, recognizes that forgiveness is a long-term process. Worthington describes several ways to sustain forgiveness, which we paraphrase: (1) remember that it is not "unforgiving" to remember the hurt you experienced, (2) try not to dwell on negative emotions, (3) remind yourself why you chose forgiveness over revenge, (4) seek reassurance from outside parties, and (5) review journals or other expressions of your decision to forgive.

As does Enright's model, Worthington's approach provides specific guidance for those seeking a path to forgiveness. Worthington effectively simplifies a complex process and identifies useful tools for the forgiver (e.g., journaling). Worthington's model is accessible to the layperson and has apparently been used with some success in therapeutic settings.

❖ COMMUNICATION TASKS OF FORGIVENESS (CTF): A NEW PRESCRIPTIVE MODEL

In proposing a communication-based approach to the practice of forgiveness, we embrace the work of Enright, Worthington, and their colleagues, even as we shift attention away from individual psychology to the communicative behaviors used by families, work teams, or romantic couples to "perform" forgiveness. We find considerable practical value in Enright's four stages and Worthington's five steps, but we are more comfortable with a framework based on communicative *tasks*.

By focusing on tasks, we ease assumptions about linear sequencing. In our view, forgiveness is a process comprising multiple tasks, but they needn't be completed in a particular order (even if they frequently are). A comparison of the other two models reveals sequential variability. For example, empathy has a pivotal role at the beginning of Worthington's process; Enright places empathy at phase three, *working on forgiveness,* after the decision to forgive. We would agree that developing empathy is an essential element, but we view it as a task that may be repeated at various points in the process.

We see forgiveness behaviors as potentially multifunctional, as when the act of confessing ("I bought a new computer because it was on sale, even though we usually talk about large purchases before deciding.") functions to acknowledge a transgression even as it helps the partner make sense of the reasons behind it. In other words, forgiveness tasks can be addressed simultaneously. Moreover, we recognize that certain communication tasks may be partially accomplished, returned to later, or simply repeated until the partners "get it right." The anecdote Jill shared in the introduction of this chapter conveys the sometimes messy and halting nature of forgiving communication.

As each communicative task is introduced, we identify examples of potentially effective communicative behaviors (for more detailed descriptions, see Chapter 4). These include acts that should be initiated or avoided by individuals and patterns of interaction. We also reference psychological processes, with particular emphasis on those proposed by Enright and Worthington. We remind the reader that we are suggesting these tasks on the basis of our own reading of the literature, our preliminary studies of the communication behaviors associated statistically with positive outcomes, and our discussions with experienced romantic couples. We have not yet systematically tested the suggestions provided here, and readers should apply them to their own relationships cautiously.

Task 1: Confront the Transgression

Most forgiveness models start with the recognition of wrongdoing. Responsibility for the wrongful act may be shared, but the key for both

Task 1: Confront the Transgression

Brief description: Both parties must acknowledge that wrongdoing has been committed and that at least one partner has been badly hurt. Responsibility for the transgression must be taken and (sometimes) shared.

Communication behaviors: Question unethical behavior; confess; request self-disclosures; truth telling; make suspicions explicit; question insincerity; describe offensive behavior; discuss violated rules and moral values; demand/claim responsibility.

Psychological processes: Acknowledge hurt; assess magnitude of violation; decide relational and personal impact; identify violated rules and values.

parties is to acknowledge that rules have been broken, values have been flouted, and harm has been done. In our model, denying, minimizing, or evading responsibility for the act is considered ineffective.

Task 2: Manage Emotion

Emotion is an individual experience, but its meaning and relational importance must be socially negotiated. "Managing emotion" involves such communicative tasks as listening, expressing, labeling, and reciprocating emotion (or choosing not to). Extreme emotion may hamper the performance of other forgiveness tasks, so the partners must cooperate in an effort to absorb the emotional impact of the transgression.

Task 2: Manage Emotion

Brief description: Strong negative emotion must be expressed, labeled, acknowledged, legitimized, accepted, and deintensified. Emotions may include shock, anger, and fear, among others.

Communication behaviors: Give voice to strong emotion; ask about emotions; listen for emotions; avoid interruption; curtail defensive communication; assess nonverbal emotional cues; affirm the right to be emotional; use labels for emotional states; resist the tendency to reciprocate negative emotions; request a "cooling off" period; allow time for emotions to dissipate; edit destructive emotional expressions.

Psychological processes: Become aware of emotions; identify source of emotion; classify emotional reactions; legitimize emotional response; give yourself permission to express emotion.

Task 3: Engage in Sense-Making

Transgressions are disruptive events that create uncertainty, call moral values into question, and force partners to reconsider relational assumptions. As a communication process, sense-making refers to efforts to "make meaning of" and "manage uncertainty about" the transgression. This information feeds psychological assessments of the magnitude of the act, attributions about why it occurred, and what the act means for the future of the relationship. This task may involve an initial assessment of whether or not the act is "forgivable" given the value system governing the individuals and their relationship. As most psychological models note, the information gathered from these interactions can help parties reframe the offense, sometimes in a manner that reduces its perceived magnitude.

Task 3: Engage in Sense-Making

Brief description: The wounded partner invites information-sharing about motives, situational details, and explanations, all in an effort to manage uncertainty and assess the magnitude of the offense. The offender provides an honest explanation. The parties jointly construct the meaning of the offense by considering it in the context of past behavior, current relational understandings, and implications for the future.

Communication behaviors: Seek/offer explanations and accounts; manage uncertainty through open questions, examples, honest answers, and paraphrasing; explore motives for the offense; question intent; engage in perspective taking; discuss extenuating circumstances; construe the relational meaning of the offense; jointly assess personal and relational harm; consider offense in context of relational past (is the offense part of a larger pattern?); create a vision for the hypothetical future (could we maintain our relationship in light of this offense?).

Psychological processes: Assess motives and intent; make attributions about the cause of the offense; weigh mitigating circumstances; contrast magnitude with value of the relationship; understand the offender's perspective; reframe the offense; determine if offense is "forgivable" within your value system; assess predictability of the relational future.

Task 4: Seek Forgiveness

Table 5.2 summarizes common forgiveness-seeking and forgiveness-granting tactics and their association with relational outcomes. These are based on reports from romantic partners (see Kelley & Waldron, 2005; Waldron & Kelley, 2005). Explicit acknowledgement (including apology and expressions of remorse), nonverbal assurances (which communicated sincerity), and offers of compensation were the approaches associated with positive outcomes. Task 4 requires both parties to agree that forgiveness is at least a possibility and to communicate in a manner that advances the process. The forgiveness seeker may accept responsibility, express regret, and apologize. The wounded party typically expects such behavior and assesses the degree to which the message sufficiently redresses the transgression. Negotiation or delay may follow (as in Jill's interaction reported above) until the issues are resolved.

A central component in the Enright and Worthington models is the development of *empathy*. Empathy is "an active effort to understand another person's perception of an interpersonal event as if one were that other person." (Malcolm & Greenberg, 2000, p. 180). The wounded

Table 5.2   Self-Reported Forgiveness Strategies and Romantic Relationship
Outcomes

Strategy	Examples	Outcome
Forgiveness-seeking strategies		
1. Explicit acknowledgement	Apology; remorse	Positive
2. Nonverbal assurance	Eye contact; hugs	Positive
3. Compensation	Gifts; repeated efforts	Positive
4. Explanation	Reasons; discuss offense	None
5. Humor	Joking; humoring	None
Forgiveness-granting strategies		
1. Explicit	"I forgive you"	Positive
2. Nonverbal displays	Facial expressions; touch	Positive
3. Conditional	"I forgive you, but only if . . ."	Negative
4. Discussion	Talking about the offense	Positive
5. Minimize	"No big deal"; "Don't worry"	None

SOURCE: From Kelley, D. L., & Waldron, V. R. (2006). Forgiveness: Communicative implications in social relationships. In C. S. Beck (Ed.), *Communication Yearbook 30* (pp. 303–341). Mahwah, NJ: Lawrence Erlbaum Associates. Table reprinted by permission.

partner may develop empathy by considering the frailty of human nature or recalling his or her own transgressions, thus identifying with the offender. Empathy can foster a more open response to forgiveness requests. Ultimately this openness can be communicated verbally (e.g., "I accept the apology") or nonverbally (e.g., through a hug, a nod, or a cessation of defensive posture).

Task 4: Seek Forgiveness

Brief description: The wounded partner convincingly apologizes, expresses regret, and (where appropriate) offers to make amends. The forgiver assesses the request for forgiveness, develops empathy, and communicates openness to the possibility of forgiveness.

(Continued)

(Continued)

> *Communication behaviors:* Explicitly acknowledge fault (apology, remorse); grant control to the offended party; offer nonverbal assurance; offer compensation (make amends); express openness to forgiveness request; listen nondefensively; acknowledge offender's communicative effort; express empathy if appropriate; when appropriate, explain why initial forgiveness-seeking efforts are inadequate (e.g., fails to fully acknowledge blame); let mutual friends know of your culpability and desire for forgiveness (when appropriate).
>
> *Psychological processes:* Decide that forgiveness is possible and potentially desirable; weigh the relative benefits of revenge and the benefits of mercy; identify with the offender; develop empathy; assess offender's behavior in light of one's own past failures; focus on learning, not defending; see offender as a person, not an object of anger; assess offender's sincerity; assess the likelihood of a repeat offense; determine if compensation is necessary; assess "fit" between forgiveness-seeking behavior and seriousness of the transgression; assess one's willingness to take a risk.

Task 5: Grant Forgiveness

Granting forgiveness is the task that Enright and Worthington refer to as "giving a gift." The gift metaphor apparently stems from the sense that the wounded partner can legitimately choose to withhold forgiveness, but chooses instead to exercise mercy. As with gifts, forgiveness is often granted as an expression of love. As indicated in Table 5.2, explicit statements of forgiveness, nonverbal displays, and willing to discuss the path to forgiveness were associated with positive relational outcomes.

> ### Task 5: Grant Forgiveness
>
> *Brief description:* The wounded partner indicates a willingness to forgive. Forgiveness may be extended immediately and unequivocally or a long-term process may be initiated. To reduce risk, conditional forgiveness may be offered and third parties may be involved.
>
> *Communication behaviors:* Extend mercy to the offender; use explicit forgiveness statements where warranted ("I forgive you"); use conditional forgiveness statements to enhance psychological safety and reduce risk; use nonverbal behavior (e.g., hugs, eye contact) to supplement the verbal message; resist the temptation to minimize serious offenses; offer to discuss the possibility of forgiving; suggest seeking assistance from third parties to increase chances of success (when appropriate).
>
> *Psychological processes:* Decide to "give a gift" of forgiveness; decide what kind of mercy is appropriate (e.g., does it include a change in relationship

status along with forgiveness?); consult your personal values (e.g., religious or moral principles); accept the gift of forgiveness; release negative feelings; clarify reasons for forgiving (e.g., in a journal), such as love for the partner, commitment to the relationship, and personal well-being; make public commitments to forgiveness if appropriate; let go of the grudge; focus on the relationship, not the self; decide to replace negative emotions with positive; find reasons for hope.

Task 6: Negotiate Values and Rules

As we suggested in Chapter 3, forgiveness can be conceptualized as a process of negotiating relational morality. As Hargrave (1994) suggests, forgiveness often leads to a new "relational covenant." Task 6 makes this process explicit, as the partners reaffirm their commitments to one another, negotiate new values that will inform their future behavior, and agree to behavioral and communication rules that will guide them. For example, in negotiating forgiveness after a serious curfew violation, parents and children may agree that (1) safety and predictability are important values, (2) "home by 11:00 p.m." is a standard they can agree to, and (3) a phone conversation should precede any decision to change the rule on a given evening. Ultimately, the task is to create a system of justice and moral responsibility that will govern the relationship in the future. Completion of this task may require the parties to reinvent their relationship; third-party assistance may be needed to imagine new ways of relating.

Task 6: Negotiate Values and Rules

Brief description: Clarify the values and rules that will govern the relationship during the postforgiveness period. Renegotiate the "relational covenant." Create the moral structure that ensures fairness and justice in future interactions (see Chapter 3 for a discussion of the Negotiated Morality Theory of Forgiveness).

Communication behaviors: Clarify existing communication rules by proposing hypothetical applications and paraphrasing; affirm and recommit to relational values and beliefs; propose new rules and ways of relating; discuss a mutual plan for rebuilding trust; communicate respect for your efforts to forgive; discuss the shared values that will define your relationship in the future (e.g., the courage to confront problems head-on).

(Continued)

(Continued)

> *Psychological processes:* Reimagine your future in this relationship; anticipate possible roadblocks and setbacks; decide which relational changes are needed to enhance psychological safety and maintain an acceptable relationship; clarify the conditions that would lead to relationship termination; learn about improved methods of relating (e.g., via therapy, books, experienced friends and family members).

Task 7: Transition: Monitor, Maintain, or Renegotiate

In Chapter 4, we imagined a transitional period between the forgiveness episode and the resumption of a stable (if redefined) relationship. The key objectives here may be to monitor the success of new relational agreements, to maintain new behavior patterns, and to rebuild trust and hope. Partners must actively create positive relational experiences to replace negative emotions. Part of this process may involve constructing a new relational narrative that celebrates the relationship's perseverance in the face of great difficulty. A focus on the future replaces rumination about the negative experience in the past. Resolve, relational stability, and confidence may be cultivated by resuming familiar rituals (like meeting regularly over lunch), reviewing the reasons for forgiveness (consulting a journal), and seeking continued support from friends, spiritual leaders, or professionals. It should be expected that the process may cycle back to an earlier forgiveness task that has yet to be completed (e.g., managing emotions). This may be the period when it becomes clear that, regardless of forgiveness, the relationship must be terminated or deescalated because of recurring transgressions, irresolvable moral differences, or concerns about the psychological safety of the relationship.

> **Task 7: Transition: Monitor, Maintain, or Renegotiate**
>
> *Brief description:* Monitor and maintain relational agreements; build trust, confidence, and hope; derive meaning from the experience; focus on the future; consider a redefined relationship if the process fails.
>
> *Communication behaviors:* Note successes in complying with new relational agreements; return to previous communication tasks as needed (e.g., manage resurgent emotions); jointly reconstruct "lessons learned" from the forgiveness episode, but edit discussions of bitterness and blame; discuss whether forgiveness is "holding" and why; adjust your relational narrative to

incorporate the forgiveness episode (i.e., create a subnarrative about surviving the hardest of times); add forgiveness to discussion of relational identity (e.g., "forgiveness makes our relationship last"); use positive communication experiences to replace negative feelings (e.g., offer compliments); talk about increases in trust, hope, and stability as they are experienced; resume comforting relational rituals (e.g., regular dinner dates); seek continued support from friends and professionals.

Psychological processes: Be mindful of your behavior and that of your partner; allow oneself to experience renewed trust (when warranted); accept appropriate levels of uncertainty about the relational future; (re)affirm oneself for seeking/granting forgiveness; remind oneself of the reasons for seeking or granting forgiveness (e.g., review journals); add forgiving to one's self-identity; focus on future benefits of the relationship; build a psychological safety net with counselors and friends; consider deescalation or termination of the relationship (if new agreements are violated).

❖ RECONCILIATION: A POSSIBLE OUTCOME OF FORGIVENESS

Forgiveness can lead to reconciliation, or what is often called *relationship repair*. In fact, the desire to reconcile sometimes drives the decision to forgive. However, as do many scholars, we find value in separating these related processes. It is quite possible to forgive without fully reconciling. In fact, reconciliation may be a poor choice in relationships marked by abuse or codependence. In our own research, we find that some parties intensify and strengthen their bonds after negotiating forgiveness, others just "return to normal," and still others choose to change their relational status (e.g., from friends to "just coworkers"), lower the level of intimacy (e.g., from lovers to friends), or terminate the relationship altogether. Nevertheless, forgiveness scholars have speculated about why and how forgiveness might lead to reconciliation. We find some helpful suggestions in our discussion with long-term married couples. In this section, we draw on both of these sources to develop guidance for those seeking reconciliation.

Contributions From Forgiveness Scholars

Several scholars have theorized about how forgiveness might facilitate relationship repair. For example, Rusbult et al. (2005), operating from an interdependence theory perspective, argue that reconciliation is dependent on restoring commitment and trust. *Commitment* is defined as "the extent to which each partner intends to persist in the relationship, feels psychologically attached to it, and exhibits long-term orientation toward it" (p. 187), whereas *trust* is defined as "the strength of each partner's conviction that the other can be counted on to behave in a benevolent manner" (p. 187). Practically speaking, commitment is the motivation to act in a prosocial manner, such as accommodating, sacrificing, or affirming one's partner. Trust is the degree to which one believes the other person will act prosocially. Thus, in order to effect lasting repair, both partners must make mutual prosocial investments in the relationship. For example, the offended party may act with goodwill, setting aside accusations in the hopes of starting anew, while the offender simultaneously decides to take responsibility for the transgression and tries to make amends. From Rusbult et al.'s work, we conclude that forgiveness is a process that cultivates prosocial action, creating the conditions for reconciliation in turn.

Gordon and colleagues (Gordon & Baucom, 2003; Gordon et al. 2000) describe a three-stage process that may facilitate reconciliation after an extramarital affair or other major betrayal. The first stage, *impact,* is characterized by feelings of uncertainty, violated trust, and increased risk. Often with the help of a therapist, during this stage the wounded partner places boundaries on his or her interactions with the offender, practices self-care, uses time-out and venting strategies, copes with flashbacks, and discusses the impact of the transgression with the offender (Gordon & Baucom, 1999). The second stage, *meaning,* is characterized by communication behavior intended to reduce uncertainty and increase mutual understanding. A goal is to restore losses of control and security while determining whether the relationship can be safely reconciled. This phase is characterized by (1) explanations and accounts, (2) questions, and (3) assurances and promises (Kelley & Waldron, 2005). The third stage is *recovery* or *moving on.* The understanding that has been developed at the *meaning* stage hopefully leads to a "nondistorted view" (Gordon & Baucom, 2003, p. 182) and less intense negative emotion. The offended party may recognize that forgiveness is preferable to revenge because the latter will not "rebalance" the relationship. During this stage, the pair may negotiate forgiveness and work through problematic issues that could affect their reconciliation. For these authors, the task of forgiveness is embedded within a larger process of reconciliation.

Hargrave's (1994) reconciliation model contains two central components: exoneration and forgiveness. *Exoneration* is a process of gaining insight into the causes of one's emotional pain while also understanding the offender's fallibility. The offended party may learn to identify with the offender and ultimately reduce feelings of superiority and blame. Hargrave emphasizes that acknowledging the offender's fallibility does *not* release her or him from responsibility.

In his therapeutic approach, Hargrave (1994) argues that *forgiveness* is relevant only after the offended party is willing and ready for healing and perceives that the offender is ready to act in a responsible and trustworthy manner. At that point, the forgiver offers the *opportunity for compensation.* The forgiver does not demand an apology or restitution, but communicates a willingness to explore possibilities for reconciliation. Ultimately this process culminates in an *overt act of forgiveness.* As Hargrave (1994) puts it, this act "is unique in the work of forgiveness because it focuses immense effort and importance on one point in time between the innocent victim of family violation and the perpetrator of the violation" (p. 346). This act can be the result of the hard work of rebuilding love and trust or can begin the process. In either case, making forgiveness an overt act can "facilitate acts of compassion, courage, and commitment between family members" (p. 346).

Thus far we can see that forgiveness is closely intertwined with reconciliation, although its placement varies in these therapeutic approaches. For Rusbult et al. (2005), forgiveness provides the foundation for the prosocial behavior that may facilitate reconciliation. For Gordon and Baucom (2003) along with Hargrave (1994), forgiveness is predicated on the decision to reconcile. However, a key element of each of these approaches is the transformation of negative emotion into positive affect and/or prosocial acts. Malcolm et al. (2005) argue that this emotional transformation process is central to both forgiveness and reconciliation. Individual Emotion-Focused Therapy (EFT; Greenberg, Warwar, & Malcolm, 2003) posits that "the suppression or blocking of primary biologically adaptive emotions subverts healthy boundary setting, self-respectful anger, and necessary grieving" (Malcolm et al., 2005). From this perspective, engaging in forgiveness requires the forgiver to acknowledge the legitimacy of emotions, such as hatred and resentment, in response to a relational transgression. Even the desire to retaliate is seen as part of a normal response to being hurt. This approach encourages individuals to work through their emotions, rather than avoiding them by excusing or condoning the offender's behavior or by focusing all of their energies on blaming the offender. Eventually, "a maladaptive emotion state is transformed best by replacing it with another, more adaptive emotion" (Malcolm et al., 2005, p. 383).

We suggest that reconciliation is also facilitated by communicative processes that cultivate more adaptive emotional expressions. One practice long-term married couples described to us involves the initiation or resumption of familiar relational rituals. One couple resumed their practice of joining friends for a night out once each week, even though it felt awkward at first. Several couples used joint prayer to regenerate positive feelings. As one wife told us, "We prayed and the next day we felt different, you know." Another couple resolved to attend family gatherings together. In each case, the renewal of ritual seemed to stimulate some degree of positive feeling and reduced the tendency to dwell on negative emotion.

As discussed at length in Chapter 3, we believe that values must be renegotiated as part of the forgiveness/reconciliation process. Successful renegotiation of values should result in a new moral structure for the relationship, if the relationship is to continue. This moral structure identifies *right* and *wrong* behavior within the confines of the relationship. In addition, it may define consequences for following or breaking these new or reinstated relational rules. The ability to renegotiate this new moral structure will influence the extent to which relationships are reconciled, weakened, or strengthened. As discussed later, renegotiating values is also central to reestablishing meaning in the relationship.

❖ CONTRIBUTIONS FROM LONG-TERM COUPLES

Before leaving our discussion of reconciliation, we would like to share some of the advice long-term couples offered us. This section is adapted from a chapter we are preparing for a book on effective interpersonal communication (Waldron et al., in press). Of course, most couples bother little with theoretical distinctions between forgiveness and reconciliation. However, we view them as "forgiveness experts" in the sense that their relationships persevered through very difficult circumstances. These couples survived affairs, financial irresponsibility, business failures, drug and alcohol abuse, serious difference in parenting, public embarrassments, vicious arguments, and other major transgressions. We well know that longevity is only one measure of relational success, as it is possible to maintain a dysfunctional relationship for a very long time. Moreover, the forgiveness practices learned by older couples, in this case those married in the 1930s–1960s, may not be entirely applicable to younger couples. The forgiveness attitudes and practices of these couples were shaped by the cultural values of their generations. For example, couples married before the 1960s sometimes felt compelled to forgive their spouses, in part because divorce was a cultural or religious taboo. Despite obvious "cohort differences," we found cross-generational consistencies in the interviews. We focus on these as we share their prescriptions for staying together after serious transgressions.

Acknowledge wrongdoing

Nearly all couples agreed that a key to negotiating forgiveness was taking responsibility for hurting your partner. The sufficient *acknowledgment* of wrongdoing is both a necessary part of forgiveness (in our communicative view) and an important step in reasserting relational justice. As a communication process, forgiveness expresses, changes, or reinforces the moral order of our relationships. It is the process by which injustice is identified and "owned up to." In some cases, offenders are forgiven unconditionally. Admitting wrongdoing and taking responsibility for transgressions are often enough to assure our partners that commonly agreed-on values will be respected in the future— that "justice will prevail."

In many cases, the responsibility for a transgression is mutual. As an example, Judith admitted continually overspending the family budget and hiding the creditor notices from her husband, Adam. As they discussed the matter, Adam realized that his sometimes harsh criticism encouraged Judith to be evasive about financial problems. Only when they both acknowledged their culpability could they move the forgiveness process along.

Apologize sincerely

Apology is the form of communication most likely to be associated with successful forgiveness. Usually issued with words such as "I am sorry," apologies communicate remorse and acknowledge a shift in conversational power to the wounded partner. Only the victim can "accept" an apology. Whereas transgressions can shatter the victim's sense of control, apologies put them in a position to determine the nature of the relationship. As previously indicated, apologies must be authentic to advance the forgiveness process. Jill's scenario, which started this chapter, illustrates the consequences of an apology that was insufficiently sincere.

Address emotion explicitly

Serious transgressions result in shock, embarrassment, anger, and hurt. Communicating these emotions is an important part of the early stages of forgiveness. Communication is the means by which emotion is vented. "Get it out on the table," one wife advised, "don't hold it in." The offender's acknowledgement of the type and depth of emotion is important as well: "I know I hurt you badly." Sometimes couples help each other label emotions: "I didn't realize how ashamed I was until he asked why I hid the bills from him." For many couples, honest discussion of emotion was a prerequisite for progress.

Request outside assistance

Many couples recommended outside assistance as an important step in the forgiveness process. Particularly during the early stages of relationships, serious transgressions overwhelmed the couples' relational skills. Pastors, counselors, and older family members were among those consulted, particularly when the partners found it impossible to resolve issues of accountability or manage volatile emotions. One couple described the grudges that developed over repeated financial problems. They finally made progress by "talking with some of the other people that I've been very close to. How do they handle it? We'd go ask other people who have done these things." Friends helped identify the reasons for their financial distress and urged the partners to release feelings of resentment.

Forgive and remember

Some couples claimed that the key to a successful marriage was to "forgive and forget," to simply excise past transgressions from current discourse. However, as they discussed the history of their relationships, it became clear that forgetting was selective for most couples. Couples "actively forget" in the sense that they no longer experience the emotional pain when remembering the transgression, and they put discussions of blame in the past. Yet they "actively remembered" the lessons learned from past transgressions as they negotiated through a long-term process of forgiveness.

Use time to advantage

An advantage of interviews with long-term couples is their appreciation for the importance of time. They told us that forgiveness can be an ongoing negotiation, one that sometimes takes months, years, and in some cases, even decades. In Chapter 3, we introduced Ray (married to Doris for 32 years), who recalled a time when he brawled with some local "punks." Doris was humiliated when she was forced to bail him out of their small town jail, but as a traditional wife, she believed she should suffer in silence. As Doris told us, she had nurtured a grudge over the incident until recently. In fact, the couple revealed that only weeks before (nearly two decades after the event) had Doris shared her feelings with Ray. In response, Ray belatedly acknowledged that he was wrong. Even as we interviewed them, the couple seemed to be mulling over the event and how it affected their marriage. Doris has not fully released her feelings of resentment, but she feels the couple is on stronger emotional footing now. "With time" Doris feels she can fully forgive Ray. She feels more hopeful about the retirement years, because she is putting the past behind her.

In addition, time may be used strategically in forgiveness negotiations. Angry partners sometimes "need time" to cool off before deciding if and how to forgive. "Taking time" to think and reduce high arousal levels sometimes helps partners put a transgression in a larger relational perspective. Hal described how he sometimes left the house briefly before realizing he needed to ask for forgiveness. "It gave us time to cool off . . . I jump in the car and go raring off and drive around a little bit and come back and realize that I was really [a] stupid idiot for doing that, you know."

Invoke spiritual values

For some couples, the difficulty of forgiveness is eased by shared spiritual values. In some interpretations of Christian theology, forgiveness is viewed as a mandate from God. For these couples, the discourse of forgiveness involves a revisiting of sacred teachings. As one Christian wife said to her husband in a joint interview, "if God forgave all of our sins, I guess I can forgive you for being a jerk sometimes." In some cases, couples seemed overwhelmed by the gravity of the offense. Together they sought insight, comfort, and guidance from shared religious texts and spiritual principles. The invoking of "higher order" values and a "higher power" may have allowed them to transcend the emotions and confusions that accompanied the relational crises. One couple was originally overwhelmed when the husband admitted his infidelity and alcoholism:

"I'm sorry," he said, "I want [you] to read the book of Mormon with me every day," so we did. We read it every day together for at least three years . . . And we would read it every day and honestly it was bringing the Lord into our life and that's what brought us together.

Revisit communication rules

Transgressions often call into question the implicit agreements that govern relationships and make them predictable. Forgiveness often involves a reassertion of those rules. The offender must assure the wounded party that rules will be followed in the future. One young woman told us she greatly distressed her parents by staying out all night and not checking in by phone (as was the custom in her family). She apologized for the upset she caused and pledged to "never do it again." In other cases, new rules are proposed. A wife felt she could forgive her husband for an affair only if he pledged to let her "know where he was at every minute of the day." By complying with this new rule, the husband would reduce her uncertainty and gradually restore her trust.

The Role of Outside Assistance in Forgiveness and Reconciliation

Although to this point we have made few references to outside influences, these older couples recognized the important role that third parties play as individuals manage their relationships. Every relationship is embedded within a broader context of relationships. For example, a married couple is embedded within a network of in-law, child, and work relationships. This relational embeddedness has two important ramifications for managing relational transgressions. First, when transgressions become public they must be managed within the larger social network. For example, when a couple experiences marital problems due to one partner's affair and the affair becomes known within the social network, each individual is now faced with new communication tasks as they seek to manage their identity goals (e.g., save face for self or partner) and place appropriate boundaries on potential involvement from third-party individuals. Toward the end of the forgiveness and reconciliation process, the disputants may circulate individual or co-created narratives that provide a final public account of the process and what it means for the relationship, the individual participants, and their future involvement in the social network.

Our couples often called on third parties for help when working through forgiveness and reconciliation: counselors, clergy, family, and friends. Third-party assistance may be needed with any of the forgiveness tasks presented earlier in this chapter. For example, one wife who left her husband early in their marriage described her mother's invaluable assistance with sense-making, as she struggled to understand the reasons for her spouse's apparently insensitive behavior. Others used counselors to help them articulate their emotions, negotiate responsibility, and create new relationship rules as they worked on reconciliation. As one wife remembered

We went into counseling after that. We did go in for, you know, marriage counseling and we had assignments even, you know, to learn to communicate and learn the cause of our problem— communication. And so we just learned through that process.

Another emphasized how her counselor taught her "how to confront him (her husband). And then he finally went to one session and since that, things have really gone well. That was another turning point in our marriage."

❖ CONCLUDING THOUGHTS

As individuals seek or grant forgiveness, and possibly move toward reconciliation in their relationships, they operate within a moral worldview. These moral assumptions inform beliefs about respect, justice, and how relationships *should* work. They are important components of personal identity and links to larger communities and cultures. It is because relationships are a primary site for the enactment, testing, and collision of values that we view forgiveness as a process of moral negotiation. For us, the nature and degree of reconciliation achieved between parties is largely a function of the extent to which they can agree on the moral framework that will guide their future interactions. This is perhaps the most fundamental communication task in the process of relational repair.

Our perspective is consistent with Flanigan's (1998) insight regarding victims of intrafamilial trauma. She argues that forgiveness is most difficult when the transgression undermines one's fundamental system of beliefs and values, when "people's beliefs in personal control and rules of justice are shattered along with their self-worth and belief in the goodness of others" (p. 99). Flanigan goes further: "Forgiveness is not given to events, but to people who have altered a person's perceptions of his [sic] internal or external world and of how this world will be in the future" (Flanigan, 1998, p. 100). In essence, recovering from severe relational transgression means finding a way to reconstruct one's moral worldview, restoring a sense that one's actions can lead to just outcomes, and creating confidence in the potential goodness of the other, even as we accept the fallibility of all humans. The resolve to forgive comes not from the simple need to fix a relational problem but also from a willingness to address the moral positions that allow us to respect ourselves and those we relate with.

In this chapter, we have proposed a series of practical forgiveness tasks. Although they certainly are shaped by the behaviors of individuals, their accomplishment ultimately stems from cooperative interaction. In our view, forgiveness tasks are not strictly sequential. They mutually influence one another in their development, can progress in parallel, and may be revisited repeatedly. We also made distinctions between forgiveness and reconciliation, although these processes clearly can overlap. Through the identification of both forgiveness tasks and reconciliation tasks, we hope to provide important insight into the debate concerning the relationship between these two important concepts. It is simply impossible to chart a single psychological or communicative path through the complicated landscape of distressed human relationships. The process of forgiving a serious transgression is an intensely personal and trying relational journey. We hope we have provided useful navigational assistance by describing key tasks, providing examples of concrete communication behaviors, and sharing the advice of experienced travelers.

6

Studying Forgiveness

*Methodological Conundrums and
Transformational Experiences*

This chapter differs from the earlier ones in that it reports, in a personal way, our decisions and experiences as forgiveness researchers. The chapter is intended for students of research and those who want to look behind the standard "Methods" section to understand the subjective experiences and methodological tradeoffs that make research a fascinating and sometimes transformational human activity. Forgiveness research offers the perfect excuse for writing this somewhat unconventional chapter. It is a complicated social process; difficult to measure in any conventional sense; ripe with personal relevance; energized by its cultural, political, and religious significance; and subject to differences in disciplinary perspective.

Between us, we have accumulated some 30 years of social science research experience. Yet our research on forgiveness has been, by far, the most engaging and rewarding of our careers. We have been privileged to hear about some of the darkest and most private of relational crises. We have been heartbroken by tales of betrayal and relationship decay and heartened by stories of forgiveness and relationship renewal. The many people who shared these stories helped us appreciate the *transformational* nature of research. By that we mean that research is not just about carefully observing and describing what *is*. It is also about *changing*. Our participants changed. In their discourse about forgiveness, couples reinterpreted its role in their relationship and sometimes practiced it, right in front of our eyes. We changed. We altered some of our ideas about the nature and importance of forgiveness. Thanks to our participants, we grew more insightful about our own families and marriages. Our friendship was deepened and energized by the long discussions we shared on our drives to and from interviews. Finally, we believe the readers of this book will change as they expand their understanding of forgiveness and the means by which it is enacted in their own relationships.

In peering at the "dark side" of personal relationships, communication researchers face difficult methodological questions. How can we shed light on communication processes that are so often private and hidden? How do we protect from emotional harm those who agree to share these painful moments? How can we measure a process that is so complex and varied? How do our own relational experiences shape the questions we ask about forgiveness and our interpretations of the data we collect? As its title "Studying Forgiveness" suggests, this chapter shares our personal efforts to address methodological questions such as these. Researchers concerned with issues of reliability and validity will find references to measurement procedures and instruments used by us and others. However, as suggested by the subtitle, the chapter is also intended for readers who seek a better understanding of the "lived experience" of forgiveness research. We highlight methodological conundrums as well as some of our more memorable mistakes, serendipitous discoveries, and rewarding experiences. We describe some of these in the textboxes labeled "On the Drive Home," because some of our best methodological discussions took place in the car as we returned from interviews with long-term married couples. We should note that the chapter is not intended to be a research primer. Excellent texts are available for those seeking a comprehensive review of the methods communication researchers use (see, for example, Baxter & Babbie, 2004; Frey, Botan, & Kreps, 2000).

We view research as a process of asking questions and then devising methods that help us find the answers—or at least refine the questions. For this reason, much of the chapter is organized in a question-and-answer format. The questions are those we asked ourselves and those raised by others as they heard about our research. Those "others" included our students, faculty colleagues, reviewers at academic journals, family and friends, curious acquaintances, and, of course, some of the many people who agreed to be part of our studies.

The chapter refers to several of our own research studies, details of which are provided in Table 6.1 and the appendices. The "interview" study involved 90–120 minute interviews of 60 couples married more than 30 years (mean = 44 years), including Ola and Doc, the subject of the textbox below. The interviews were completed in their homes. See Appendix A for interview questions.

On the Drive Home #1: Forgiveness in the Garden of Eden: Interviewing the World's Longest-Married Couple

Our decision to interview couples in their homes yielded logistical challenges on the one hand, and wonderfully rich interviews on the other. We spent countless hours on the road but found that most couples were comfortable talking about their relationships while sitting on a couch in their own living room. Inviting couples to our research space, phone interviews, surveys—none of these approaches would have yielded the same rich data. We navigated some challenges, particularly when additional family members were present. But as was the case with Doc and Ola, on-site interviews yielded a rich sense of the relational and cultural context that shapes forgiveness episodes.

We left early that winter morning on the long drive from our homes in the Phoenix area. Forecasters had predicted a rare desert snowstorm, and sure enough, white powder dusted the huge saguaros that stood along our route through rocky mountain passes. Three hours later, through a windshield clouded by steam from third cups of coffee, we caught our first glimpse of Eden, a tiny, remote, exhausted-looking farm town gasping for life along a dry riverbed. We were here to interview Ola and Doc, offspring of the rugged Mormon settlers who wrestled this small valley away from the native Apaches in the late 1800s. They scraped out farm fields; built a church, a general store, and stage stop; and periodically gathered at a community dance hall, built by hand from local wood and preserved today by the town's few residents, most of whom are directly related to Ola and Doc. Aged 94 and 98. Married 80 years. And, as confirmed by a certificate from the Guinness Book of World Records, the longest-married couple living on earth.

The physical decline of old age had only recently taken its toll on this contented and obviously loving couple. Until a recent leg injury, Doc drove more than 10 miles every day, just to share a cup of coffee with old friends in a nearby town. But the act of communicating was hard work at their age. Despite their determined efforts, many of our questions went unheard. We

---

(Continued)

(Continued)

> could see they were tiring quickly, so we simply listened as they regaled us with stories of their turbulent, and by the standards of Eden, even scandalous, relationship. Protective and loving, their sons and daughters (who still work the family cotton farm despite being in their 70s) hovered nearby, goading the couple to reveal the "juiciest" tales and laughing with delight when they obliged.
>
> We developed no radical new insights about forgiveness that memorable day. But we did learn that Ola was only thirteen when she and Doc married ("She will try to tell you she was fourteen," her daughter whispered to us, "but the record is pretty clear on that one."). Against the advice of their parents, under cover of darkness, the young pair snuck across the border to Mexico, where they could be married legally. We learned that Doc and Ola were by no means completely compatible, even now, and that he frequently tried her patience. A favorite story recalled by Ola and met by hoots of laughter from family members concerned Doc's tendency to spend the evenings at his parents' home rather than with his new bride. Ola cooked up a plan to extract revenge from her inconsiderate husband, "to set him right." Upon his return one night, she offered him a freshly baked pie—one of his favorite treats. Unbeknownst to Doc, she had stuffed the pie with cotton, in the belief that it would make him sick (and presumably repentant). The punch line was that Doc consumed the whole pie with relish and happily crawled into bed, suffering no ill effects whatsoever. The moral of the story seemed to be that effort spent on vengeance was wasted on Doc. Over time, Ola simply learned to talk with Doc, rather than poison him! She recruited his family to help her understand his sometimes odd ways. They are still helping.
>
> As Eden disappeared in the review mirror, obscured by dust from the unpaved road, we talked excitedly about our good fortune in meeting the unique members of this pioneering family. More than any other, our interview with Ola and Doc helped us realize that forgiveness can be conceptualized not just as an event, but as a lengthy process, sometimes very lengthy indeed. We were reminded just how important family support can be and came to appreciate how forgiveness may be promoted through the telling and retelling of family stories. Eden turned out not to be a garden, just a sprawling cotton farm. But our conversations with Ola and Doc bore fruit nonetheless, in the form of a richer and deeper conceptualization of forgiveness.

In addition to interview data, we reference three studies based on questionnaires. Doug's original survey (Kelley, 1998) asked participants to write narratives of forgiveness episodes (see Appendix B for questions and instructions). Two additional published studies (Kelley & Waldron, 2005; Waldron & Kelley, 2005) are based on a comprehensive survey that asked participants to provide open-ended descriptions, likelihood of use ratings, and effectiveness ratings for various communication tactics. The nature of the transgression, relationship quality, and relational outcomes were also assessed (see Appendix C). Finally, some of the examples presented in this book are drawn from Vince's studies of emotional episodes in the workplace. He analyzed accounts obtained from over 800 employees, including factory workers, corrections officers, attorneys and judges, government agency staffers, and private-sector managers (see Waldron, 1994, 2000). We drew most heavily on employee reports of relational transgressions and subsequent experiences of forgiveness and revenge.

❖ WHY DO WE STUDY FORGIVENESS?

"So, what do you study?" As university researchers, we hear that question often. Reactions are mixed when we explain that forgiveness is one of our keenest research interests. Some are puzzled. "Forgiveness about *what?*" they want to know. Others register a look of skepticism. "I am not the forgiving kind," one of our colleagues growled, "so I don't think I would find it interesting." Still others warm to the topic immediately. They give us knowing looks and affirming nods. "Been there, done that," they seem to be saying. A surprising number of this group offers a spontaneous prescription: "You can't hold a grudge," they say, or "To forgive is divine," or "Forgive and forget—that's the key thing," or yet again, "You know. It's not really forgiveness if you wait for the other person to apologize."

So why *do* we study forgiveness? One answer is that the study of forgiveness was a natural next step in our research programs. Doug has long had an interest in marital communication. One of his research themes since the late 1980s has been relationship expectancies (see Kelley & Burgoon, 1991). What happens when our partner's communication is less intimate or more controlling than we expect it to be? What are our communicative reactions and how does the violation make us feel about the relationship? Forgiveness is one possible reaction, but as Doug soon learned, very few researchers had studied it. Vince has studied the role of communication in maintaining work relationships since 1990 (Waldron, 1991, 2000). In a series of papers on the expression of emotion at work, he documented the emotional nature of hurtful relational events, such as coworker betrayals, public humiliations, and supervisor abuse (e.g., Waldron, 1994, 2000). Vince wondered how communication processes could be used to promote repair and healing in damaged work relationships. Forgiveness appeared to be one such process.

A related question concerns how we came to study forgiveness *together.* We have been down-the-hall colleagues at Arizona State University's west campus in Phoenix, Arizona, since the mid-1990s. We helped design the curriculum and shared the teaching duties in interpersonal communication and research methods courses. We have become friends over the years—discussing our kids, marriages, students, and research interests, sometimes over a game of racquetball at the university's courts. Starting in 1996, Doug and his group of undergraduate research assistants started collecting forgiveness stories. The original survey asked participants to describe in detail forgiveness episodes they had experienced. Vince read early drafts of the paper, and the two of us engaged in lively discussions about the meaning of forgiveness in relationships and the best ways to present the data. Subsequently, Doug published what (to our knowledge) was the first data-based paper focused on the communication of forgiveness (Kelley, 1998). In the meantime, Vince had started a study in a nearby retirement community that included a large number of long-term married couples. Questions about the role of forgiveness in these long-term marriages were of mutual interest. The partnership grew from there.

A second reason we studied forgiveness was its resonance in our personal lives. Like most people, we had made mistakes in our relationships with family, friends, and coworkers. We knew the tiresome feeling of holding a grudge and the relief that comes from letting it go. Vince remembered a time years ago when a good friend had failed to pay back a sizable loan. After months of smoldering resentment, he forgave the debtor on the advice of a second friend. The emotional liberation associated with this act remains a strong memory. Doug's interest in forgiveness is an integral component of his identity as a Christian. For him, the Bible is clear on the importance of forgiveness ("Forgive us our debts, as we also have forgiven our debtors," Matt. 6:12, NASB); however, it is sparse on specific information on how to actually communicate forgiveness. So, for somewhat different reasons, both of us knew from personal experience that forgiveness has important implications in relationships.

A final motive we call "currency." We mean this mainly as a comment on the timeliness of the topic. As noted in Chapter 1, interest in forgiveness was growing in popular culture, among therapists, and even in international relations. Yet, few researchers were studying it from a communicative point of view. The time was right for researchers like us to influence the conversation by publishing articles and books on communicative aspects of the topic. Of course, currency also means *money*. Vince had drummed up some corporate financial support for the research with local retirees, and Arizona State University pitched in some modest grant funds to help with that project. More important, Doug discovered that the Templeton Foundation, a philanthropic organization supporting research at the intersections of science and religion, was funding projects on forgiveness. We are grateful to the foundation for the $30,000 they contributed. These monies allowed us to buy recording equipment, pay research assistants, and use one whole summer to conduct interviews with long-term married couples.

❖ CONCEPTUAL DEFINITION:
   WHAT IS FORGIVENESS ANYWAY?

The first stage in any research project, and the most difficult one for many of our students, is defining an appropriate research topic. The initial topic is often undefined, too broad, or too obvious. The "so what?" question lingers. Is this topic really important enough to deserve months and even years of research effort?

Answering the "So What?" Question

In the case of forgiveness, the "so what?" question was easy to answer. Clinicians, theologians, justice studies researchers, and social scientists were making persuasive arguments for its importance in human relationships. It was also receiving considerable attention in the popular media. As we mentioned previously, we could make a good case that the study of forgiveness would advance existing research on the maintenance and repair of personal relationships. In addition to this external evidence, we knew intuitively, from experiences in our social networks, that forgiveness was an important, if poorly understood, relational process.

Defining What Forgiveness Is (and What It Isn't)

Despite its importance, it turns out that defining forgiveness has been a daunting task (see Sells & Hargrave, 1998). We quickly recognized that most existing definitions view forgiveness as psychological decision made by *individuals*. We fully accepted the importance of that perspective even as we noted that psychologists were calling for transactional approaches (e.g., Fincham & Beach, 2002). As communication researchers, we started with the assumption that forgiveness arises from social *interactions* between two or more parties, that it involved the creation of *meaning*, and that it could be a *process* that unfolded over time. The definition provided earlier in this book embraced these features. In short, we intentionally adopted a *communication-based* definition of forgiveness. We wanted to narrow the definition as much as possible so it could be distinguished from broader communication processes such as conflict management or relationship maintenance. We also knew that existing research was focused on distressed married couples or abuse victims, often in the context of therapy or even divorce mediation. However, believing that the bulk of forgiving communication is experienced in nontherapeutic relationships, we directed our research attention to more "ordinary" relationship contexts.

In defining forgiveness, we also considered what forgiveness *is not* (see Chapter 1). As with so many social concepts, forgiveness is related to, and overlaps with, numerous other concepts. For that reason, we compared forgiveness definitions with those associated with terms such as *reconciliation, acceptance, justice, remorse,* and *atonement.* This process helped us sharpen our conceptualization. For example, on one hand, we concluded that reconciliation could be an outcome of forgiveness, but it was not a *necessary* component of the process. (Forgiving someone needn't mean that you wish to continue a relationship with them.) On the other hand, forgiveness definitions nearly always involved the explicit recognition of wrongdoing, letting go of legitimate feelings of hostility, and forgoing vengeance or retribution. We included those elements in our conceptual definition.

On the Drive Home #2: Letting Participants Self-Define

Our interview questions allowed couples to define forgiveness for themselves. This decision yielded insights on "lay definitions," even as it created its own challenges.

"That was like pulling teeth!" Vince winced as he pulled away from the driveway. Doug just closed his eyes and nodded. We had just completed a 90-minute interview with Milt and Shelley, a perfectly gracious couple, married more than 40 years. We had intended to "pilot test" our interview questions, including a series of questions about forgiveness. When Doug delicately asked if the couple had ever experienced a time when they needed forgiveness, Milt glanced at Shelley, who smiled warmly and said, "No. We can't really think of anything." And Milt added, "We pretty much just work things out. We have a strong marriage." This line of conversation repeated itself over several minutes as the couple looked increasingly puzzled and we grew increasingly flustered. Finally, with a more than a hint of desperation in his voice, Vince exclaimed, "Forty years of marriage and you never had a serious problem! Never had a fight?"

On the way home, we recognized two problems that would be confirmed with subsequent experience. First, for this couple (and many others in their age cohort) the word "forgiveness" was emotionally loaded. Forgiveness was required only for only the most grievous of sins, most notably an affair. From their point of view, the couple had experienced no affairs, so forgiveness was irrelevant to them. Second, couples in this age group had a vested interest in appearing happy. Admitting to past marital problems could be a threat to this shared identity. Two methodological changes resulted: (1) We adjusted our interview questions, so we asked couples about "challenging times" or those requiring "extra understanding," rather than jumping right to the forgiveness theme. (2) We realized that a limitation of our interview method was its advantaging of couples who were willing to "talk in public" in detail about their relationship. We knew that Doug's earlier study of forgiveness narratives would be a valuable alternative source of qualitative data, particularly from people who preferred to write their stories while remaining anonymous.

❖ PICKING OUR PARADIGM: WHICH QUESTIONS MATTER MOST?

As any research methods text would suggest, the kinds of research questions we asked about forgiveness were determined in part by the assumptions we made about the purposes of research and the nature of knowledge—our research paradigm (see the textbox below). Because the *communication* of forgiveness is relatively unstudied, our earliest questions were descriptive (Kelley, 1998). What kinds of communication behavior trigger forgiveness episodes? Which motives lead people to seek and grant forgiveness? Which behaviors are used to seek forgiveness? To grant forgiveness? How does forgiveness interaction unfold over time? How do people make sense of forgiveness experiences?

On the Drive Home #3: Choosing Our Paradigm

As we chatted informally about the purposes of our forgiveness research, the language of the *scientific/positivist* paradigm frequently slipped into our speech. In this tradition, researchers assume that regularities in human

(Continued)

(Continued)

behavior can be "uncovered"—that, for example, certain kinds of forgiveness-granting communication leads to predictably positive or negative outcomes. But as we debriefed after our long conversations with couples, the language of science, with its emphasis on detachment, variables, and objectivity, just didn't describe what we were doing in the interview study. We were *creating* knowledge in conversation with these often very wise and experienced couples; to do so we had to put aside our preconceptions and see the world as much as possible from their point of view. In fact, as our colleagues working from an *interpretative* paradigm could have told us, we loosened our structured interview format (Appendix A) and tried instead to have authentic conversations about forgiveness. Of course, as colleagues working from a critical paradigm are right to note, our approach advances a certain ideology, a set of assumptions that really need to be questioned by scholars (including us), because they may privilege certain people over others. For example, is forgiveness necessarily a "good" thing? Does forgiving an abusive person, church, or government simply increase the likelihood that victims will be abused again? Needless to say, this ongoing discussion left us ambivalent, although happily so, about our paradigm of choice!

At the same time, we realized that forgiveness might vary considerably across relational contexts. The kinds of transgressions that trigger forgiveness episodes in coworker relationships might be quite different from those in dating couples or extended family relationships. That insight led us to questions about how relationship context shapes forgiving communication (Kelley, 1998). Of course, the interviews with long-term married couples allowed us to pursue context-specific questions in considerable depth. Over the course of a long relationship, what kinds of transgressions require forgiveness? How do long-term married couples communicate forgiveness? How long do forgiveness episodes last? How are younger and older cohorts similar or different in their approach to forgiving communication?

As we developed preliminary answers and consulted various theories of communication (see Chapter 3), we asked questions, and even offered hypotheses, about the relationships between elements of the forgiveness process. For example, uncertainty management theories led us to expect that uncertainty-reducing forgiveness tactics would be used more extensively with severe transgressions (Waldron & Kelley, 2005). Identity management theories suggested to us that face-protecting tactics would be perceived as having larger positive effects on the preservation of relationships. So we expected that explicit acknowledgments of wrongdoing would relieve the perpetrator of blame and thus be perceived more favorably (Kelley & Waldron, 2005).

❖ HOW DO YOU MEASURE FORGIVENESS?

Having defined forgiveness and identified research questions, we faced conundrums of measurement. As communication researchers, we prefer to *observe* interaction as it unfolds in natural settings. However, outside of therapy sessions or contrived communication "experiments," observational techniques were pretty much off-limits to us. Forgiveness is largely a private and spontaneous relational activity. It would be neither practical, nor ethical, to observe people 24 hours a day, waiting for forgiveness to happen. Moreover, by our very presence, we would presumably encourage *artificial* forgiveness behavior. Imagine asking your partner for forgiveness while a team of researchers looked on.

Given that we couldn't be there when forgiveness happened, our best bet was to consult with those who were. Therefore, all of our studies used some version of *self-report* techniques, although we used multiple approaches to maximize the usefulness of the data. Self-reports, usually responses to items on a written survey or questions asked by an interviewer, are the personal recollections of those who participated in a social event. In our case, we asked people to describe what they remembered from a concrete forgiveness episode (e.g., "Describe the situation that required forgiveness."). In a variation called *observer reports*, we also asked respondents to describe behavior that they had observed in romantic partners, coworkers, or family members (e.g., "What did they say or do, if anything, that indicated you were forgiven?").

The usefulness of self-report data has been debated for years (see, for example, Metts, Sprecher, & Cupach, 1991). Its limitations are well known. Respondents may not clearly remember the past, or may not want to. Particularly problematic for us, the details of communication behavior are often replaced in memory by general impressions or conjectures about what plausibly "could have" occurred. To avoid embarrassment, respondents sometimes edit reports of the past to make their behavior appear more "socially desirable" and the behaviors of others less so. Finally, individual self-reports about communication are necessarily one-sided and incomplete reconstructions of what is essentially a *relational* phenomenon.

Of course, self reports have their advantages. They help researchers understand what is happening now "inside the heads" of relational partners—the meanings, memories, and emotions that help them make sense of past relational events. Even if technically "inaccurate," these recollections may be important indicators of how past forgiveness episodes shape current relational practices. Fortunately, researchers have offered extensive guidelines for increasing the accuracy of self-reports (Ericsson & Simon, 1980). Table 6.1 lists the steps we took to increase the accuracy of the self-reports we collected through interviews and surveys.

Table 6.1   Techniques Used to Increase the Accuracy of Self-Reports

---

All Studies

1. Describe concrete situations rather than summarizing across many situations

2. Describe situations that are clearly remembered and considered important

3. Ask participants to rate the clarity of their recollections

4. Use open-ended questions before closed-ended questions to encourage full descriptions

5. Assure anonymity and/or confidentiality; use aliases in research reports

6. Address the same concept with multiple questions

Interview Studies

7. Build rapport before asking sensitive questions

8. Use a conversational approach to encourage authenticity

9. Question partners individually and together; explore inconsistent accounts

10. Check understandings through rephrasing and feedback

11. Record interviews and review transcripts; keep note-taking to a minimum

Written Surveys

12. Pilot-test questions to assure they can be answered accurately

13. Inductive development; questions are grounded in qualitative reports of lived experiences

14. Allow "not applicable" responses

15. Distinguish between plausible and actual behavior

For example, we found long-term couples to be more forthcoming after we took the time to really build rapport through small talk, self-disclosure, and humorous exchanges. We interviewed couples together and individually, finding that sensitive memories were sometimes discussed more frankly when the partner was absent. On surveys, we used open-ended questions to encourage participants to describe communication in their own words, before responding to our list of researcher-determined survey items.

On the Drive Home #4: Getting Participants to Talk

Doug's counseling experience should have given us a clue that couples would often wait until the last minute to raise the really important issues. In addition, we found it difficult to "probe," and stir up past hurtful memories, when sitting with really likeable people who had invited us into their homes.

We glanced at each other with raised eyebrows as we walked down the driveway toward the car. "Could she have waited any longer?" Vince groaned as Doug pulled his truck away from the curb. We had just completed one of our more pleasant, if uneventful, interviews. On the drive home, we recounted the sequence of events. Stan and Barb had been reticent at first; they had difficulty locating a challenging moment in their long relationship. We patiently persisted, joking about some of our marital challenges, encouraging them to share stories about their kids and their retirement in our area. Eventually they revealed that, yes, now that they thought about it, minor parenting differences *had* been a source of occasional conflict some years ago. We delicately probed the role of forgiveness during that period, and thanked the couple, feeling some smugness about our rapport-building prowess. As she led us to the door, Barb glanced around discreetly and whispered, "Maybe next time we will talk about Stan's drinking problems. Talk about needing forgiveness!"

What Were the Interviews Like?

To be honest, we never had so much fun doing research. In addition to sharing intimate details of their long marriages, these couples offered us drinks and food, toured us through their homes, and shared pictures and treasured memories of their closest family and friends. But there were difficult moments. As couples struggled through painful stories of extramarital affairs, we felt empathetic and sometimes uncomfortably voyeuristic. Did we have the right to peer into the darkest corners of these relationships? Needless to say, we felt privileged by the experience.

We arranged most interviews by phone after couples (or family members) responded to a mailed solicitation, media report, or notice posted at a neighborhood center. The phone call followed a written description of the purposes and procedures of the study. The interviews lasted approximately 60–120 minutes with an average of about 90 minutes. They were conducted in each couple's home, usually seated in their living room or around the kitchen table. Many of the couples owned houses, some of which were quite well appointed. But we also interviewed couples of modest means who lived in apartments, trailers, and small bungalows.

We followed a format similar to the oral history interviews conducted by other marriage researchers (e.g., Buehlman & Gottman, 1996). Interviews began with a written description of the study, discussion of informed consent and confidentiality issues, and a request for permission to record the interviews. Both Doug and Vince were present during many interviews, although some we conducted alone. We realized early on that two pairs of ears and eyes, as well as the discussion immediately after the interviews, were helpful in processing the interview experience. Using the protocol in Appendix A as a loose guide, we questioned the couple together for 20–25 minutes, then each partner alone for 15 minutes, and finally, we brought them together again so they could share any final thoughts as a couple.

The interview began with small talk and questions about how the couple met. Having established rapport, the interviewer asked the couple to identify particularly challenging times in their relationship. The most important, clearly remembered challenge, the episode that most required understanding and forgiveness, was then discussed in detail with each individual. We asked about antecedents to the incident, the nature of the transgression or trying incident, the kind of communication used to seek and grant forgiveness, and the short- and long-term relational effects. When rejoined, the pair discussed additional details of the event and then answered questions about the longevity of their marriage and their advice to younger couples. We ended the interview by affirming the couple and their long relationship and thanking them for the privilege of hearing their story.

On the Drive Home #5: How Do You Know the Stories Are True?

As we began to create a structure for our interviews, we contemplated whether the couples would speak openly and honestly with us. To ensure we were getting valid information, we decided to interview each couple together and each partner separately. This way, we were able to assess co-created narratives as well as individual perspectives.

Vince recalls an interview with Wanda, an 82-year-old woman who revealed in whispers her lifelong struggle to forgive her husband Earl for his extramarital affairs during their early years together. For his part, Earl merely mentioned that his wife had become upset about his "friendship" with a nurse during a long hospitalization. Neither partner mentioned the affair during their joint interview. As we expected, we found that in the individual interviews partners yielded detailed disclosures, some of which were never hinted at in the presence of their spouse, whereas in the joint interviews couples offered their story in a way that brought meaning to the experience and protected face for each partner.

Couples in the first part of our data collection were solicited from a database of long-term couples and received a gift certificate as a token of our appreciation. Other participants joined the study later in response to media coverage. We also shared contact information of several local marriage counselors and encouraged the couples to contact them or us if the interviews raised any troubling issues.

We transcribed the interviews. The process resulted in literally thousands of pages of recorded conversation. The data have been analyzed by us and our students using qualitative data analysis techniques, including the constant comparative method (Glaser & Strauss, 1967). The primary purposes of this work has been to identify and classify types of transgressions, forgiveness dialectics, motives for forgiveness, and communication tactics used for forgiveness-seeking and -granting.

What Were the Surveys Like?

Our interviews yielded rich data about forgiveness as it was practiced in a particular relational context, but some of our research questions called for a different kind of methodology. Certain questions drew on mathematical concepts such as correlation and magnitude. Do people who rely more heavily on certain forgiveness-granting tactics, such as "explicit forgiveness," report more improvement in the quality of their relationships? We could answer this question by establishing statistical relationships between these two variables. In fact, we used a two-step process to collect what we hoped would be more *precise* forms of data, the kind that could be subject to statistical analysis. First, Kelley's (1998) survey used opened-ended questions (Appendix B) to collect detailed descriptions of forgiveness episodes in a variety of relational contexts, including coworkers, friends, families, and romantics. Second, drawing from these descriptions, we narrowed our focus and attempted to develop survey items to describe each communication behavior. Survey respondents rated these items using a numerical scale. (See examples in Appendix C.) We then identified patterns in the quantitative responses, using statistical procedures (e.g., factor analysis). That is how we identified the general types of forgiveness tactics reported in Chapter 4. Of course, in creating quantitative measures of forgiving communication, we were forced to filter out much of the rich but imprecise information produced through interviews and narratives (see the textbox below).

On the Drive Home #6: Unforgivable Information Loss? From Qualitative to Quantitative Measurement

The narratives provided by participants in Doug's study (Kelley, 1998) described numerous approaches to seeking forgiveness, including relatively noncommunicative tactics such as enlisting the help of mutual friends or simply letting time pass. Much of this variety was lost as we tried to create concise survey items for use in subsequent studies. This information loss is illustrated by comparing a passage from a forgiveness narrative shared by one of our students and a survey item, both of which represent "conditional" forgiveness granting. The survey item is rated on two 1–7 scales indicating the extent to which this behavior was used and the degree to which it was effective.

Narrative:

I told Raul that he needed to know that I was scared about the future and needed him to promise never to do it again. I said, "I forgive you, but only if things are different." No flirting with other girls. No pretending he is a free man with no rules. He needs to show he respects me if this is going to stick.

Survey item:

I told them I would forgive them, but only if things changed.

The survey studies yielded some potentially important quantitative results. For example, correlations indicated that the tendency to offer explicit forgiveness (as opposed to, say, conditional forgiveness) was associated with more positive relational outcomes. We don't know if the use of explicit forgiveness *caused* relationships to improve. Our data don't allow us to address that question. We simply know that those who experienced improved relationships after a transgression also said they used explicit forgiveness tactics.

As indicated in Appendix C, our survey questions concerned relationship qualities, severity of the transgressions, forgiveness motives, post-transgression relationship changes, relationship outcomes, and a variety of demographic variables, including sex, age, and religion. But our primary focus was on items describing forgiveness-granting and forgiveness-seeking communication, which we derived from Kelley's (1998) narratives. The survey was designed to be anonymous (to protect respondents and encourage honest reporting) and to take roughly 20 minutes to complete (to avoid respondent fatigue and increase response rate). The survey was "self-administered." Participants completed it privately and returned it to us in a sealed envelope.

We used 7-point Likert-type scales to measure the *extent* (1 = slight use, 7 = extensive use, 0 = not applicable) to which a given communication tactic was used during a forgiveness episode and its *usefulness* in communicating forgiveness in that episode (1 = not at all useful, 7 = very useful).

Why not use an existing survey measure? As we reviewed the literature, we found that existing forgiveness measures had significant limitations when it came to the questions that most interested us. As Ross et al. (2004) noted, most were developed for highly specific purposes, and in some cases their validity had yet to be tested extensively. Most important to us, none of the measures were extensively concerned with the *communication* of forgiveness. For researchers seeking more information about existing measures, Table 6.2 presents the name of the measure, its authors, and its measurement focus. Full citations are found in the reference list. As noted in the table, existing surveys measure attitudes toward forgiveness, the disposition to be forgiving, motives for forgiveness, and the decision to forgive (rather than seek revenge or practice forbearance). Those measures that consider the behaviors used in forgiveness negotiations tend to be vague ("I would try to avoid interacting with him/her.") and oriented to general tendencies rather than situation-specific behaviors (see Brown & Phillips, 2005).

Sampling: Who participated and why? Kelley's original survey was completed by 107 student volunteers who produced 307 forgiveness narratives. The students received a small amount of extra credit for their work. The sample was 69% female, and the average age was 26 years.

In contrast, the written survey items used in two of our studies (Kelley & Waldron, 2005; Waldron & Kelley, 2005) were distributed by students to nonstudent friends, family members, and coworkers. Students received a small amount of course credit for their participation in this optional project. Participants were informed about the

Table 6.2   Selected Existing Measures of Forgiveness

Scale Name	Authors	Focus
Attitudes Toward Forgiveness	Brown, 2003	Pro-forgiveness attitudes
Enright Forgiveness Scale	Subkoviak et al., 1995	Forgiveness judgments/affect
The Forgiveness Scale	Rye et al., 2004	Forgiveness decisions
Forgiveness of Self/Others	Mauger et al., 1992	Forgiveness dispositions
Interpersonal Relationship Resolution Scale	Hargrave & Sells, 1997	Forgiveness affect/stages
Tendency to Forgive	Brown & Philips, 2005	Forgiveness disposition
Transgression Narrative Test of Forgiveness	Berry et al., 2001	Forgiveness disposition
Transgression-Related Interpersonal Motivations Inventory (TRIM)	McCullough, Fincham, & Tsang, 2003	Forgiveness motives

purpose of the study and given the opportunity to receive study results. They returned the surveys to the researchers in sealed envelopes and agreed to be contacted by phone for follow-up and verification.

This "network sampling" approach extended our reach beyond the typical college student sample, as indicated by demographic data describing these respondents and their relationships. Average age of the 187 respondents was 31 years old, although age varied from 18 to 83 years. Respondent sex was almost evenly split; 52% were males. Respondents had participated in a romantic relationship for approximately three years. The forgiveness episode had occurred approximately two years into the relationship. When asked to rate the intimacy of the relationship immediately prior to the transgression on a 1 (lowest) to 7 (highest) scale, 93% of participants selected 6 or 7. In short, we felt confident that our sample was mature enough to have experienced forgiveness in the context of a meaningful romantic relationship.

Sampling for the interview study was purposive in the sense that we "went looking" for heterosexual romantic couples who (1) had been married more than 30 years, (2) had experienced significant relationship challenges, and (3) were willing to be interviewed in detail by university researchers. We interviewed mostly couples in our geographic area (metropolitan Phoenix). However, the fact that many of our couples retired to Arizona from various locations across the United States provided great geographic diversity. Most of the couples who originally volunteered were white, middle class, and of Judeo-Christian religious background, so we modified our sampling strategy to increase ethnic, socioeconomic, and religious diversity.

We began by sending written solicitations to couples who had participated in Vince's earlier study of retirees and then following up with phone calls. We explained the purpose of the study in general terms (learning about long-term marriages) and how the results might be used (in a book for students, researchers, or the public). This process yielded roughly 30 couples. We expanded the pool by advertising at senior centers. Then television reporters got wind of the study and visited the campus to interview us. We promoted the study on the air, and the resulting coverage yielded numerous phone calls from family members and couples. We even appeared on an early morning newscast. More phone calls followed. All of this resulted in an interview sample of 54 couples, all of whom were married more than 30 years, with an average of around 44 years (age range = 30–80 years). Of these, 95% were in their first marriage and 95% were parents.

"Cohort effects" were on our minds as we interviewed couples of different generations. The largest group of our couples was married under relatively humble circumstances between 1935 and 1945. World War II weighed heavily on their generation. Some married quickly days before the husband shipped out for military duty. For these inexperienced couples, the return from war sometimes marked a period of relational stress. Another subsample married during the prosperous 1950s, when the roles of men and women remained restricted. All of these couples came of age when divorce was largely taboo in our culture, as was the acknowledgment of marital distress. Most knew little about the art of marital communication during their early years together. In contrast, some of our younger couples were married in the turbulent 1960s, when norms were questioned, marital expectations changed, and self-help books filled bookstore shelves. They spoke willingly and frankly about their relationship challenges. These differences made us cautious in applying what we learned across generations. For example, older couples seemed less likely to "negotiate" relational issues, particularly early in their marriages, because expectations were simply assumed to be clear. We learned to appreciate how forgiveness perceptions and practices could be shaped by the larger cultural context. The model provided in Chapter 2 was adjusted to acknowledge these contextual factors.

On the Drive Home #7: Why Do Couples Share Their Stories With Total Strangers?

Because forgiveness stories often involve very private and potentially hurtful memories, we thought long and hard about how to create a climate in which people would be willing to share. As such, the way that we began each interview was critical to the process. We made certain that couples knew this was university-sanctioned research and that the information was confidential (even though it was being tape recorded). Many couples weren't willing to share until we had established rapport.

On the drive home, we often marveled at the difficulties these couples had overcome over the course of their long marriages. Extramarital affairs. Alcohol abuse. Bankruptcy. Serious illness. The death of a child. These troubles made our own concerns seem small by comparison. Yet we also wondered *why* they were so willing to talk to us in such intimate detail. Doug guessed that these couples were eager to share their expertise with younger couples. We did hope to incorporate the interview data in classes and publications that might be read by younger people. Couples expressed concerns about rising divorce rates and thought they might help. Vince agreed, but also wondered if some couples were simply proud of what they had accomplished over the years. A few seemed to genuinely enjoy the fact they were selected to be part of a university research project. Still others found pleasure in the opportunity to put their experiences into words. We gathered that some partners rarely talked about the relationship between themselves or to others.

Whatever their motivations, most of these couples invited us into an *authentic conversation*, as indicated by their intimate disclosures, spontaneous emotions, back-and-forth dialogue, and even their probing questions about our own wives and families. The dialogue itself yielded a subjective sense of validity, a confidence in the honesty and sincerity with which our interviewees spoke about the role of forgiveness in their relationships.

Are the Data Accurate?

As we hope this chapter makes clear, the limitations of interview and questionnaire research make us cautious about our interpretations. But by using multiple methods and different kinds of samples, we have increased the breadth of our data and possibly countered some of the error associated with any one methodology.

We do provide the usual statistical support in our research articles. For example, Cronbach's reliability statistics for our forgiveness-seeking and forgiveness-granting measures were acceptable (above .70). This is an indication that the underlying concepts are stable and the items are answered consistently. However, we are cautious about "reifying" our survey measures. We aren't intending them to be used "whole" by other researchers at this point. Our scales are clearly works in progress, and they need to be adjusted and tested. We also know that the richness of forgiving communication is lost when researchers reduce it to a few quantitative survey items. We can report that at least one study has attempted to produce similar measures based on the narrative reported in Doug's study. In an as yet unpublished survey of romantic couples, O'Riordan and Yoshimura (2005) analyzed forgiving and vengeful responses to hurtful events. Their forgiveness-granting items are similar to ours, but they combined them on a single 15-item measure of forgiving/unforgiving behavior, rather than the five distinct approaches that we embrace currently.

We think our work gains most of its credibility from listening to and reading numerous accounts of forgiveness episodes. Long exposure to these stories has yielded an appreciation for the complexity of the process, but also revealed patterns and similarities across our many respondents. In short, forgiveness discourse speaks for itself. We just tried to listen as closely as possible; to understand as best we could.

On the Drive Home #8: Do People Really Do What They Say?

One of the problems with any kind of self-reported data is determining the degree of confidence the researcher has that the information is truly representative of participants' behavior. Although we have no way of testing naturally occurring forgiveness behavior, we have taken numerous steps to ensure the validity of our findings.

We had stopped for coffee one day and the conversation turned to the issue of validity. We had recently submitted one of our papers to a journal, where a reviewer questioned one of the survey items we used to describe forgiveness-granting tactics. The item asked respondents to indicate whether they used the words "I forgive you." The reviewer questioned the ecological validity of the item. People don't *really* say those words, the reviewer argued. To be honest, we were both taken aback. Those words had been directed to us many times by our own wives and kids. Probably too many times! But what evidence could we provide to a skeptical reviewer? It was clear that our personal experiences were not enough. So, we concocted a validation procedure right there, over a second cup of coffee and one chocolate donut and an organic blueberry oatbar. We would conduct a "mini-study" in which we would ask a sample of our students to read all of our survey items. For each they would indicate (1) whether they believed that behavior was plausible ("used by people you know") and (2) whether

---

(Continued)

(Continued)

they had personally used this behavior to forgive a romantic partner. In the end, 47 people completed the rating task. Results supported the ecological validity of the forgiveness-granting measures, including the item in question. A large percentage of respondents considered the behavior plausible (91%), and most had actually used the behavior themselves (81.5%). The reviewer was convinced.

How Did You Protect the People You Studied?

As do all ethical researchers, we followed procedures to protect human participants from harm. For example, we obtained informed consent, guaranteed confidentiality, and made all procedures optional. But the private and emotional nature of many forgiveness episodes called for additional precautions. For example, in our interview procedure we ensured that private stories shared with us by one partner were not made known to the other. In such situations, we often wondered what the other partner's "take" was, but curbed our desire to ask. When the couples were rejoined for the end of the interview, we sometimes found ourselves carefully editing our comments, so as not to reveal a confidence.

Couples often revealed details to us that were unknown to their families. Offspring may never have been told about Dad's affair or Mom's drinking problem. How could we write about the interviews in a way that would keep these secrets? We ended up altering names and places and editing the stories so that the gist of the story was preserved but identifying details were altered.

As we mentioned previously, forgiveness is most required only when relationship partners experience serious emotional hurt. As interviewers and communication professors, we played a potentially influential role as individuals and couples recounted difficult events. We felt a moral obligation to listen respectfully, refrain from judgment, and offer human warmth when couples were obviously suffering. On some occasions, we encouraged distressed couples to consider counseling or other forms of support. The couples we interviewed were almost always generous with their time, respectful of our work, and unflinchingly honest. We have done our best to honor their contributions and protect their interests.

❖ TRANSFORMATIONS

Both of us have memories of interviews that changed us in some way. We were surprised that a research project could move us so deeply, shake our assumptions so fully, teach us so much.

For Vince, these memories include an interview with a former World War II pilot—a truly courageous man who survived the war even as many of his best friends burned to death in the skies all around him. Late in life he realized how the war had hardened him. How he had viewed forgiveness as a sign of weaknesses, something he would never seek from his wife or anyone else. More than 60 years later he has come to view things differently. He sees now that failing to ask for forgiveness in those early years created unresolved tensions and long periods of distance in his most valued relationship. Knowing he was soon to die, he had only recently gathered the courage to ask her forgiveness.

Doug remembers a couple of former teachers from New York State. Because of their limited incomes, they waited 20 years to buy their first home. The couple spoke with energy and excitement about one another and about life. He emphasized that if you expect life to bring difficulties you are not so disappointed when they come—and it's easier to forgive. If they never come, it's icing on the cake! With all of the negative press about marriage, it was so refreshing to talk to people who really loved each other after 70 years.

Vince reevaluated his assumptions about the potential for couples to recover from an affair. Marta, the Hispanic women profiled in Chapter 3, convinced him that an episode of sexual infidelity was just one part of a complex relational history. Her quiet faith and love for family, her unfailing belief that her husband was ultimately a good man, her determination to make a marriage work, all permeated the tiny house they shared in a dusty Phoenix barrio.

Doug was moved by a husband who had taken hold of an idea that seldom is championed in our culture. After a fight with his wife, he and she completely disagreed about what had actually happened. However, he decided that his "being right was less important than her being hurt." To this day they still disagree over what initially happened, but forgiveness is no longer a problem as she is absolutely convinced of his love for her and his commitment to their relationship.

These are the lasting legacy of this research project: our indelible memories of the power of forgiveness in personal relationships.

Appendix A

Interview Questions/Instructions for Long-Term Married Couples Study

Note: Start with the broadest questions in each section. Cover all sections, but not all questions need to be asked. Many answers will be provided without asking. Use conversational style. Encourage partners to talk to each other and to you. Remember to change tapes if needed.

Introduction

1. Introduce yourself

2. Express appreciation

3. Review purposes of the study (including understanding the role of forgiveness)

4. Preview the process
   "For some of these questions we would like to talk with you as a couple. For some of them, we would also like to talk with you individually. We do this because some of these issues might still be sensitive or you might have different individual memories of the event."

5. Explain tape-recording process; get permission to tape

6. Obtain permission to continue interview
   —— state the couple number, date, time
   —— explain informed consent and confidentiality
   —— explain uses of the data (book)
   —— explain how their words will be used and the interpretation-checking process
   —— obtain permission to continue and to tape
   —— turn on tape recorder!

Background Questions

"First, tell me a little bit about yourselves . . ."

1. How long have you lived here?

2. Where did you live before?

3. Are you retired or employed?

4. Do you have children?

5. What is your religious background?

General Relationship Questions

1. Is this your first marriage?

2. How long have you been married?

3. What is your anniversary date?

4. How did you meet?

5. How has your marriage changed over the years?

Forgiveness Event

"*Most couples know how to get along when times are easy. But all couples experience challenges that require understanding and forgiveness.*"

1. How is forgiveness important to maintaining your marriage?

2. How important has forgiveness been in keeping your relationship going?

3. Can you describe two or three times when forgiveness was needed in your relationship?

Note: Prompt couples to come up with some specific times, events, or themes.

"*Specific examples will be most useful to other couples.*"

Note: If multiple themes emerge, ask the couple to focus on the one that had the greatest impact on their relationship.

Nature of the Event

1. What happened in this situation? Please describe the event that required forgiveness.

2. When did the event happen? How long had you been married?

Individual Interviews

Note: Completely separate the partners. Introduce this section, review confidentiality procedures, and emphasize that partners will *not* see these interview responses without explicit permission.

Additional Description of the Event

1. Is there anything that you would like to add to the description of the event?

Probes: Was this a short or long-term event? Explain.
Had such an event occurred before? Has it occurred since?

2. What were your feelings at this time?

Probes: How long did they last? Did they change during this time?

Immediate Impact on the Relationship

1. At the time, what did you expect the impact of the event would be on the relationship?
2. How serious or severe was this event in terms of its immediate impact on your marriage?

Probe: Did you experience other immediate effects or changes in your relationship?

Motivations/Reasons for Forgiving

Note: Pick question A or B as appropriate, then go to C

A. What made you ask for forgiveness in this situation? (*Probe for motives*)
B. What made you grant forgiveness in this situation? (*Probe for motives*)
C. Some couples would have chosen not to forgive in this situation. What made you choose to forgive?

The Forgiveness Process

Please describe what you actually *said* or *did* in the forgiveness process. Consider the beginning, middle, and end of the process.

Beginning:

What was said or done?

What was the "key" to successfully completing this part of the process?

Possible Probes:

How did you know that it was time to begin the process of forgiveness?

How long did it take to begin?

What or who helped you during this time?

What was said or done to start this process (if anything)?

Do you recall any critical events or conditions that made it possible to begin forgiving?

Were there any false starts or difficulties that you recall?

Middle:

What was said or done during this time?

What was the "key" to successfully completing this part of the process?

Possible Probes:

How long did the forgiveness process continue?

Were there any important understandings or insights that were important as the process unfolded?

What kinds of communication were important at this time?

What behaviors or words kept the forgiveness process going?

End:

What was said or done during this time?

What was the "key" to successfully completing this part of the process?

Do you feel the forgiveness process was resolved/completed?

How did you know the forgiveness process was complete?

Did you do or say anything to indicate that the forgiveness process was complete?

Probe: Have you completely forgiven? How long did it take (if you have)?

What do you think the long term effects of this process were on your relationship?

Probes: Returned "to normal"? Positive effects? Negative effects? Increased understanding? Lingering feelings?

What would you say or do differently if you could "redo" the forgiveness process?

What would you keep the same?

Reconciliation

1. Do you feel you have reconciled over this event? (*Explain the meaning of the term if necessary*)

Couple Is Rejoined for the Conclusion

Concluding Questions

What other advice would you give couples facing this kind of situation?

Describe how your belief system and/or religious faith affect the practice of forgiveness in your marriage (if at all).

What have you gained in _____ years of marriage that you would have missed if you had only been married 20 years?

Note: End with thanks and affirmation. Provide counseling contacts. Explain next steps. Provide gift certificates.

Appendix B

Instructions for Three Types of Forgiveness Narratives

1. Describe a time when you were *forgiven by someone else.* Please describe the situation in as much detail as possible. What elements stand out as most important in this interaction? For instance: Why did they forgive you? Was the forgiveness requested or offered spontaneously. How was the forgiveness expressed? (What, if anything, did you do or say?) What occurred within the relationship after you were forgiven?

2. Describe a time when you *forgave someone else.* Please describe the situation in as much detail as possible. What elements stand out as most important in this interaction? For instance: Why did you forgive them? Was the forgiveness requested or offered spontaneously. How was the forgiveness expressed? (What, if anything, did you do or say?) What occurred within the relationship after you forgave them?

3. Describe a time when you believed that you *needed forgiveness from someone.* Please describe the situation in as much detail as possible. What elements stand out as most important? For instance: Overall, what happened? How did you let the other person know you/ needed/wanted forgiveness (or did you let them know of your desire)? How did the other person respond?

SOURCE: From Kelley, D. (1998). The communication of forgiveness. *Communication Studies, 49*(3), 255–271. Reprinted with permission of Taylor & Francis. http://www.tandf.co.uk/ journals.

Appendix C

*Abbreviated Survey Questions
and Selected Instructions*

(details available from the authors)

1. Nature of the relationship

   The items below refer to the relationship (described previously) **before** the offense that required your forgiveness, immediately **after the offense**, and **after you gave them forgiveness**. Use the numbers below to indicate how much you agree with each statement. Use 0 if you think the question is not applicable to your situation.
   Sample items:

   - We had an intimate relationship before the offense.
   - We had an intimate relationship immediately after the offense.
   - We had an intimate relationship after I forgave them.

2. Need for forgiveness
   - Please describe the actions performed by you that created a need for forgiveness. What did you say or do? In other words, what did you need to be forgiven *for*?

3. Motives for seeking forgiveness
   - Please describe in your own words *why* you sought forgiveness.

4. Forgiveness-seeking strategies (Note: Same structure was used for forgiveness-granting.)
   - Before proceeding, please describe in your own words *how* you sought/granted forgiveness from the other person. What did you say or do?

- Below are some things people might say or do when seeking/ granting forgiveness. Think about the situation where you sought forgiveness. For each item, give two ratings. First, indicate the extent to which you used the described behavior by writing a number next to the item. Write a *zero* if you did not use the behavior. If you did use the behavior, pick a number from 1 to 7 (scale was provided) to indicate how extensively you used the behavior during this situation. If you used it extensively, pick a number toward the "7" end of the scale. If you used it only slightly, pick a number toward the "1" end of the scale. (Note: Effectiveness ratings were requested using similar instructions.)

5. Relational consequences
   - Did the other person forgive you? (*Yes/No*)
   - To what extent did you feel forgiven? (*1–7 scale*)
   - Are you still in the process of seeking forgiveness form this person? (*Yes/No*)
   - Indicate your agreement (*1–7 scale*) with these items.

After the forgiveness process . . .

I felt the situation was resolved

Our relationship was strengthened

Our relationship ended

Our relationship was weakened

Things went back to normal in our relationship

- Please describe any changes in the roles played by you and the other person in the six months after you sought forgiveness. For example, from boyfriend to friend; from friend to enemy.

- Please consider how your relationship changed as a result of the situation you have been describing. A "0" (*scale was presented visually*) means no change, –1 means a small amount negative change, +1 means a small amount of positive change, and so on. Circle the appropriate number for each item (*selected items presented here*).

Trust

Emotional closeness

Amount of time spent together

Sharing information about our day

References

Afifi, W. A., Falato, W. L., & Weiner, J. L. (2001). Identity concerns following a severe relational transgression: The role of discovery method for the relational outcomes of infidelity. *Journal of Social & Personal Relationships, 18*(2), 291–308.

Afifi, W. A., & Weiner, J. L. (2004). Toward a theory of motivated information management. *Communication Theory, 14,* 167–190.

Al-Mabuk, R. H., Enright, R. D., & Cardis, P. A. (1995). Forgiveness education with parentally love-deprived late adolescents. *Journal of Moral Education, 24,* 427–444.

Antaki, C. (1994). *Explaining and arguing: The social organization of accounts.* Thousand Oaks, CA: Sage.

Aquino, K., Grover, S., Goldman, B., & Folger, R. (2003). When push doesn't come to shove: Interpersonal forgiveness in workplace relationships. *Journal of Management Inquiry, 12,* 209–216.

Aristotle, Roberts, W., Bywater, I., & Solmsen, F. (1954). *Rhetoric. English; rhetoric; translated by W. Rhys Roberts. poetics; translated by Ingram Bywater. introduction by Friedrich Solmsen.* New York: Modern Library.

Babrow, A. S. (2001). Uncertainty, value, communication, and problematic integration. *Journal of Communication, 51,* 553–574.

Backman, C. W. (1985). Identity, self-presentation, and the resolution of moral dilemmas: Towards a social psychological theory of moral behavior. In B. R. Schlenker (Ed.), *The self and social life* (pp. 261–289). New York: McGraw-Hill.

Bakhtin, M. M. (1981). *The dialogic imagination: Four essays by M. M. Bakhtin* (C. Emerson & M. Holquist, Trans., M. Holquist, Ed.). Austin: University of Texas Press.

Baxter, L. A. (2003). A tale of two voices: Relational dialectics theory. *Journal of Family Communication, 4,* 181–192.

Baxter, L., & Babbie, E. (2004). *The basics of communication research.* Belmont, CA: Wadsworth.

Baxter, L. A., & Bullis, C. (1986). Turning points in developing romantic relationships. *Human Communication Research, 12*(4), 469–493.

Baxter, L. A., & Montgomery, B. M. (1996). *Relating: Dialogues and dialectics.* New York: Guilford.

Baxter, L. A., & West, L. (2003). Couple perceptions of their similarities and differences: A dialectical perspective. *Journal of Social and Personal Relationships, 20,* 491–514.

Baxter, L. A., & Wilmot, W. W. (1984). "Secret test": Social strategies for acquiring information about the state of the relationship. *Human Communication Research, 11,* 171–201.

Berger, C. R., & Calabrese, R. (1975). Some explorations in initial interaction and beyond. *Human Communication Research, 1,* 99–112.

Berger, C. R., & Kellermann, K. (1994). Acquiring social information. In J. Daly & J. Weimann (Eds.), *Strategic interpersonal communication* (pp. 1–32). Hillsdale, NJ: Erlbaum.

Berry, J. W., Worthington, E. L., Parrot, L., O'Connor, L. E., & Wade, N. G. (2001). Dispositional forgiveness: Development and construct validity of the transgression narrative test of forgiveness (TNTF). *Personality and Social Psychology Bulletin, 27,* 1277–1290.

Botcharova, O. (2001). Implementation of tract two diplomacy: Developing a model of forgiveness. In R G. Helmick, S. J. Peterson, and R. L. Petersen (Eds.), *Forgiveness and reconciliation: Religion, public policy, and conflict transformation* (pp. 279–304). Radnor, PA: Templeton Foundation Press.

Bradfield, M., & Aquino, K. (1999). The effects of blame attributions and offender likableness on forgiveness and revenge in the workplace. *Journal of Management, 25,* 607–631.

Brashers, D. E. (2001). Communication and uncertainty management. *Journal of Communication, 51,* 447–498.

Brown, D. (2003). *The Da Vinci code.* New York: Doubleday.

Brown, P., & Levinson, S. (1978). Universals in language usage: Politeness phenomena. In E. Goody (Ed.), *Questions and politeness: Strategies in social interaction* (pp. 56–289). Cambridge: Cambridge University Press.

Brown, R. P. (2003). Measuring individual differences in the tendency to forgive: Construct validity and links with depression. *Personality & Social Psychology Bulletin, 29,* 759–771.

Brown, R. P., & Phillips, A. (2005). Letting bygones be bygones: Further evidence for the validity of the tendency to forgive scale. *Personality & Individual Differences, 38*(3), 627–638.

Buehlman, K., & Gottman, J. M. (1996). *The oral history interview and the oral history coding system.* Mahwah, NJ: Erlbaum.

Canary, D. J., & Dainton, M. (2003). *Maintaining relationships through communication: Relational, contextual, and cultural variations.* Mahwah, NJ: Erlbaum.

Canary, D. J., & Stafford, L. (1992). Relational maintenance strategies and equity in marriage. *Communication Monographs, 59,* 243–267.

Chai, M., & Chai, W. (2001). *The girl from purple mountain: Love, honor, war, and one family's journey from China to America.* New York: Thomas Dunne.

Cody, M. J., & McLaughlin, M. L. (1988). Accounts on trial: Oral arguments in traffic court. In C. Antaki (Ed.), *Analyzing everyday explanation: A casebook of methods* (pp. 113–126). London: Sage.

Cody, M. J., & McLaughlin, M. L. (1989). *The psychology of tactical communication.* Philadelphia: Multilingual Matters.

Cody, M. J., & McLaughlin, M. L. (1990). Interpersonal accounting. In H. Giles & W. P. Robinson (Eds.), *Handbook of language and social psychology* (pp. 227–255). Chichester, UK: Wiley.

Cupach, W. R., & Spitzberg, B. H. (1994). *The dark side of interpersonal communication.* Hillsdale, NJ: Erlbaum.

Dainton, M., Zelley, E., & Langan, E. (2003). Maintaining friendships throughout the lifespan. In D. Canary & M. Dainton (Eds.), *Maintaining relationships through communication: Relational, contextual, and cultural variations* (pp. 79–102). New York: Erlbaum.

Dindia, K. (2003). Definitions and perspectives on relational maintenance communication. In D. J. Canary & M. Dainton (Eds.), *Maintaining relationships through communication: Relational, contextual, and cultural variations* (pp. 1–30). Mahwah, NJ: Erlbaum.

Dindia, K., & Baxter, L. A. (1987). Strategies for maintaining and repairing marital relationships. *Journal of Social and Personal Relationships, 4,* 143–158.

Dorff, E. N. (1998). The elements of forgiveness: A Jewish perspective. In E. L. Worthington, Jr. (Ed.), *Dimensions of forgiveness* (pp. 29–55) Radnor, PA: Templeton Foundation Press.

Duck, S. (1990). Relationships as unfinished business: Out of the frying pan and into the 1990s. *Journal of Personal and Social Relationships, 7,* 5–28.

Dunne, E. A. (2004). Clerical child sex abuse: The response of the Roman Catholic Church. *Journal of Community & Applied Social Psychology, 14*(6), 490–494.

Emmers, T. M., & Canary, D. J. (1996). The effect of uncertainty reducing strategies on young couples' relational repair and intimacy. *Communication Quarterly, 44*(2), 166–182.

Emmers-Sommer, T. M. (2003). When partners falter: Repair after a transgression. In D. J. Canary & M. Dainton (Eds.), *Maintaining relationships through communication: Relational, contextual, and cultural variations* (pp. 185–208). Mahwah, NJ: Erlbaum.

Enright, R. D. (2001). *Forgiveness is a choice: A step-by-step process for resolving anger and restoring hope.* Washington, DC: American Psychological Association.

Enright, R. D., & Coyle, C. T. (1998). Researching the process model of forgiveness within psychological intervention. In E. L. Worthington (Ed.), *Dimensions of forgiveness* (pp. 139–161). Radnor, PA: Templeton Foundation Press.

Enright, R. D., Eastin, D. L., Golden, S., Sarinopoulos, I., & Freedman, S. (1992). Interpersonal forgiveness within the helping professions: An attempt to resolve differences of opinion. *Counseling and Values, 36*(2), 84–103.

Enright, R. D., & Fitzgibbons, R. P. (2000). *Helping clients forgive: An empirical guide for resolving anger and restoring hope* (1st ed.). Washington, DC: American Psychological Association.

Enright, R. D., Freedman, S., & Rique, J. (1998). The psychology of interpersonal forgiveness. In R. D. Enright, & J. North (Eds.), *Exploring forgiveness* (1st ed., pp. 46–62). Madison: University of Wisconsin Press.

Enright, R. D., Gassin, E. A., & Wu, C. R. (1992). Forgiveness: A developmental view. *Journal of Moral Education, 21,* 99–114.

Enright, R. D., & the Human Development Study Group. (1991). The moral development of forgiveness. In W. Kurtines & J. Gewirtz (Eds.), *Handbook of moral behavior and development* (pp. 123–152). Hillsdale, NJ: Erlbaum.

Ericsson, K. A., & Simon, H. A. (1980). Verbal reports as data. *Psychological Review, 87,* 215–251.

Exline, J. J., & Baumeister, R. F. (2000). Expressing forgiveness and repentance: Benefits and barriers. In M. C. McCullough, K. I. Pargament, & C. E. Thoresen (Eds.), *Forgiveness: theory, research, and practice* (pp. 133–155). New York: Guilford.

Fehr, B. (1988). Prototype analysis of the concepts of love and commitment. *Journal of Personality and Social Psychology, 55*(4), 557–579.

Fincham, F. D. (2000). The kiss of the porcupines: From attributing responsibility to forgiving. *Personal Relationships, 7*(1), 1–23.

Fincham, F. D., & Beach, S. R. H. (2002). Forgiveness in marriage: Implications for psychological aggression and constructive communication. *Personal Relationships, 9*(3), 239–251.

Fincham, F. D., Beach, S. R. H., & Davila, J. (2004). Forgiveness and conflict resolution in marriage. *Journal of Family Psychology, 18*(1), 72–81.

Fincham, F. D., Hall, J. H., & Beach, S. R. H. (2005). "'Til lack of forgiveness doth us part": Forgiveness and marriage. In E. L. Worthington, Jr. (Ed.), *Handbook of forgiveness* (pp. 207–225). New York: Routledge.

Flanigan, B. (1998). Forgivers and the unforgivable. In R. D. Enright & J. North (Eds.), *Exploring forgiveness* (pp. 95–105). Madison: University of Wisconsin Press.

Foss, S. K., & Griffin, C. L. (1995). Beyond persuasion: A proposal for an invitational rhetoric. *Communication Monographs, 62,* 2–18.

Freedman, S., Enright, R. D., & Knutson, J. (2005). A progress report on the process model of forgiveness. In E. L. Worthington, Jr. (Ed.), *Handbook of forgiveness* (pp. 393–406). New York: Routledge.

Frey, L. R., Botan, C. H., & Kreps, G. L. (2000). *Investigating communication: An introduction to research methods* (2nd ed.). Boston: Allyn & Bacon.

Glaser, B. G., & Strauss, A. L. (1967). *The discovery of grounded theory: Strategies for qualitative research.* Chicago: Aldine.

Goffman, E. (1955). On face-work: An analysis of ritual elements in social interaction. *Psychiatry: Journal for the Study of Interpersonal Processes, 18,* 213–231.

Goffman, E. (1959). *The presentation of self in everyday life.* Garden City, NY: Doubleday.

Gordon, K. C., & Baucom, D. H. (1999). A multitheoretical intervention for promoting recovery from extramarital affairs. *Clinical Psychology: Science and Practice, 6*, 382–399.

Gordon, K. C., & Baucom, D. H. (2003). Forgiveness and marriage: Preliminary support for a measure based on A model of recovery from A marital betrayal. *American Journal of Family Therapy, 31*(3), 179–199.

Gordon, K. C., Baucom, D. H., & Snyder, D. K. (2000). The use of forgiveness in marital therapy. In M. C. McCullough, K. I. Pargament, & C. E. Thoresen (Eds.), *Forgiveness: Theory, research, and practice* (pp. 203–227). New York: Guilford.

Gordon, K. C., Baucom, D. H., & Snyder, D. K. (2005). Forgiveness in couples: Divorce, infidelity and couples therapy. In E. L. Worthington, Jr. (Ed.), *Handbook of forgiveness* (pp. 407–421). New York: Routledge.

Greenberg, L. S., Warwar, S., & Malcolm, W. (2003). *Differential effects of emotion focused therapy and psychoeducation for resolving emotional injuries.* Paper presented at the International Society for Psychotherapy Research, Weimar, Germany, June 2003.

Hargrave, T. D. (1994). Families and forgiveness: A theoretical and therapeutic framework. *The Family Journal: Counseling and Therapy for Couples and Families, 2*, 339–348.

Hargrave, T. D., & Sells, J. N. (1997). The development of a forgiveness scale. *Journal of Marital and Family Therapy, 23*, 41–63.

Harvey, J. (2004). *Trauma and recovery strategies across the lifespan of long-term married couples.* Phoenix: Arizona State University West Press.

Hebl, J., & Enright, R. D. (1993). Forgiveness as a psychotherapeutic intervention with elderly females. *Psychotherapy, 30*, 658–667.

Helmick, R. G. (2001). Does religion fuel or heal conflicts? In R. G. Helmick & R. L. Petersen (Eds.), *Forgiveness and reconciliation* (pp. 81–95). Philadelphia: Templeton Foundation Press.

Heschel, A. J. (1996). *Moral grandeur and spiritual audacity: Essays.* (S. Heschel, Ed.). New York: Farrar, Straus & Giroux.

Hill, P. C., Exline, J. J., & Cohen, A. B. (2005). Social psychology of justice and forgiveness in civil and organizational settings. In E. L. Worthington, Jr. (Ed.), *Handbook of forgiveness* (pp. 477–490). New York: Routledge.

Johnson, M. P. (1999). Personal, moral, and structural commitments to relationships: Experiences of choice and constraint. In J. M. Adams & W. H. Jones (Eds.), *Handbook of interpersonal commitment and relationship quality* (pp. 73–87). New York: Plenum.

Kachadourian, L. K., Fincham, F., & Davila, J. (2005). Attitudinal ambivalence, rumination, and forgiveness of partner transgressions in marriage. *Personality and Social Psychology Bulletin, 31*, 334–342.

Kanz, J. E. (2000). How do people conceptualize and use forgiveness? The forgiveness attitudes questionnaire. *Counseling & Values, 44*(3), 174.

Kearns, J. N., & Fincham, F. D. (2004). A prototype analysis of forgiveness. *Personality and Social Psychology Bulletin, 30*, 838–855.

Kearns, J. N., & Fincham, F. D. (2005). Victim and perpetrator accounts of interpersonal transgressions: Self-serving or relationship-serving biases? *Personality and Social Psychology Bulletin, 31*, 321–333.

Kelley, D. L. (1998). The communication of forgiveness. *Communication Studies, 49*(3), 255–271.

Kelley, D. L. (2001). *Common perspectives of forgiveness.* Paper presented at National Communication Association conference, Atlanta, Georgia, November 2001.

Kelley, D. L., & Burgoon, J. K. (1991). Understanding marital satisfaction and couple type as functions of relational expectations. *Human Communication Research, 18*, 40–69.

Kelley, D. L., & Waldron, V. (2005). An investigation of forgiveness-seeking communication and relational outcomes. *Communication Quarterly, 53*, 339–358.

Kelley, D. L., & Waldron, V. (2006). Forgiveness: Communicative implications in social relationships. *Communication Yearbook, 30*, 303–341.

Kelley, H. H. (1971). *Attribution in social interaction.* Morristown, NJ: General Learning Press.

Kirkup, P. A. (1993). Some religious perspectives on forgiveness and settling differences. *Mediation Quarterly, 11*, 79–94.

Mahoney, A., Rye, M. S., & Pargament, K. I. (2005). When the sacred is violated: Desecration as a unique challenge to forgiveness. In E. L. Worthington, Jr. (Ed.), *Handbook of forgiveness* (pp. 57–71). New York: Routledge.

Malcolm, W. M., & Greenberg, L. S. (2000). Forgiveness as a process of change in individual psychotherapy. In M. E. McCullough, K. I. Pargament, & C. E. Thoresen (Eds.), *Forgiveness: Theory, research, and practice* (pp. 179–202). New York: Guilford.

Malcolm, W., Warwar, S., & Greenberg, L. (2005). Facilitating forgiveness in individual therapy as an approach to resolving interpersonal injuries. In E. L. Worthington, Jr. (Ed.), *Handbook of forgiveness* (pp. 379–392). New York: Routledge.

Mallin, I., & Anderson, K. V. (2000). Inviting constructive argument. *Argumentation & Advocacy,* (36), 120–133.

Mauger, P. A., Perry, J. E., Freeman, T., & Grove, D. C. (1992). The measurement of forgiveness: Preliminary research. *Journal of Psychology and Christianity, 11*, 170–180.

McCullough, M. C., Fincham, F. D., & Tsang, J. A. (2003). Forgiveness, forbearance, and time: The temporal unfolding of transgression-related interpersonal motivations. *Journal of Personality and Social Psychology, 84*, 540–557.

McCullough, M. E., Pargament, K. I., & Thoresen, C. E. (Eds.). (2000). *Forgiveness: Theory, research, and practice.* New York: Guilford.

McCullough, M. E., & Worthington, E. L. (1995). Promoting forgiveness: A comparison of two brief psychoeducational group interventions with a waiting-list control. *Counseling and Values, 40*, 55–68.

McCullough, M. E., Worthington, E. L., Jr., & Rachal, K. C. (1997). Interpersonal forgiving in close relationships. *Journal of Personality and Social Psychology, 73*, 321–336.

Metts, S. (1994). Relational transgressions. In W. R. Cupach & B. H. Spitzberg (Eds.), *The dark side of interpersonal communication* (pp. 217–241). Hillsdale, NJ: Erlbaum.

Metts, S., Cupach, W. R., & Lippert, L. (2006). Forgiveness in the workplace. In J. M. H. Fritz & B. L. Omdahl (Eds.), *Problematic relationships in the workplace* (pp. 249–278). New York: Peter Lang.

Metts, S., Sprecher, S., & Cupach, W. R. (1991). Retrospective self-reports. In B. M. Montgomery & S. Duck (Eds.), *Studying interpersonal interaction* (pp. 162–178). New York: Guilford.

Montville, J. V. (1990). *Conflict and peacemaking in multiethnic societies.* New York: Macmillan.

Mullet, E., Girard, M., & Bakhshi, P. (2004). Conceptualizations of forgiveness. *European Psychologist, 9,* 78–86.

North, J. (1987). Wrongdoing and forgiveness. *Philosophy, 62,* 499–508.

O'Riordan, C. K., & Yoshimura, S. (2005). Reactions of forgiveness and revenge after hurtful events in romantic relationships. Paper presented at the Western States Communication Association conference, San Francisco, February 2005.

Paleari, F. G., Regalia, C., & Fincham, F. D. (2005). Marital quality, forgiveness, empathy, and rumination: A longitudinal analysis. *Personality and Social Psychology Bulletin, 31,* 368–378.

Planalp, S. (1999). *Communicating emotion: Social, moral, and cultural processes.* New York: Cambridge University Press.

Prager, D. (1997, December 15). The sin of forgiveness. *Wall Street Journal,* p. 1.

Prager, K. J. (1995). *The psychology of intimacy.* New York: Guilford.

Reid, B. (2000). The way to harmony: A father's death pulls at Navajo's faith. [Electronic version]. *Reid, B.,* Retrieved April 1, 2006, from http://www.poynter.org

Ross, S. R., Kendall, A. C., Matters, K. G., Wrobel, T. A., & Rye, M. S. (2004). A personological examination of self and other-forgiveness in the five factor model. *Journal of Personality Assessment, 82,* 207–214.

Rusbult, C. E., Hannon, P. A., Stocker, S. L., & Finkel, E. J. (2005). Forgiveness and relational repair. In E. L. Worthington, Jr. (Ed.), *Handbook of forgiveness* (pp. 185–205). New York: Routledge.

Rye, M. S., Folck, C. D., Heim, T. A., Olszewski, B. T., & Traina, E. (2004). Forgiveness of an ex-spouse: How does it relate to mental health following a divorce? (author abstract). *Journal of Divorce & Remarriage, 41*(3–4), 31(21).

Rye, M. S., Loiacono, D. M., Folck, C. D., Olszewski, B. T., Heim, T. A., & Madia, B. P. (2001). Evaluation of the psychometric properties of two forgiveness scales. *Current Psychology: Developmental, Learning, Personality, Social, 20,* 260–277.

Rye, M. S., Pargament, K. I., Ali, M. A., Beck, G. L., Dorff, E. N., & Hallisey, C., et al. (2000). Religious perspectives on forgiveness. In M. E. McCullough, K. I. Pargament, & C. E. Thoresen (Eds.), *Forgiveness: Theory, research, and practice* (pp. 17–40). New York: Guilford.

194   COMMUNICATING FORGIVENESS

Schonbach, P., & Kleibaumhuter, P. (1990). Severity of reproach and defensiveness of accounts. In J. Cody & M. L. McLaughlin (Eds.), *The psychology of tactical communication* (pp. 229–243). Philadelphia: Multilingual Matters.

Scobie, E. D., & Scobie, G. E. W. (1998). Damaging events: The perceived need for forgiveness. *Journal for the Theory of Social Behaviour, 28,* 373–401.

Sells, J. N., & Hargrave, T. D. (1998). Forgiveness: A review of the theoretical and empirical literature. *Journal of Family Therapy, 20,* 21–36.

Sharpsteen, D. J. (1993). Romantic jealousy as an emotion concept: A prototype analysis. *Journal of Social and Personal Relationships, 10,* 69–82.

Simons, H. (2000). A dilemma-centered analysis of Clinton's August 17th apologia: Implications for rhetorical theory and method. *Quarterly Journal of Speech, 86*(4), 438–453.

Smith, S. L., Smith, S. W., Yoo, J. H., Ferris, A., Downs, E., Pieper, K. M., et al. (2005). Altruism on American television: Examining the prevalence of and context surrounding such acts. Paper presented at International Communication Association conference, New York, May 2005.

Subkoviak, M., Enright, R., Wu, C-R., Gassin, E., Freedman, S., Olson, L., & Sarinopoulos, I. (1995). Measuring interpersonal forgiveness in late adolescence and middle adulthood. *Journal of Adolescence, 18,* 641–655.

Tutu, D. (1999). *No future without forgiveness.* New York: Doubleday.

Vangelisti, A. (1994). Messages that hurt. In W. R. Cupach & B. H. Spitzberg (Eds.), *The dark side of interpersonal communication* (pp. 53–82). Hillsdale, NJ: Erlbaum.

Vangelisti, A. (2006). Family communication theories: Variations and challenges. In D. O. Braithwaite & L. A. Baxter (Eds.), *Engaging theories in family communication: Multiple perspectives* (pp. ix–xvii). Thousand Oaks, CA: Sage.

Vangelisti, A. L., & Young, S. L. (2000). When words hurt: The effects of perceived intentionality on interpersonal relationships. *Journal of Social and Personal Relationships, 17,* 393–424.

Vogl-Bauer, S. (2003). Maintaining family relationships. In D. Canary & M. Dainton (Eds.), *Maintaining relationships through communication: Relational, contextual, and cultural variations* (pp. 31–50). New York: Erlbaum.

Volf, M. (2001). Forgiveness, reconciliation, and justice: A Christian contribution to a more peaceful social environment. In R. Helmick & R. L. Petersen (Eds.), *Forgiveness and reconciliation: Religion, public policy, and conflict transformation* (pp. 27–49). Philadelphia: Templeton Foundation Press.

Wade, N. G., Worthington, E. L., Jr., & Meyer, J. E. (2005). But do they work? A meta-analysis of group interventions to promote forgiveness. In E. L. Worthington, Jr. (Ed.), *Handbook of forgiveness* (pp. 423–439). New York: Routledge.

Wagoner, R., & Waldron, V. R. (1999). How supervisors convey routine bad news: Face-work at UPS. *Southern Communication Journal, 64,* 193–210.

Waldron, V. R. (1991). Achieving communication goals in superior-subordinate relationships: The multi-functionality of upward maintenance tactics. *Communication Monographs, 58,* 289–306.

Waldron, V. R. (1994). Once more, *with feeling:* Reconsidering the role of emotion in work. *Communication Yearbook, 17,* 388–416.

Waldron, V. R. (2000). Relational experiences and emotion at work. In S. Fineman (Ed.), *Emotion in organizations* (2nd ed., pp. 64–82). Thousand Oaks, CA: Sage.

Waldron, V. R. (2003). Relationship maintenance in organizational settings. In D. Canary & M. Dainton (Eds.), *Maintaining relationships through communication: Relational, contextual, and cultural variations* (pp. 163–184). New York: Erlbaum.

Waldron, V. R., & Kelley, D. (2005). Forgiveness as a response to relational transgression. *Journal of Social and Personal Relationships, 22,* 723–742.

Waldron, V. R., Kelley, D., & Harvey, J. (in press). Forgiving communication and relational consequences. In M. Motley (Ed.), *Studies in applied interpersonal communication.* Thousand Oaks: Sage.

Waldron, V. R., & Krone, K. (1991). The experience and expression of emotion in the workplace: A study of a corrections organization. *Management Communication Quarterly, 4*(3), 287–309.

Ware, B., & Linkugel, W. (1973). They spoke in defense of themselves: On the general criticism of apologia. *Quarterly Journal of Speech, 59*(3), 273–283.

Weick, K. E. (1969). *The social psychology of organizing.* Reading, MA: Addison-Wesley.

Wiesenthal, S. (1997). *The sunflower: On the possibilities and limits of forgiveness* [Die Sonnenblume] (H. J. Cargas, Trans.). (Rev. and expanded ed.). New York: Schocken. (Originally published 1969).

Witvliet, C. V. (2001). Forgiveness and health: Review and reflections on a matter of faith, feelings, and physiology. *Journal of Psychology and Theology, 29,* 212–224.

Witvliet, C. V., Ludwig, T. E., & Vander Laan, K. L. (2001). Granting forgiveness or harboring grudges: Implications for emotion, physiology, and health. *Psychological Science, 12,* 117–123.

Worthington, E. L. (1998). *Dimensions of forgiveness: Psychological research & theological perspectives.* Philadelphia: Templeton Foundation Press.

Worthington, E. L. (2001). Unforgiveness, forgiveness, and reconciliation and their implications for societal interventions. In R. G. Helmick & R. L. Petersen (Eds.), *Forgiveness and reconciliation* (pp. 171–192). Philadelphia: Templeton Foundation Press.

Worthington, E. L., Jr. (Ed.). (2005a). *Handbook of forgiveness.* New York: Routledge.

Worthington, E. L. (2005b). Initial questions about the art and science of forgiving. In E. L. Worthington, Jr. (Ed.), *Handbook of forgiveness* (pp. 1–14). New York: Routledge.

Worthington, E. L., Jr., Kurusu, T. A., Collins, W., Berry, J. W., Ripley, J. S., & Baier, S. N. (2000). Forgiving usually takes time: A lesson learned by studying interventions to promote forgiveness. *Journal of Psychology & Theology, 28,* 3–20.

Worthington, E. L., Jr., & Scherer, M. (2004). Forgiveness is an emotion-focused coping strategy that can reduce health risks and promote health resilience: Theory, review, and hypotheses. *Psychology and Health, 19,* 385–405.

Worthington, E. L., & Wade, N. G. (1999). The psychology of forgiveness and unforgiveness and implications for clinical practice. *Journal of Social and Clinical Psychology, 18,* 385–418.

Zechmeister, J. S., & Romero, C. (2002). Victim and offender accounts of interpersonal conflict: Autobiographical narratives of forgiveness and unforgiveness. *Journal of Personality and Social Psychology, 82,* 675–686.

Index

About the Authors

Vincent R. Waldron received his PhD in 1989 from Ohio State University. After several years at the University of Kentucky, he became a founding member of the new Communication Studies department at Arizona State University's west campus in Phoenix. He teaches courses in interpersonal and organizational communication, communication and aging, and research methods.

Dr. Waldron researches the communication practices that shape personal and work relationships. His early work focused on such cognitive processes as conversational planning. Later studies focused on communication tactics used in "problematic" communication situations, such as discussing safe sex, persuading reluctant supervisors, expressing strong emotion, obtaining sensitive information, and requesting social support. With Douglas Kelley, Vince studies how forgiveness is negotiated in various relationship types, including long-term marriages. His work has appeared recently in the *Journal of Social and Personal Relationships, Communication Yearbook*, and the *Journal of Applied Gerontology*.

Dr. Waldron takes pride in his teaching and leadership accomplishments. At ASU, he implemented a learning communities program for first-year students, co-founded a public-speaking laboratory, and serves as faculty director of the Osher Lifelong Learning Institute, which provides educational experiences for roughly 1,000 older learners. Vince is a past recipient of the Arizona *Professor of the Year* award from the Carnegie Foundation for the Advancement of Teaching. He serves on the editorial boards of several journals, including *Human Communication Research* and *Communication Monographs*.

An avid backpacker, Vince lives in the Phoenix area with his wife Kathleen, their two teenaged daughters Emily and Laura, and their golden retrievers, Zella and Zoe.

Douglas L. Kelley received his PhD in 1988 from the University of Arizona. He spent five years at Seattle Pacific University before settling in at the west campus of Arizona State University. Doug teaches relationship-based courses such as Family Communication, Conflict and Negotiation, Relational Communication, and Inner-City Families.

Dr. Kelley studies interpersonal communication processes. Most of this research has focused on marital communication, including how couples negotiate privacy and relational expectations. His 1998 study on *The Communication of Forgiveness* launched a decade's worth of work with his colleague, Vince Waldron, focusing on various forgiveness processes.

Dr. Kelley considers teaching a primary focus of his work at ASU. He has been nominated for various teaching awards and takes great pride in the creation of a service-learning course in which students work with children and youth in inner-city contexts. In addition, he puts in numerous hours each week as faculty advisor to the college Young Life club on campus. He has served on the editorial boards of various journals including, most currently, the *Journal of Family Communication*.

Doug loves to spend time with his wife, Ann, and sons, Jonathan and Daniel. He enjoys kayaking and swimming, and running with his beagle/lab, Allen.